ARCHITECTURE AND GEOMETRY IN THE AGE OF THE BAROQUE

ARCHITECTURE
AND GEOMETRY
IN THE AGE OF THE
BAROQUE

GEORGE L. HERSEY

The University of Chicago Press
Chicago and London

GEORGE HERSEY was
born in 1927 in Cam-
bridge, Massachusetts.
After World War II service
in the army (as a French
horn player) and merchant
marine, he attended Har-
vard College and gradu-
ated in 1951. He then at-
tended Yale Drama School
and thereafter taught
scene design until his return to Yale in 1961 to get
a Ph.D. in art history. He
taught at Yale until his re-
tirement in 1998.

The University of Chicago Press, Chicago 60637
The University of Chicago Press, Ltd., London
© 2000 by The University of Chicago
All rights reserved. Published 2000
Printed in Hong Kong
09 08 07 06 05 04 03 02 01 00   1 2 3 4 5

ISBN (cloth) 0-226-32783-3
ISBN (paper) 0-226-32784-1

Library of Congress Cataloging-in-Publication Data
Hersey, George L.
Architecture and geometry in the age of the Baroque / George Hersey.
        p. cm.
Includes bibliographical references and index.
ISBN 0-226-32783-3 (cloth : alk. paper) —ISBN (paper) 0-226-32784-1 (pbk. : alk. paper)
1. Architecture, Baroque—Europe. 2. Architecture, Modern—17th–18th centuries—Europe.
3. Architectural design—Mathematics. 4. Geometry in architecture—Europe. I. Title
NA956.H47 2000
724¢.16—dc21
00-037791

This slide show of a book is dedicated to
my valuable colleagues and invaluable advisers,
Michael Frame and the late Claude V. Palisca,
and to the dear years when I made my
living with a magic lantern.

CONTENTS

ACKNOWLEDGMENTS

I am indebted, for inspiration, advice, and corrections, to Mark Wilson Jones (in architectural matters); to Michael Frame and David Park (in mathematical and physical matters); to Marty Golubitsky (ditto, and for special help with chapter 5); to Victor Bers and Alice Falk (for Greek and Latin); to Claude V. Palisca (for the musicology, and especially for laboring with me over the tune that Bernini's baldacchino plays); to Joseph Connors (for architecture, especially Borromini's); to Carter Wiseman for help with the Modulor; and to Alberto Pérez-Gómez, Cesar Pelli, and John Beldon Scott (more generally). But above all I want to thank the many generations of Yale undergraduates who took my Architecture and Geometry course. Over these years the fundamental skeleton of this book was constructed, fleshed out, dressed, and groomed for publication in the classroom.

Particular thanks go also to the two anonymous readers of the manuscript for the University of Chicago Press, to Susan Bielstein, senior editor for art and architecture, and her staff, whose always-helpful enthusiasm was of the greatest assistance in the process of publication. I owe further thanks to my copyeditor, Jennifer Moorhouse, who, to adopt the epithets of Jupiter, is in all ways optima and maxima.

ARCHITECTURE

AND GEOMETRY

IN THE AGE

OF THE BAROQUE

ONE

INTRODUCTION

This book deals, in what I hope is a refreshing and useful way, with a well-worn subject: European architecture in the seventeenth and eighteenth centuries. I will not be attempting a geographical survey, nor will I be interested in style, iconography, patronage, or urbanism; nor in such juicier matters as deconstruction, commodification, gender studies, or body imagery.

My interests will be centered on something equally fundamental to architectural design, if not more so: geometry. I will look at the ways in which designs were laid out on paper and at building sites, and at the geometric figures that stand behind or within those designs. I will be interested in what the likes of Bernini, Borromini, Blondel, Guarino Guarini, and Wren learned from, or had in common with, the likes of Descartes, Galileo, Kepler, Desargues, and Newton.

The book consists of separate episodes of forgotten lore. This means that the book is not a summation of what is known about Baroque architecture, plus a summation of what is known about geometry in the period, with the two then somehow interwoven. Nor is it even limited to the specific ways in which architecture and geometry interacted. Given the advanced state of research now at the turn of the twenty-first century, these approaches would have produced a book that was almost more than massive. Instead, my "episodes" are exactly that—brief independent units that make up a longer narrative. Each episode, whether it has to do with epicycles or with "pregnant" Platonic solids, is sharply focused on a specific problem in architectural design: in these two cases, first, the geometric matrix of architectural spirals, and second the way one basic type of solid relates to another. The episodes are grouped into chapters based on their themes—for example, the idea that architecture is musical, or that it involves principles derived from optical instruments. I will readily admit that another author might write with equal justification about different episodes.

I also need to explain my idea of geometry itself. Partly this will be a matter of the science as we study it today; but it also comes out of a wider, less "scientific" geometry that was known and practiced in the seventeenth and eighteenth centuries. Not only geometry proper but geometrics (number and shape games) and geomancy (number and shape magic, prophecy) held sway during most of the period I write about. It is almost a truism to complain that in the 1600s the leading lights of the "century of genius" wrote as much about astrology, numerology, and alchemy as about what we would call science. Rather than decrying such beliefs, however, I will be showing how they could condition and guide both "science" and architecture. These wider kinds of geometry make up much of the book's "forgotten lore."

An important aspect of this geometry, as I hope to show right here in this introduction, is that some shapes and numbers were considered better than others. Johannes Kepler used the word "effable"—capable of speaking, of being expressed—to describe this aristocracy. Using a more common word for the same thing, the Modenese architect Guarino Guarini called these nobler shapes and numbers "rational."[1] Such effable or rational shapes and numbers dominated Baroque architecture. I will also look at other forgotten Baroque terms for geometric and architectural forms. These too were hierarchical. I conclude this chapter by looking at another phenomenon deeply connected with these ideas, and that helped justify them: the invisible architecture of the heavens. This preeminently embodied effability and rationality. It was often advocated as a model for buildings on planet Earth.

BAROQUE ARCHITECTURE AND BAROQUE GEOMETRY

Though few modern scholars make use of the fact, or even seem to realize it, Baroque architecture was above all mathematical.[2] It comes from an age when architects and patrons could think of buildings as "studies in practical mathematics," to use Virgilio Spada's phrase about a proposed Pamphilj villa in Rome.[3] Any number of the major architects of the period were as much mathematicians as architects, and this when all of architecture itself could well have been called a subset of geometry. In this same spirit the preface to Guarino Guarini's posthumous *Architettura Civile* says that the book shows how "excellent a geometer Father Guarini was, how versed and profound in all parts of mathematics, and especially the part that constitutes civil architecture."[4]

Once again the mathematics of architecture, after a lapse of several centuries, is beginning to fascinate people. In writing the following chapters I have been particularly aware of my debts to three recent magnificent studies. The first, by the late Robin Evans, is *The Projective Cast: Architecture and Its Three Geometries* (Cambridge: MIT Press, 1995). As its title indicates, this is about projective geometry in architectural design. The second book is *Architectural Representation and the Perspective Hinge,* by Alberto Pérez-Gómez and Louise Pelletier (MIT Press, 1997). This deals with more or less the same things as Evans's book (linear perspective as a form of projective geometry), but with instructive differences. The third book is Lionel March's *Architectonics of Humanism: Essays on Number in Architecture* (London: Academy Editions, 1998). This, more than any previous publication that I know of, makes the architectural geometry of the Italian Renaissance crystal clear to non-mathematicians. And it does so in a completely visual way. It is my hope, in the following pages, to do the same for Baroque architecture.

All three books, in short, attack the same mountains of unstudied material that I do, and do so with finesse and learning. My approach, however, will be different from those of Evans, Pérez-Gómez, and Pelletier. They take in wide swaths of architectural history. I limit my undertaking to the European Baroque, much as March limits his to the Italian High Renaissance. In addition I will be making new inroads into these mountains, into rocky and forbidding terrain. I go inside the geometrical principles, I anatomize the theorems, I work out (at least some of) the problems. And I think I say things—in the field of architectural analysis—that have not been said before, and do things not done before, at least not in the last 250 years or so.

More specifically, the following chapter, "Frozen Music," is predicated on the ways in which heaven-derived musical sounds, and music itself, can be translated into visual form. The chapter concentrates on the geometry of the heavens and on the idea that this geometry can be read musically and, indeed, that it actually embodies the unheard melodies that Keats wrote about. As a corollary, we will see how the geometries of architectural structures, such as Bernini's baldacchino in St. Peter's, may be musically understood. I go so far as to write out sample chords and tunes.

Chapter 3, "The Light of Unseen Worlds," fastens on optics, the science of light. Here again, heaven, the main source of earthly light, is the key. Light-projection, conic sections, and projective geometry were studied as heavenly emanations. These studies determined the shapes of the lenses and reflectors used in optics. We will see how, in architecture, domed structures also used these forms—how in a way they were telescopes for imaging their painted vaults—and how the instruments designed to exploit light (the camera obscura, the magic lantern, the microscope, and the telescope) had architectural as well as scientific influence.

The fourth chapter, "Cubices Rationes," deals with the Baroque mystique of the cube. The cube was considered the parent—literally—of all other forms. More curiously still, theorists like Kepler and Athanasius Kircher interpreted the reproduction of geometric forms, notably the Platonic solids, sexually. Like lusting gods and goddesses these shapes (which were particularly effable) kiss, have intercourse, and above all give birth—though some of them are gay. These geometrical joinings and unions lead onward to Kepler's ideas about tiling. Tiling is the interlocking and interpenetration of exactly fitting plane and solid shapes. It is, we will see, an important Baroque architectural phenomenon.

We also find intensive development of what at the time was turning into the modern science of symmetry. Architectural examples of reflective, translatory, and glide symmetries will be investigated, by themselves and in architectural settings. Spiral symmetry, especially, was of key importance in the design of buildings. And it spoke out with special strength in that characteristic piece of Baroque decor, the Solomonic or twisted column. All this constitutes the fifth chapter, "Symmetries."

Chapter 6, "Stretched Circles and Squeezed Spheres," investigates the beauties of distortion. For all its reverence for effable shapes, Baroque architecture loved to pull, push, squeeze, and stretch those shapes. We look at some of the results in the work of Borromini, Bernini, and Blondel. And then, returning to the subject of tiling, we look at the ways in which these "distorted" shapes, usually unstable in themselves, could be packed or tiled into stable lattices to form buildings or parts of them.

Chapter 7, "Projection," deals with one of the great mathematical achievements of the French seventeenth century: projective geometry. This was discovered or invented by Girard Desargues but has a lot to do with earlier concepts such as Descartes's picture of physical reality as a geometrical and algebraic lattice; and, indeed, with Renaissance perspective, which, as I will note, *is* a form of projective geometry. I will deal with this latter subject, emphasizing the so-called *costruzione legittima;* with Desargues's treatises on perspective and geometry; and in a wider context with Desargues's architecture, showing how spiral staircases are projective.

In chapter 8, "Epicycles," we turn to a type of planetary movement that was ultimately rejected by Baroque astronomers but that continued to have plenty of fallout in earthly geometry. We look at simple epicycles, epicycloids, eccentric epicycles, elliptical epicycles, and related forms of broken symmetry. These serve to analyze and explain several further aspects of Baroque architecture.

The last chapter, "Unforgotten Lore," considers how all this plays into the earlier twentieth-century architectural "modernism." This happens, first, when the Baroque ideas survive, unsuspectedly, into later periods. I instance two giants, Frank Lloyd Wright and Le Corbusier. These men were geometers—neo-Baroque geometers, I will claim—in an architectural world that was decidedly antigeometric.

EFFABLE SHAPES

I have said that in the age of the Baroque people believed in hierarchies of number and form. Indeed it was claimed that only these number-aristocrats, these rational or effable numbers, were "real" in the mathematical sense.[5] Or as Guarino Guarini put it: "Some proportions are effable, and can manifest themselves by [rational] numbers, for example the proportion of an inch to a foot, 1:12. But other proportions are ineffable and cannot be expressed in [rational] numbers, but are called irrationals, for example the side of a square with its diagonal, as proved by Euclid Book 12, Proposition 4."[6] In other words, the ratio 2:3 is effable but the ratios $1:\pi$ and $1:\sqrt{2}$ are ineffable. Of course, given the complexities of putting up a building, ineffable numbers and shapes could hardly be avoided entirely. They were, however, avoided as much as possible, and certainly so when the architect was laying out a building's principal proportions. People saw effable or rational shapes as part of a divine order involving all the regular or geometric solids—not only cubes but spheres, certain parallelepipeds, the Platonic and Archimedean solids, and other select two- and three-dimensional shapes. Add to this the fact that it was much easier to measure the area or volume of a "perfect" solid, such as a sphere, than those of an irregular shape. A sphere's volume can be neatly stated:

$$v = \tfrac{4}{3}\pi r^3.$$

The volume of an irregular sphere-like form, on the other hand, depends entirely on its particular irregularities and distortions. To paraphrase Tolstoy on happy and unhappy families: all regular spheres are the same; each irregular one is different in its own way. This sense of the perfect sphere's greater measurability, and therefore superiority, applies to all the other effable forms.

The perceived superiority of easy-to-measure shapes still lurks in the language we use today. For example, we now know, thanks to Newton, that Earth is not a sphere but an oblate spheroid—a squashed sphere (see chapter 6). And the very word "spheroid" implies something that has degenerated from an earlier perfection. A spheroid is like a humanoid or a factoid—not the real thing, not effable.

Presumably we would feel a similar weakness, a similar decay from some original simple beauty, if, for example, a Renaissance prototype for any number of Baroque churches, the Gesù, instead of being built up of double squares and perfect circles, had been composed of square-oids and circle-oids like a twentieth-century building. Nevertheless, I repeat, just such squeezed and distorted shapes will play their role in the following pages; but often they do it to set off, to express more forcefully, some effable beauty, present or implied. We are told that in the eighteenth century a beautiful lady, as the ultimate touch in her toilette, would carry a tiny pug dog. This enhanced her own beauty by setting it off with a contrasting piece of ugliness. In the same way square-oids and circle-oids, in the lesser or marginal spaces of a Baroque building, enhance by contrast the perfect shapes in its main areas.

Then let us look at the Gesù—at its plan by Giacomo Vignola (fig. 1.1).

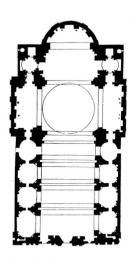

Fig. 1.1. Plan of the Gesù (Rome, 1568ff.). Courtesy Bildarchiv Foto Marburg/Art Resource, New York.

TABLE 1.1 *Component Shapes in the Gesù*

Area	Shape
Site	Double square
Transept	Double square
Nave	Double square
Choir bay (in front of apse)	Double square
Completed circle of apse (which meets the front of the choir bay)	Dome's circle
Nave	Two dome-diameters
Width of aisle chapel areas	½ dome/apse diameter

If you measure it with a pair of compasses you will find that it possesses, packed tightly together edge to edge, the effable, rational shapes listed in table 1.1. In other words, the plan of the Gesù is what I will call a tiling of squares and double squares. The circles of its dome and apse correspond to the squares of the nave and transepts. The diameters of these circles equal the squares' sides. Two mutually interlocked geometries, one of circles and one of squares, subdivided, clustered, and overlapped, create just about everything that exists in this plan. Not every one of the Gesù's innumerable offspring have just these shapes and just these clusterings, but those things are the genetic pool of that progeny.

SQUARE-BASED PROPORTION

Effable shapes had other special names. In the age of the Baroque, proportions like 3:2 and 5:4 were not written out that way—at least not before Newton at the end of the seventeenth century.[7] Instead, a cumbersome but revealing Latin terminology was used. Each author had his own variations, but the basics are the same. Though hard to grasp, the system opens the door to a really different way of thinking about numbers and forms—different from our way, yes, but it was Bernini's, Blondel's, and Wren's way.[8]

We begin by looking at a Latin word for which there is no English equivalent: *sesqui*. It means "more by a half." We still say sesquicentennial to mean a 150th anniversary. A sesquicentennial is a centennial plus "more by a half." But sesqui can be used in other ways. Sesquitertial means the ratio of 4:3. In this case the "sesqui" is modified by the "tertial" to mean: "more by ⅓." That is, 3 plus ⅓ of 3. (That number, of course, would more commonly be known as 4.) Or you can say that a rectangle is ⅔ × ⁴⁄₃. (But, in this pe-

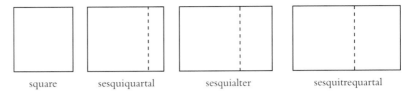

square   sesquiquartal   sesquialter   sesquitrequartal

Fig. 1.2. Square-based
rectangles

riod, you do not write 3:4. You can see why recent generations have considered this system problematic.) To continue: sesquiquarta means "more by
¼," sesquioctava "more by ⅛," and so on.

In short, the classical and early modern tradition thinks of rectangles that
are some unit along one side, and then, on the other side, that same unit plus
a specific fraction of itself. The terminology can be applied to many other
shapes besides rectangles.

This is why I call the whole business a square-based system. It will introduce my chapter on *cubices rationes*, chapter 4. The centrality of the square, so
clear in the age of the Baroque, becomes much vaguer when we resort to
today's way of stating ratios and say 3:2 or 8:7. A sesquiquartal rectangle is a
square plus another slice of that same square, a slice equal to one vertical
quarter of the original square. The names of the rectangles in figure 1.2
mean, from the left: 1 square, 1¼ squares, 1½ squares, and 1¾ squares. Such
are the geometric building blocks we'll be examining.

Other traditional terms are based on the word *partiens,* "sharing, dividing." Thus *tripartiens quartas* means something "divided into four quarters
plus three more of those quarters"—for example, a rectangle formed of a
four-quartered square extended in one direction by three more of those
same quarters. This makes a 7:4 (4 × 4 plus 3) rectangle. *Superbipartiens tertias*
means three thirds along one side and, along the other, two more of those
same thirds (*superbipartiens,* two parts beyond), to make five of them altogether. *Sesqui-bitertial* means 1:1⅔. Or you can say superbipartiens tertias:
three thirds, and then two more.

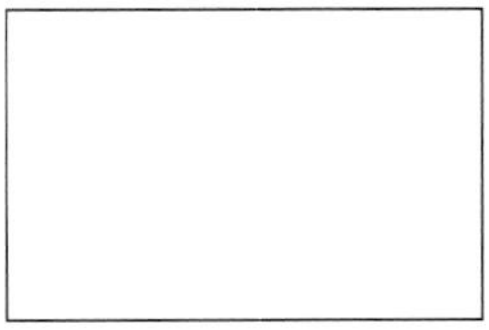

The system gets really fancy. *Dupla undecupartiens duodecimus* (fig. 1.3)
means "double elevenths [to] twelfths": twelve twelfths related to a number
that equals twice twelve (24), on one side, and this same number plus eleven
twelfths (35) on the other.

The more elaborate the system gets, the more irrational and ineffable it
becomes. Indeed, any proportion—good, bad, or indifferent, effable or inef-

Fig. 1.3. A dupla undecu-
partiens duodecimus
rectangle (24:35)

fable—can be described with this terminology, at least if you're willing to get sufficiently complicated. But the clumsiness of the more arcane ratios, as above, made people prefer the simpler ones. (We don't suffer from this sensitiveness. The rectangle in figure 1.3 would look ugly to Blondel or Wren; to us, of course, since we have abandoned Baroque geometry, it looks perfectly fine.) But it is exactly these principles that make up the introductory matter in the most influential of Baroque architectural treatises, François Blondel's *Cours d'architecture enseigné dans l'Académie Royale d'Architecture*, first published in 1675 and frequently reprinted.

EFFABLE NUMBER SEQUENCES

Obviously, if ratios can be effable so can longer sequences of numbers. (Here, by the way, is the place to distinguish a sequence from a series. A sequence is simply a sequence: short, long, whatever. It must be recursive—each new number must derive somehow from its predecessor—but simply as a sequence it doesn't have to get anywhere. A series, on the other hand, is a number sequence that culminates in a specified sum. In other words, arithmetical, geometric, harmonic, and other sequences become series if their totals or end-points within a given design also figure in that design itself.)

One of the most important recursive number sequences is the arithmetical, where each new number is the previous one plus some constant amount. For example, the sequence

2, 4, 6, 8

could be written

2, (2+2), (4+2), (6+2),

which makes it clear that the added constant is 2. A geometrical sequence adds not a constant number but a constant proportion, so a formula could be

2, (2 + 50% of 2), (3 + 50% of 3), (4.5 + 50% of 4.5),

which would work out to

2, 3, 4½, 6¾.

This shows the mechanics of the sequence. If, like a Baroque architect, you think fractions are ineffable, you can multiply all the numbers in the set by 4, at which point it becomes

8, 12, 18, 27.

This was known as rationalizing the fractions. Finally, a harmonic sequence is one whose *reciprocals* form an arithmetic sequence. Since a number's reciprocal is that number divided into 1, a harmonic sequence normally goes from high to low. For example,

2, 4, 6, 8

would become

.5, .25, .16, .125,

which for architectural purposes can be stated by moving the decimal point to get

50, 25, 16, 12½.

I have semi-rationalized it. In an architectural or urbanist setting these sequences can go in any direction—left-right, right-left, up-down, down-up. They can even spiral. In figure 1.4 I have arranged squares that are related to one another in each of the three different sequences. One could use rectangles or circles instead of squares—for example, creating a set of 2:4, 4:6, and 6:8 shapes out of the arithmetical sequence. In the language of the time one would speak of a dupla, a sesqui, and a superbipartiens tertias ratio. Or else one could combine the three types together, as shown on the right in figure 1.4, which can be the plan of a domed building made from the largest of the harmonic shapes on the left together with four side chapels made from the second-smallest of the arithmetic shapes.[9]

Another kind of sequence is called the self-similar. It is the principle of Chinese boxes and Russian dolls. We will see in chapter 7 that this concept covered a biogeometric theory that takes Chinese boxes, Russian dolls, and their geometric and architectural cousins all the way from molecular scale to the cosmic. In a way, too, even the number and shape sequences I have been discussing are a bit self-similar. Each increase involves the same previous number plus some constant. The same goes, obviously, for the shapes associated with these numbers.

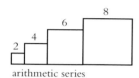

arithmetic series

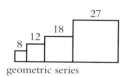

geometric series

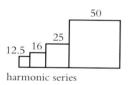

harmonic series

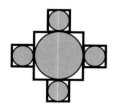

Fig. 1.4. Clustered squares in arithmetic, geometric, and harmonic sequence; and an architectural plan that clusters them

THE GOLDEN SECTION SEQUENCE

Two of the most famous ways of generating self-similar sequences lie in the golden section and its companion, the Fibonacci sequence. Most simply, the golden section is the relationship (as in the height versus the width of a rectangle, ellipse, or other shape) of 1:1.618.[10] Now it must be said right off that this ratio is ineffable. Never mind. It can be rescued. But I also have to say that the golden section has caused a lot of trouble. It has fanatical adherents and fanatical, or at least steely-eyed, detractors—and all across an astonishing variety of fields. Transposed from space to time, for example, the ratio is used to determine such things as the frequencies and proportions of medical treatments; and then, transposed from time to quantity, to determine dosages. In literature it is found in the ratios of line numbers and word-counts. It appears in a long list of other venues. [11]

In antiquity, and oftentimes since, the golden section was known as the doctrine of extreme and mean ratios. In other words, in a line, a rectangle, or just about any shape (visual shape or shape of time) the relation of the smaller (mean) to the larger (extreme) division is the same as that between the larger division and the whole. Another way of writing this is

$$\tfrac{1}{2}(1+\sqrt{5}).$$

In figure 1.5 I illustrate the golden section principle stripped to utter visual simplicity. In it, *PB* (yellow, the shorter segment) is to *AP* (red, the larger segment) as *AP* is to *AB*—the whole. To repeat: the greater is to the lesser subdivision as that same greater subdivision is to the whole thing.

The golden section, usually in the form of a rectangle (i.e., below, with the red line, *AP*, as the width and the yellow, *PB*, as the height), has been spotted, or at least claimed, for all sorts of structures such as the front elevations of the Parthenon, Notre-Dame, and any number of other masterpieces.

More appropriately for this book, the main front of St. Peter's (by Carlo

Fig. 1.5. A line in golden section: *AP:PB :: AB:AP*

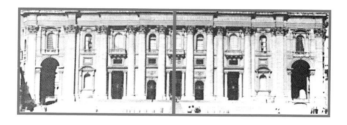

Maderno, 1604–17), measuring from the bases of the columns up to the top
of the main cornice, makes an approximate double golden section rectangle
(two of them lying horizontally together; in red in fig. 1.6). Yet this proves
very little. Maderno may have arrived at this proportion not because he
wanted golden sections but for any number of other reasons. Anyway, if we
thicken these rectangles and measure from the base of the steps instead of
the column bases, we get a double sesquiquadroquintal (fig. 1.6, in blue)—
in other words, a 5:9 rectangle, not one of the preferred ratios. Maybe this is
why Bernini complained that Maderno's facade was too low.

So here's an important point: in the absence of documentation, there is
absolutely no way of proving that Maderno worked from the one shape and
not from the other. To make geometric analyses by trying to get inside the
head of a long-departed architect is folly. To paraphrase Aristotle on mater-
nity versus paternity, we'll say that the shapes an architect chooses are matters of fact; how he arrived at them is a matter of opinion.[12]

But in any event I don't want to go hunting for golden section rectangles.
They are too easy to find and don't mean much when found. For one thing,
1:1.618, by the standards of the time anyway, is close to 1:1.666 (1:1⅔).
Given the period's possibilities for drafting and site errors, one is quite right
to suspect that the architect was not really after a golden section at all, but
rather had chosen that workshop standby, the superbipartiens tertias.

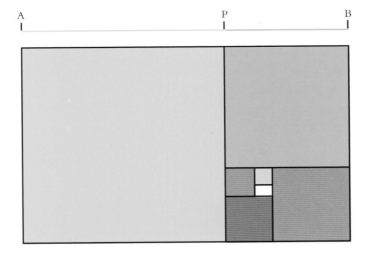

A   P   B

For us, then, the golden section, simply as a shape, has little intrinsic importance. Instead, I take a leaf from Michael Frame and Theodore Bick's new book and say that it is a unique method for producing what we have just been talking about—a self-similar sequence that grows bigger or smaller as it goes along.[13]

What I mean is this: in figure 1.7 the outer rectangle or perimeter of the whole is a golden section rectangle. That is, the ratio of length to width is 1:1.618. Within this, the largest square, in yellow (or shall I call it gold?) has sides that equal the rectangle's height, which we will call 1, with the length of this outer rectangle being 1.618. The next smallest square, colored light pink, is 0.618 percent as large as the yellow one. Each still-smaller square diminishes by that same percentage. At the same time the proportion 1:1.618 is maintained in all the rectangles formed by these squares as they curl up into a sort of spiral.

Thus does a double sequence of ever-shrinking self-similar shapes—one sequence of squares and the other of rectangles—come to be. Note that once again, as with our "sesqui" system, we have a square-based or square-parented technique. Each new shape not only possesses the ratio 1:1.618 but is also just 61.8 percent of its parent.

In our period the golden section ratio was often discussed as I discuss it here—as a way of creating self-similar progressive sequences. In figure 1.8,

Fig. 1.7. A golden section rectangle subdivided with a square. With each new division, the remainder will be another golden section rectangle. The procedure can be repeated ad infinitum, always maintaining the same shapes.

for example, Guarino Guarini tries to show how to use a semicircle to cre-ate line segments that will make up the heights and lengths of two differently sized golden section rectangles.[14] The two rectangles, in turn, are also golden section in proportion to each other. In other words, not only does each rectangle have the height-width ratio of 1:1.618, the larger rectangle is 1.618 times the size of the smaller.

In Guarini's diagram, you draw out the line *AC* and swing a semicircle from its center, marked at *E*. Halfway between that center and point *A* you place point *F*. You then draw *FH* up to where it meets the perimeter of the semicircle: point *H*. *FH*, *AF* will respectively be the height and the width of a golden section rectangle, *AFBH*. Furthermore,

CH:*FH* :: *FH*:*FA*.

And *CF*, *FH* are respectively the height and width of the second golden sec-tion rectangle (which Guarini doesn't bother to draw out). Once the system is thus set up one can go on using it to reproduce golden section rectangles at ever smaller or ever larger scales. This capacity appears to be unique to this particular proportion.

THE FIBONACCI SEQUENCE

The golden section's cousin is the Fibonacci sequence. This governs the arrangement of leaves and petals on practically all plants.[15] In the sequence, each new number is the sum of the two preceding numbers. So the simplest Fibonacci sequence would be 2, 3, 5, 8, 13, 21. If you start calculating, you find that the ratios between any two of these numbers approximate the golden section without ever actually reaching it. Approximate golden sec-tions are much more common in architecture and art than exact ones. Thus, too—because its golden sections are all approximate—the Fibonacci se-quence remains effable throughout its course. Anyway, the sequence's lower numbers (2, 3, 5, 8, etc.) are all components of standard ideal ratios in Baroque architecture.

And, in architecture, not just carved leaves and petals but columns, niches, bays—any repeated feature—can obey Fibonacci distributions. In other words, just as we look for arithmetical sequences like 2, 4, 6, 8, we can look for the Fibonacci values of 3, 5, 8, 13, and so on. Figure 1.9 shows the

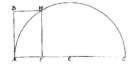

Fig. 1.8. Guarino Guar-ini's scheme for deriving two golden section rec-tangles from a semicir-cle. From Guarini, *Ar-chitettura civile* (1737).

Fig. 1.9. Lower half of the facade of SS. Vincenzo e Anastasio (Martino Longhi the Younger, Rome, 1650). Photograph courtesy of Alinari/Art Resource, New York.

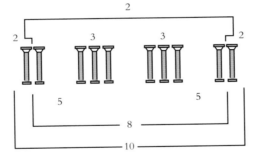

Fig. 1.10. Column distribution in SS. Vincenzo e Anastasio

lower half of the facade of the Roman Baroque church of SS. Vincenzo e Anastasio (dating from about 1650) near the Trevi Fountain. The building's architect, Martino Longhi the Younger, is famous, when he groups his columns, for avoiding normal classical spacings, which are usually more or less equal. He prefers arrangements that are arbitrary, albeit bilaterally symmetrical.

Is there a Fibonacci sequence here? The facade has a total of ten Corinthian columns grouped on each side of the central door and its multiple nested coaxial edicules. Immediately on each side of the door are three columns. Pairs of columns then decorate the extreme ends of the facade—the inner column on the plane of the more central columns; the outer one stepped back, introducing the building's front corners.

There are two ways to describe Longhi's distribution. We could call it a decastyle portico. But then we would have to redefine "decastyle" to mean columns with highly irregular distributions rather than, as would be normal for a decastyle portico, fairly regular. Or we would take our cue from the column-groups themselves. We supplant the notion of the portico with two groupings of 2 and 3, with these two groups of 5 in mirror symmetry. Figure 1.10 demonstrates each side of the facade.

Note that 2, 3, and 5 are Fibonacci numbers. One cannot say the same about the 10-column total, though one can say it of the central group of 8. And, furthermore, one can say that Longhi's facade, in its exact bilateral mirror symmetry, is a double Fibonacci cluster, just as the lower part of Maderno's facade at St. Peter's is a double golden section rectangle.

I would be the last person, however, to claim that Longhi employed these groupings and subgroupings *as* Fibonacci numbers—though the sequence was well-known, we are told, in Baroque Rome.[16] Longhi could equally well have chosen his groupings from a simple gut feeling. But then, of course, to this one might respond that a geometrically aware architect's gut feeling, like the gut feeling of a rosebush, favors Fibonacci sequences.

HEAVENLY FABRICS

In the age of the Baroque all these geometrical principles and practices were gathered into a set of transcendent beliefs about the architecture of the cosmos. Human geometric activity, whether in building design or anything else, and whether dealing with effable shapes, effable sequences, the golden section, or the Fibonacci sequence, was encompassed and presided over by a gigantic vision of similar shapes and ratios—those of the universe itself. In contrast to our current vision of space as a vast emptiness, people in the seventeenth century assumed that Earth and its fellow planets were embedded in translucent spheres and framed by other geometric presences, shapes that were invisible and impalpable but nonetheless real, and that conformed to the principles we have been discussing. In most of these visions, in fact, the cosmos consists of a self-similar sequence of concentric or coaxial spheres progressing from small to large. These structures will sail like a vision over the pages of this book—as "frozen music," as sources of projected cosmic light, and as ideal shapes that churches and palaces should embody.

What substances composed these great shapes? There was much speculation. Each planet had its own brand of matter. Often this was a heavenly version of some earthly metal—iron for Mars, gold for Venus, silver for the Moon. Another cosmic building material was "influence"—yes, our earthly noun with its varied associations of peddling, anxiety, and politics began life as one of the building materials (or immaterials) of Heaven's fabrics. Like other down-siftings from that place, influence affected human affairs.[17] Other heavenly substances included light itself and what was thought to be its vehicle—which Descartes called plenum and Newton ether.[18] Ether, a fluid or gas, was in turn said to fill the universe's every interstice. Yet it was also a sturdy building material, in the words of Sidney Perkowitz "firmer and more elastic than steel, yet completely penetrable."[19]

Still another celestial substance was the crystal from which, according to many natural philosophers, the planetary spheres were made. Most often this crystal was formed into the immense domes in which each planet was embedded like a ruby or an emerald on the surface of an enormous glass globe. Yet crystal, too, was penetrable. Quintessence, however—in ancient and scholastic philosophy (known to Aristotle as *ousia*) the magical fifth element after earth, water, fire, and air—was immaterial. It could be found on Earth as well as throughout the universe.[20] One of the aims of alchemy was to extract it from other substances.

These beliefs were powerful. When the great Danish astronomer Tycho Brahe saw a comet coursing through the sky, apparently unimpeded by crystalline barriers, he did not therefore conclude that these crystalline barriers, these spheres, must not exist—not at all. On the contrary, he said, the spheres did exist but, obviously, the supernal substance of which they were formed allowed meteors to pass through it. (On the other hand, Kepler renounced his belief in the spheres because of this same observation of Brahe's. But only eventually, and with great reluctance.)[21]

As noted, many of these heavenly substances were shed or projected down onto Earth. Speaking of Atlas's daughters, who had been turned into stars, Milton writes: "The Pleiades before him danced, shedding sweet Influence" (*Paradise Lost* 7.375). Kepler writes about the phenomenon in *Har-*

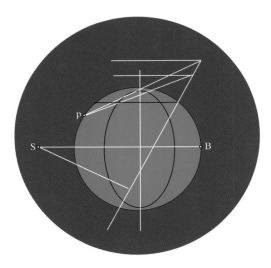

Fig. 1.11. Newton's dia-
gram of the motions of
the Moon's nodes. From
Isaac Newton, *Mathe-
matical Principles of
Natural Philosophy and
His System of the World*,
1729.

monices mundi. He is concerned not only with the fact of the projected matter but with the angles of the rays along which it traveled. These rays, he
thought, were mathematically harmonic and could be consonant or dissonant musically.[22]

Nor are these ideas about cosmic projections all that absurd or out-
moded. After all, as we know today, we actually are bombarded with cosmic
rays and other heavenly projections or sheddings. The imaginary cosmic
building materials of the age of the Baroque are mythic ancestors of the different kinds of matter that current astronomy sees or senses out there: dark
matter and whatever it is that makes up black holes; or even the antigravity
force that is said to flood the cosmos, much as ether, plenum, and quintessence once did.

There is another way in which we may see the Baroque cosmos as being
filled with unseen geometric presences. Although the nested concentric
crystalline spheres gave way to more accurate views of what was happening,
these more accurate views nonetheless filled space with geometric forms.
That is, in order for Kepler to propose his elliptical planetary orbits it was
necessary for him to "construct" huge ellipses circling through space. Some
of his diagrams fill space with architectural, indeed hyper-architectural,
complexes. The latter are unseen and unseeable, only calculable. But they are
nonetheless there, and they determine the shapes, positions, and motions of
everything else.

Newton was an enthusiastic contributor to this state of affairs. Figure 1.11 presents his diagram of the hourly motion of the Moon's nodes (points where its orbit intersects the ecliptic). I will not reproduce his proof. But I will point out that in the diagram, the Moon itself is but a tiny thing: point p. Everything else—the angle rising high above the orbit, the ellipse of the orbit itself, the circle within which that ellipse is inscribed, and the vast axis running from S (the Sun) to B on the right, across the middle of the whole, is an imagined (but of course real) diagram of gravity and motion. Newton's geometric vision fills up the Moon's space, its orbit, its libration or wobble, its rotation, and all its motions with an invisible structure or building. The "layouts" of these cosmic actions and shapes have their earthly equivalent in the layouts of architecture, which take their first form as similarly unseen, but determining, calculations.

In the following chapters I shall be showing (for the first time, I think) that Baroque architecture was nourished on theories, beliefs, and practices that are now forgotten. We have already looked at a few of these forgotten things and noted how different they are from what we believe and do today. Aristocracies of shapes and numbers, effable and ineffable sequences, and the golden section and the Fibonacci sequence are forgotten lore. Nor, today, does anyone, architect or other, believe in a universe filled with invisible geometric solids made of influence, quintessence, plenum, or ether. Such things, moreover, are not mentioned, or even subliminally sensed, in the current scholarly literature on Baroque architecture. It is to reveal some of this lost world-picture and its lore—lore that, after all, helped produce some of Europe's greatest architectural masterpieces—that I write.

FROZEN MUSIC

T his chapter will address   M O D U L A R   M U S I C
some of the things that
architecture and music share, the interface being geometry.
Thanks to a suggestion and much help from my colleague
Claude V. Palisca, I can begin with an example from the writings of Vincenzo Galilei. Vincenzo is famous for being the father of Galileo Galilei (of
whom more later), but he was also a celebrated musician and music theorist.
His *Dialogo della musica antica e della moderna* (1581) contrasts with the anti-
experimental attitudes of earlier, traditional music theory. More important
for our purposes, the book includes diagrams of musical intervals—musical
ratios—that richly repay discussion.

Many earlier treatises on music had contained graphic images. The diagrams could even in a sense be considered architectural. After all, they involved rectangles, circles, and other architectural shapes; they could also involve scale and dimension; and, like Baroque architectural drawings, they
often concentrated on ratios. Above all, like architectural designs these
music diagrams could be modular.

At one point Vincenzo Galilei's treatise confronts just this question. He is
discussing the areas and volumes of square, triangular, and round organ
pipes, and how the volumes and cross-sections of these pipes affect pitch. He
does this by showing how the numerical ratio of a musical interval—what

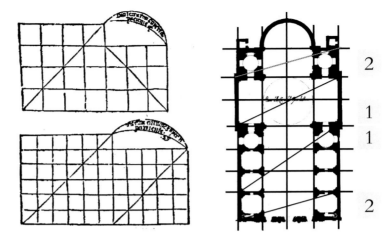

Fig. 2.1 (left). Two diagrams of the numerical ratios of musical intervals. *Above*, the "diatessaron super 7 partiente 9," or fourth (16:9, the square of 3:4); *below*, the "super 11 partiente 25," or minor third (36:25, the square of 5:6). From Vincenzo Galilei, *Dialogo della musica antica, et della musica moderna* (1581).

Fig. 2.2 (right). Plan of the Gesù (Giacomo Vignola, Rome, 1568ff.), with overlaid lattice of the plan's two different modules. From Del Pesco, *Architettura del seicento*.

today we would call the frequency of the upper as opposed to that of the lower tone—may be geometrically mapped.[1] In the upper image (fig. 2.1, top) we see 16 squares, set 4 × 4 and crossed by a diagonal to indicate that this is a distinct subgroup. There is in the same diagram a set of 9 squares, set 3 × 3 and crossed by a separate diagonal. Each of these sets of squares may be thought of as the cross-section of a square organ pipe. In the lunule at the top of the diagram are the words "diatessaron super 7 partiente 9."[2] In the jargon of the music profession at the time, this means a musical fourth, C–F. The blocks of squares—the cells in the lattices—show that this interval has the ratio of 9:16: in Vincenzo's terminology, 16 is 7 more than (super) 9, which is his basic division (partiente).

Vincenzo has squared the numbers in the ratio so he can create square cross-sections for the organ pipes. This 9:16 ratio reduces to 3:4, which ordinarily cannot be represented as a square.[3] The lower diagram in figure 2.1 similarly graphs two pipes that sound a minor third—for example, C–E-♭, which has the ratio 25:36 ("terza minore super 11 partiente 25" (36 is 11 more than 25). Here the area of the cross-section is the square of 5:6. Other diagrams in this passage create other standard intervals, always with their ratios squared or otherwise manipulated so that they can map out the cross-sections of pipes with the appropriate pitches.

In making these transformations (such as 3:4 into 9:16), Vincenzo is applying a module to his designs. Modules, often of two or more sizes, also constitute a common procedure in architectural design. And of course it is perfectly appropriate that organ pipes should be treated architecturally. They frequently appear, after all, as architectural elements in churches and concert halls, where, aside from making music, they can serve as ornamental screens. How might further "architectural" qualities be read in Galilei's diagrams? For one thing, they create what an architect or geometer would call subdivided modular lattices.

As to a more purely architectural version of such things, I turn back to the plan of the Gesù, discussed in the previous chapter. Vignola's plan (fig. 2.2) represents a kind of modularity that is akin to what Galilei was doing. I have indicated the lattice of modules that form the church's chapels, nave, transepts, and choir. These shapes are aliquot parts—that is, subdivisions that exactly fill up a total shape. They measure out his church plan just as Vincenzo's shapes are aliquot parts that measure out the plans or top views of his organ pipes. To complete the likeness between the two diagrams, I have drawn diagonals through the different blocks of modules in the church—demonstrating, as with Galilei, the subgroups into which Vignola's lattice divides. One might even add, more tentatively, that the arched forms of the labels in Galilei's diagrams, and of the apse in the church plan, have similar functions: they bridge across the subgroups within each lattice to emphasize the larger composite lattice constituted by those subgroups, taken together.

It is true that unlike the musical modules, Vignola's, within each of his overall lattices, are of two different sizes: 1, the smaller, is a square; and 2, the larger, is a 3:4 rectangle. But these two different shapes are strongly related to each other, since the end of the rectangle is equal to the side of the square. Vignola or Galilei would have said that the 3:4 rectangle was a superpartiens tertias or a sesquitertial (that is, a square divided into thirds, with one of those thirds added onto one side of the square, forming a rectangle with the ratio of 3:4). These terms, I repeat, mean that the square was being seen as part of the rectangle—and in fact as its origin, with the rectangle being the square's "offspring." (These ideas are pursued further, and illustrated, in chapter 4, "Cubices Rationes.")

PLANETARY MUSIC

In the previous chapter we looked at the rather fanciful ideas about the heavens that prevailed during the Baroque period. Heavenly architecture, made as it was of crystal and other substances, and shaped as it was into spheres, was thought to express this translated musicality. Cosmic shapes generated cosmic music and vice versa. And the music was not just a matter of geometry but also of various kinds of heavenly musicians. Plato (*Republic* x.617b) envisioned in the heavens a colossal seated female figure, Necessity, with a spindle on her knees. The spindle turned a set of eight vast rings, one for each planet. On each ring a siren sat, singing a single note. Together the sounds of the sirens made up the seven different notes of an octave scale (Mercury, Venus, Mars, Jupiter, Saturn, Earth, and the Moon).[4]

The belief that the planets, and/or their spheres, emitted musical tones became one of the most deeply entrenched traditions.[5] But how was this planetary music produced? Nicomachus of Gerasa (c. 100 C.E.), a neo-Pythagorean, says that all orbiting bodies, such as the planets, produce these tones. Variations in pitch are dependent on the planets' size, speed, and distances from one another.[6]

Then, in a more famous passage, Nicomachus tells how Pythagoras himself, pondering these questions, was passing a blacksmith shop where several smiths were at work. As their hammers struck the anvils, common intervals—the octave (for instance, C–C), fifth (C–G), fourth (C–F), and major second (C–D) sounded.[7] This, Pythagoras thought, was because the hammers had different weights. Sure enough, it turned out when he investigated that those weights were respectively 6, 8, 9, and 12 pounds. When the 12-pound hammer struck together with the 6-pound hammer, he claimed, a musical octave was sounded. When the 12- and the 9-pounders struck together he heard a perfect fourth. Thus, he concluded, did different intervals derive from the weights of the hammers: the two notes that constitute an octave must vibrate at the ratio of 6:12 (i.e., 1:2); the fourth must be 9:12 (or 3:4); the fifth 8:12 (or 2:3); and the major second 8:9. (He used what is now known as the Pythagorean tuning system; other tuning systems have different ratios.)

Ever since, Pythagoreans have assumed that these principles applied to the music of the planetary spheres, with their relative weights and sizes producing different musical intervals as the planets orbit and rotate. The same ratios, they thought, controlled the musical pitches of strings, pipes, water glasses, bells, and other musical devices. In other words, the specific shape and size of the music-producing element, whether metal, hollowed-out wood, or a column of air, determines pitch.[8]

However, practical experiments bring out a fallacy in Pythagoras's theory. The hammers and anvils may have produced the tones he heard, but he was wrong about the cause. The tones would have varied with the size and shape of the anvils, not the hammers. This is proved by tuned percussion instruments like xylophones and marimbas, where the pitches of the objects struck (known as the slabs) remain the same no matter what it is that strikes them.[9] Nonetheless, Pythagoras's basic insight survives.[10] Indeed the corrected version of the experiment only reinforces my point. The shapes, sizes, and materials of the anvils (not all controlled by the ratios I've given, but controlled by ratios of some sort), the compound ellipsoids of the bells, and the cylinders of the water glasses and the cylinders or parallelepipeds of the organ pipes all do indeed determine pitch. Music is in part, therefore, a matter of solid geometry.

These notions involve what, with a bow to Friedrich von Schelling, I will call frozen music—music that is somehow there but not audible, music whose sounds have been crystallized into the form of measurable visible spaces and solids. In the case of the shapes and volumes of the bells and partly filled glasses, or of the anvils, even when they are not being sounded, they would constitute what Schelling so famously said about architecture generally—that it is "music in space, as it were frozen music." And I will add here Schelling's less celebrated but, for us, crucial conclusion: that therefore "these [musical] ratios are simultaneously geometric relationships."[11] The thing that "freezes" music into architecture, in other words, is geometry.

Most traditional astronomical authorities were convinced that since heavenly bodies shine, the materials from which the cosmos was made were like glass or ice. The term "frozen music," therefore, fits the architecture of the cosmos particularly well. It suggests not just any architecture, but architecture with a crystalline substance, architecture in which light is a major interior actor. These same effects characterize any number of Baroque buildings.

ANGEL MUSIC

The cosmos produced other music. All through history we have been told that angels dwell in or on the planetary spheres and elsewhere in the heavens. Usually they are arranged in nine choirs forming great rings floating above the Earth—perhaps not too unlike the rings on which Plato's planetary sirens sat.[12] When the well-known Christmas carol bids angels to sing ("Sing, choirs of angels, sing in exultation"), the subtext involves these celestial rings. The angelic concerts are joined by the saints and other heavenly singers. Their music observes the same mathematical rules as does that of the planets and spheres. The *Musurgia universalis* of that great Baroque figure, Athanasius Kircher, is a veritable treasury of angel music, some of which he writes out—for example, on the title page—for the reader's edification. Thus do the nine moons of Jupiter constitute that planet's separate chorus, singing rounds, canons, and the like. Each planet, moreover, and its sphere is occupied by a conscious Intelligence—a singing angel, muse, or siren who acts as a sort of concertmaster. God conducts.[13]

This belief that outer space was filled with music-making angels was no mere pious opinion. "The psalmody of the Church Militant [i.e., the Church on Earth] is the daughter of the heavenly hymnody which resounds forever before the throne of God," wrote Urban VIII, one of the greatest patrons and builders of the early Baroque.[14] Anyone who didn't think so was a heretic.

Heavenly performers are not limited to angels and saints. They include souls and intelligences—the latter being needed also for, among other things, the intricate calculations governing the planets' courses. This was a theological proposition that some reformers, like Kepler, would actually embellish with new scientific knowledge.[15] In the fifth book of the *Harmonices mundi*, describing one of his dreams, Kepler saw the universe populated with singing spirits. "Of course these creatures exist!" he says in effect: why would the Creator have gone to the trouble of constructing this colossal temple, with all its distant planets and its massive central Sun, and not have peopled it?[16] Nor was all this, for Kepler, mere dream-stuff. It was a matter of contemporary musicology. "The mortal musicians who had invented [polyphony] on Earth," he writes, "had been mere 'apes of their Creator.'"[17] And he adds that the angels' music is what today we call Baroque polyphony (i.e., roughly from Monteverdi through Bach).

One particularly obvious source of visual information about angel music is in the omnipresent painted domes of the Baroque. These frequently depict the heavens, often complete with planets and almost always with rings of singing angels. Curiously enough, the domes are frequently Copernican

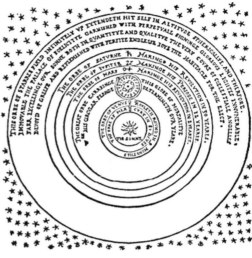

rather than Ptolemaic, with a central Sun blazing behind the figure of God the Father, Christ, or the Holy Spirit.

In Corrado Giaquinto's *Celestial Glory: The Coronation of the Virgin* in the Royal Palace, Madrid (1755, fig. 2.3), we see just such groups. Since we're discussing cosmic geometry, I will mention that the rings of angels are what mathematicians call toruses or anchor rings—i.e., doughnut-like shapes. I say this because toruses are formed by rotation and are therefore the cousins of spheres. (In architecture, the column-base moldings that resemble the outside of a doughnut are also called toruses; so the shape and its name are omnipresent in architecture. As we shall also see, Blondel gives column-base toruses a voice in his architectural music-making.)

In Giaquinto's fresco, meanwhile, the Holy Spirit is emblazoned on the central Sun, centered within a golden haze that sheds its light everywhere, a haze perhaps of influence or quintessence. Then comes an outer sphere of seraphim, then clouds of empty space, then more outer toruses—empyreans, these were called—of saints kneeling in adoration of the blue-clad Virgin as she approaches the Throne of Grace.

Fig. 2.3. Corrado Giaquinto, *The Coronation of the Virgin* (dome of chapel, Royal Palace, Madrid, 1755). Photograph courtesy of Archiv Mas, Barcelona.

Fig. 2.4. Thomas Digges's Cosmography. From Digges, *A Perfit Description of the Coelestiall Orbes, according to the Most Ancient Doctrine of the Pythagoreans: Lately Revived by Copernicus* (1569; reprinted in *Prognostication of Right and Good Effect*, by Leonard Digges [Aldburgh, England, 1592]).

As noted, one must imagine these angels all singing. We are told that their constant text is "blessedness, and honor, and glory, and power, forever and ever" (Revelation 5:11, 8:2ff.). We thus see the whole of Giaquinto's scene, and its innumerable cousins, as exercises in heavenly geometrics. The invisible spherical architecture of the empyrean is made visible to our earthly eyes by its populations of singing saints and angels.

Giaquinto's conception is clearly linked—I will not say indebted—to the pictures of the astronomical cosmos as it had long been supposed to be. As noted these visions saw the heavens as a set of concentric spheres, invisible to mortal view but nonetheless present. Often, too, the spheres are filled with angels. In Thomas Digges's view (fig. 2.4), which dates from 1592, we see a central Sun and then, successively and concentrically, the spheres of Mercury, Venus, that of Earth, which latter takes up a large swath of space mostly occupied by Luna and her orbits; and then Mars, Jupiter, and Saturn, each placed in accordance with its period (i.e., the time span of its orbit). Around the outside of these spheres is a more distant orb containing the whole. Beyond that, in turn, are the stars, unenclosed by an orb. This feature in Digges's diagram is now being interpreted as one of the earliest proposals that the universe is infinite in extent.[18]

And, we note particularly, there are angels in Digges's heavens, angels who inhabit a palace. He labels the outermost orb as follows: "The orbe of starres fixed infinitely up extendeth hit selfe in altitude sphericallye and therefore immovable the pallace of foelicitye garnished with perpetuall shininge glorious lightes innumerable farr excelling our Sonne both in quantitye and qualitye the very court of coelestiall angeles devoid of greefe and replenished with perfite endlesse joye the habitacle of the elect." The many crystal domes, in short, with their toruses of angels, compose a vast and glorious architecture.[19]

ARCHITECTURAL ACOUSTICS

Another reason for investigating musical sound in terms of architecture has to do with the spaces within which sounds are produced and heard. A church, legislative chamber, or concert hall designed to reinforce and clarify musical and spoken sound can be thought of as an enlarged version of a musical instrument's resonator, or even of the human voice box.

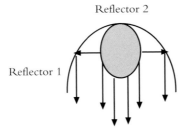

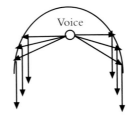

Fig. 2.5. Parabolic sound reflector with secondary reflector inside it

Fig. 2.6. Voice projection in a parabolic room. Both redrawn from Marin Mersenne, *Harmonicorum libri* (Paris: Baudry, 1636). Note that Mersenne's diagrams do not follow the rule that the angle of incidence should equal the angle of reflection.

"Architectural acoustics" is a modern term but the thing itself goes way back.[20] The Greeks and Romans had built indoor theaters for music known as odeia—rooms or halls that provided performance spaces and seating for audiences. The spaces presumably sought to channel and amplify the performers' music and speech.[21] As to outdoor structures, where the audiences were usually much larger, Vitruvius discusses the use of strategically placed sound-resonators or boosters. These were bronze vases distributed throughout an auditorium and tuned to musical intervals such as fourths and fifths (Vitruvius, *De architectura* 5.5.1). Presumably when speakers and singers sounded those pitches (and Vitruvius has in mind chanting, probably, rather than conversational speech), their notes were amplified or perhaps retransmitted to a new part of the audience.

The age of the Baroque, while almost always quoting Vitruvius, embarked on its own elaborations of these ideas. The French natural philosopher and musical theorist Marin Mersenne begins his treatise *Harmonicorum libri* (1636) with a short illustrated essay on architectural acoustics.[22] He maintains that "sonic rays" (*radios sonoros*) are projected in conical form. The rays bounce off inclined planes and can be mapped onto screens or reflectors shaped in plan like half-ellipses or parabolas. The reflectors focus and project sounds by locating the speaker or player at one of the ellipse's two foci.

In figure 2.5 is a Mersenne-derived diagram of an outer concave sound reflector; within its inner center, a bit like the ovary of a flower, is a smaller convex reflector, or re-reflector. Mersenne claims that sounds entering from the center of the open ellipse of the outer reflector, following its long axis, can be bounced twice—laterally, across part of the smaller reflector's width; and then, in a second bounce, back out toward the listeners, now with the sound broadened to fill the whole width of the outer reflector.

In figure 2.6 is another diagram redrawn from Mersenne. Now we have projection rather than amplification. The speaker's voice is located at one of the foci. The radios sonoros project outward to the sides of the ellipse, and thence to the audience beyond—that is, outward to the lower, open part of the reflector. Mersenne does not say so but he is employing the principles of light-reflection used in magic lanterns and reflector telescopes (see chapter 3)—and, indeed, he is also employing the principles described in a story Diodorus Siculus tells about Archimedes, who set enemy ships afire by focusing giant mirrors on them.[23] The younger Galileo—Vincenzo's astronomer-son—redid the mathematics behind this claim and decided that Archimedes' feat was believable.[24]

Kircher's *Musurgia universalis* (Universal Music-Making), already mentioned, contained many illustrations of architectural acoustics.[25] Kircher's phrase for them is *magia phonocamptica,* from the μαγέια, φόνο, κάμπτερ, "the magic [or technique] of sound-bending"). Much of Kircher's discussion is derived from Mersenne, by the way, whom Kircher does not adequately credit.

Nonetheless, Kircher's book is a landmark in the history of acoustic theory. He considers music and speech, indoors and outdoors. He is particularly concerned with echoes and reverberations. He writes of caves and classical buildings where strange, elaborated echoes were to be heard, and about how echoes may be bounced onward for long periods of time. He writes about the percussive power of resonance, as in the trumpets that blew down the walls of Jericho.[26]

Kircher also reinforces the analogies, so common in the Baroque period, between music and light. To him, sound, especially musical sound, is the ape of light: *sonus lucis simia est.* He diagrams the geometries of the *linea actionis phonicae,* the line or ray of "phonic action." And, indeed, as with Mersenne, his diagrams of sound reflection and refraction greatly resemble optical lens and reflector diagrams.[27] For Kircher, acoustics, like optics, is a matter of spherical and conic sections.

Also, for Kircher, the rooms in which sound best projects tend to be regular polygons, or else to have elliptical, parabolic, or hyperbolic plans. Kircher's words for these three-dimensional volumes are *ellipsoplaste, paraboloplaste, hyperboloplaste* (*plaste* = molded).[28] With such architectural resonators, says Kircher, you can make three voices sound like a hundred. (We will discuss these shapes further in chapter 6.)

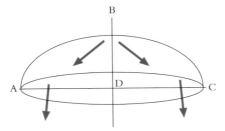

Fig. 2.7. How a dome
amplifies sound. After
Athanasius Kircher,
Musurgia universalis
(Rome: Typographicum
haeredum Fratelli Corbi-
netti, 1650). The source
of the sound is directly
beneath the center of
the dome.

Kircher shows how domes and domed buildings are particularly good for
acoustics (fig. 2.7). A room that carries the sound straight across, horizontally
from A to C, will deaden it, he says. But if the sound, shown by red arrows,
is able to leap up inside the dome, and mix together in the semicircular con-
tainer, "they will be forcefully heard all together in the polar area."[29] From
which, I presume, they descend, reinforced, to the listeners below (also
shown by red arrows). Kircher adds that if the dome interior is smooth, the
"sonic lines" will come together in it with particular unity and power.

Kircher's discussion includes an extraordinary architectural project. This
is for a palace provided with normal rectilinear rooms and courtyard but
filled with huge "acoustical instruments" shaped like Kircher's hyperbolo-
plastes, and also reminiscent of the anatomical images of the inner ear that
he prints in his book. These colossal cochleas and eardrums project voices,
even whispers, from one part of the building to another.

But Kircher's big set piece is his re-creation of Vitruvius's theater with its
bronze resonators. He calls it a theater of echoes (fig. 2.8). More or less based
on the Theater of Marcellus in Rome, it is a concave three-story edifice rising on one side of an oval orchestra space. The central part of the facade follows this oval. The facade is also divided into cells or bays. As I interpret
Kircher's text and drawing, the central three of these, on each of the theater's
three floors, are equipped with hollow bronze vessels and bells, with a vase
on the second floor representing the musical fundamental of the whole system, and with the other vases tuned to that fundamental's harmonics.[30]

Harmonics are the overtones that sound when a musically tuned note is
struck. With a C as the fundamental, for instance, the harmonics would be
the G, C, E, G, C, D, and so on, above it. Then in the successively higher octaves the harmonics become a regular scale of steps and half-steps. Kircher
calls the lower tier of openings in his theater the harmonic order. The mid-

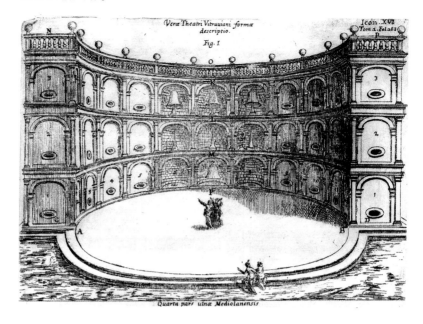

Fig. 2.8. "Theater of
Echoes" from Athana-
sius Kircher, *Musurgia
universalis*, 1650. Photo
courtesy of Beinecke
Rare Book and Manu-
script Library, Yale Uni-
versity.

dle tier is the chromatic order, and the upper the diatonic. In other words, the sounds boosted by the ground-floor vases make a chord of tonic and fifth, the second-floor vases add thirds, and the upper floor sounds a complete scale. Taken all together the three orders form a fourth order that Kircher calls the symphonic. In calling these tones "orders" and incorporating them into a building, Kircher is of course exploiting analogies between music and architecture; and, I would like to think, he is proposing a way in which that architecture may embody a fundamental and its resulting harmonics or overtones—certainly an original idea for its time.

The other cells in Kircher's theater are walled up except for their elliptical openings. These connect conduits or pipes leading from cell to cell, all of them delivering sounds and resonances from the central openings to the theater's outer curves. In short, Kircher's Vitruvian theater is a great amplifier for the actors' voices.[31]

SOUNDING BOXES FOR PREACHERS

Mersenne and Kircher were discussing important issues of their time. Particularly in Protestant countries, where the sermon ranks at least as high as the ritual, church interiors began to be built literally as resonators. Often, massive pulpits were raised above the congregation, with sounding boards behind or above them that were intended to refract, focus, and boost the preacher's voice as well as make him visibly prominent—which, of course, helped make him audible.

In Great Britain such churches were sometimes called "preaching boxes." Possibly the term was borrowed from the wind-boxes of pipe organs (or from the voice boxes of the preachers themselves). Anyway, Sir Christopher Wren and the other English Baroque architects turned out many a preaching box.[32]

In Wren's St. Andrew's-by-the-Wardrobe, London, as originally erected (fig. 2.9), the pulpit rose way up into the center of everything, a giant canopied phallus whose purpose was to propagate the seed of the Gospel ("And thy seed . . . thou shalt spread abroad to the west, and to the east, and to the north, and to the south" [Genesis 28:14]).[33] Over the preacher's head floated a huge hexagonal sounding-board—a sort of acoustical halo. Presumably the curved nave vault was also designated as a sound-reflector, while the side galleries may have worked as baffles to cut down on reverberations. That Wren's churches were conceived as theaters for the preacher's visual and sonic presence, the architect himself attests.[34]

Giant pulpits in Roman Catholic churches also acted as sound projectors. Oftentimes these pulpits were curvaceous erections reflecting Baroque ideas about acoustics.[35] In figure 2.10, for example, is a project by Charles de Wailly for a pulpit for the Paris church of St.-Sulpice. Though dating from well into the period of neoclassicism—indeed from 1789, birth-year of the Revolution—it is nonetheless a sumptuous exercise in late Baroque design. Bilaterally symmetrical stairs, like two faces of a polyhedron, mount to an immense central cylinder. The cylinder opens up in front like the lower

Fig. 2.9. Sir Christopher Wren's interior of St. Andrew's-by-the-Wardrobe, 1685–94 (before reconstruction). From J. Clayton, *The Dimensions, Plans, Elevations, and Sections of the Parochial Churches of Sir Christopher Wren* (London, 1848–49).

part of an organ pipe. Within that opening the preacher gestures to the
heavens, whose beams are bathing him in supernal light. He is the voice of
a mighty instrument. Over his head floats a huge disk filled with radiating
designs, a sun-disk. On its roof is a monumental sculptured Charity with her
infants. The Gospel suckles believers as Charity does her orphans. Other al-
legories sit, maybe a bit like Plato's planetary muses, on the staircase's massive pedestals. Enraptured auditors populate the floor.[36] The sun-disk reflects the preacher's voice downward and the cylindrical reflector behind
him bounces it outward. The great staircase, meanwhile, mimics an out-
pouring of Kircher's "radios sonoros."

BLONDEL: THE ATTIC BASS

The French architectural theorist François Blondel and his musician colleague René Ouvrard were particularly open to the analogies between
music and architecture.[37] Both believed that musical ratios—that is, tuned
intervals—lie at the origins of architectural proportions.[38] If the grand siè-
cle was characterized by the Quarrel of the Ancients and Moderns, Blondel
very much wanted to be counted as a Modern. It was in this mood that he
asserted that the unity between musical and architectural proportions is not
a matter of pure mathematics, as Renaissance Neoplatonists and their predecessors had held, but is grounded in experimental physics.[39] Here Blondel
comes close to more recent authorities—for example, Hermann Helmholtz, who based his theories entirely on the physics of musical tone, and on
the physiology of the ear, rather than a priori theory. By Helmholtz's day, in
fact, it was clear that the ear will accept musical ratios that are far from the
simple ones used in ideal or theoretical discussions. For example, the equal
temperament used in most modern keyboard instruments has double- and
even triple-digit ratios.[40]

In his *Cours d'Architecture*, however, Blondel constitutes a canon of the
most desirable shapes using the simplest ratios. There is a total of eight. In
figure 2.11, in which I redraw Blondel's scheme, I have first notated the
names of the intervals and then notated them musically.[41] Below the notes,
I give the numerical ratio that produces each interval. Beneath the number
ratios I have drawn out Blondel's eight prescribed rectangles, color-coded to
enhance their variety. These same ratios can produce many shapes besides
rectangles. But I must warn that these ratios work only with string-lengths
and the lengths of air columns, and only within the octave. However, that's
enough to account for a good-sized chunk of Baroque music.

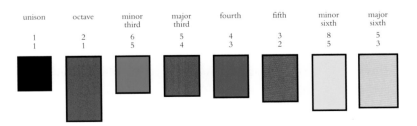

unison	octave	minor third	major third	fourth	fifth	minor sixth	major sixth
1 1	2 1	6 5	5 4	4 3	3 2	8 5	5 3

Fig. 2.11. François Blondel's scheme of eight consonant musical intervals, their numerical ratios, and their relevant rectangles. Adapted from François Blondel, *Cours d'architecture enseigné dans l'Académie royale d'architecture* (Paris: Chez l'Auteur, 1698).

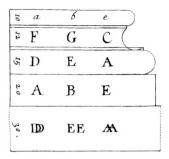

Fig. 2.12. Attic column base with its corresponding chord in three different plagal modes. From Blondel, *Cours d'architecture*.

Blondel pushes things a lot further than this, however. And it is in his more advanced musico-architectural thought that he shows his greatest originality (or modernity). People had been talking about music and architecture for centuries. Vitruvius had specified the octave, fifth, and fourth as consonances. But he never actually said that, therefore, buildings should embody the consonant intervals 1:2, 3:4, and 2:3 (though he does advocate these ratios, simply as ratios, often enough). Nor did Vignola, Palladio, Scamozzi, and Blondel's other predecessors contribute much that was new to Vitruvius's notions about music. Even Daniele Barbaro, whose 1567 edition of Vitruvius is the most elaborate to have been published so far, and who writes extensively about ancient music, does not actually make much of an analogy between musical intervals and architectural ones.[42] Blondel's *Cours* was therefore a musico-architectural landmark. And, as I have noted, it remained the main textbook for French and other architectural students for a good century after it was first published.[43]

Figure 2.12 is an example of Blondel's novel thinking.[44] He gives us the profile of an Attic base. Such a base would normally support an Ionic, Corinthian, or Composite column, and is therefore one of the most common sights in architecture. It consists of two toruses (the "doughnuts" mentioned earlier), which are the two convex moldings. They are separated by a scotia—the concave molding sandwiched between them. In a proper Attic base these larger concave or convex moldings are separated from each other by narrow flat bands called fillets, just as in Blondel's sketch. This much of the base is round in plan; but it rises from a pair of superimposed square plinths.

How do we get music out of all this? The thicknesses of these five main elements, says Blondel, increase in descending order according to a sequence of measuring-units that he has written on his image: 10:12:15:20:30. The unit here is probably a module—that is, some set fraction of the column diameter—but Blondel doesn't say. He does say that these particular proportions come from Vitruvius (I have not found them there). But note, anyhow, that the numbers form a harmonic progression or sequence, whose core version would be 3:5:8:10.[45]

Blondel points out that this sequence, and therefore the proportions of the moldings conforming to it, can be translated into musical tones that produce three different chords. He has printed the chords next to his Attic base profile: D–A–D–F–A, E–B–E–G–B, and A–E–A–C–E. (Blondel notates his three chords simply by writing three different clefs for a single set of notes.) As he notates them, the chords would be minor. However, Blondel's number sequence demands a major third with a minor third above it—not the other way round.[46] In modern notation, then, and corrected, the music of Blondel's Attic base would be as in figure 2.13.

Fig. 2.13. Blondel's three chords in modern notation (sharps added)

In this form the analogy between moldings and music works out well. Let's take the D major chord. Low D to A above it equals a fifth, which in turn equals the 3:2 ratio (i.e., Blondel's first pair of ratios, 30:20). The next interval in the chord is that same A plus the D above it, which is a fourth, or 4:3 (Blondel's 20:15). The next interval, D–F#, is a major third, or a 5:4 ratio (Blondel's 15:12). And the upper interval in the chord is F#–A, a minor third, or 6:5 (Blondel's 12:10). Thus the widths of Blondel's moldings do in fact equal his sequence 30:20:15:12:10. The two other chords, E major and A major, would have these same ratios at different pitches.

But we mustn't forget the fillet moldings. "As to the fillets," Blondel writes, "they are the notes fusées and semifusées in music. They serve to create passages that by their modulation make the essential notes of the chords (or consonances) agreeable and of greater sweetness." My musicologist colleague Claude Palisca tells me he has never seen the term *notes fusées*. Nor have I found it in any dictionary. What Blondel seems to mean is that the fillet moldings are like appoggiaturas—fleeting dissonances, grace notes, that resolve into consonances. In short, and whatever notes fusées may be, however, it is undeniable that Blondel has made a reasonable case for his analogy between architecture and music.

But now I must ruefully add that while I can find comparable "chords" in some other column bases, they are by no means universal. Keeping in

Fig. 2.14. Attic base from
Giambattista Piranesi's
funeral candelabrum,
mid-1770s.

mind how many possible ratios there are in the world of numbers, and how
few possible ratios there are in music, many molded bases have no musical
equivalents whatever. I will leave to someone else the task of making a cen-
sus. But let's look at one more case that will be instructive.

In figure 2.14 I illustrate what can only be called, by Blondel's standards,
a "dissonant" set of moldings. In the 1770s the great Italian etcher Giambattista Piranesi incorporated this base into a candelabrum for his own tomb in
Santa Maria del Priorato, Rome, dating from the mid-1770s. We have in this
base just what Blondel had: a round plan, two toruses separated by a scotia,
and intercalated fillets—though here the fillet on the top of the scotia swells
out umbrella-wise into a frieze of palmettes. Piranesi then omits Blondel's
two lower square plinths. Anyway, reading upward, as I judge from the photograph, you get proportions of 6:8:7:5. This is not a musico-mathematical
sequence, though 6:8 (i.e., 3:4) is a perfect fourth, C–F. But 7:5 is an augmented fourth or tritone—for example, F–B-natural.[47] Piranesi's Attic base
therefore produces the chord printed in figure 2.15. There is no way these
notes could be put together into a consonant chord like Blondel's.

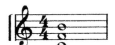

Fig. 2.15. An unresolved
dissonance

Nevertheless Piranesi's "dissonance" is perfectly musical. From the zil-
lions of possible ratios that these moldings could plausibly have, Piranesi,
consciously or not, has chosen relationships that do in fact correspond to
notes on a standard musical scale. Indeed you could hear just this sound in
any piece—though some sort of subsequent resolution would normally
occur, such as the B resolving down to the adjacent A. That would turn Piranesi's B into what you might call a note fusée, the sort of appoggiatura
that, with its temporary dissonance, sweetens the final consonance—in this
case an F major chord in its second inversion.

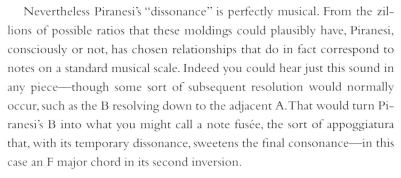

Assuming, as I will for the sake of prudence, that Piranesi was uninfluenced by the ideas of Blondel and Ouvrard, he most likely picked his ratios in purely visual terms. (It is perfectly possible to achieve all these effects by, as they say, eyeballing them. But you must have the right kind of eyeballs.) And this, paradoxically, only reinforces the idea that architectural ratios, all by themselves, might *want*, as it were, to be musical—just as architectural distributions, like rosebushes, might *want* to obey Fibonacci sequences.

CONSONANCE AND DISSONANCE

Practically all music combines dissonances and consonances. The subtitle of Kircher's *Musurgia universalis* is *sive Ars magna consoni et dissoni*.[48] As noted, however, dissonances normally resolve almost immediately, though in the seventeenth century they could sometimes be prolonged; and, sometimes, never actually resolve at all.[49]

There are different types of dissonance. One, which is by far the most common statistically, consists of all the possible "strange" ratios or intervals that are not part of any accepted tuning system. Some of these might seem innocent enough—say, for example, 17:25. A room with that shape, in plan, might look well enough, though if one was a Blondelian and could compare it with a nearby room that was fully consonant, say 16:24 (2:3, a perfect fifth), one would presumably be happier with the consonant room. In music itself, however, nonmusical ratios can create the most appalling sounds. In Italy, the horns on some sports cars and especially aggressive trucks have these cruelly raucous intervals; they seem intended to cause other motorists to have heart attacks, and probably they do. What this makes us realize, again, is that Blondel and even Piranesi, in their two bases, entirely excluded all these nonmusical intervals from their architecture. By eliminating them, and thus eliminating their associated shapes, Blondel, Piranesi, and all likeminded architects of the age were left with an extremely narrow canon within the huge pool of statistical possibilities.

Another sort of dissonance, this a fully musical one, comes with intervals such as sevenths and seconds—intervals that, like Piranesi's unresolved augmented fourth, absolutely *do* belong to accepted tuning systems. Today on ordinary keyboards this type of dissonance is heard in major and minor seconds and sevenths (B–C, C–C#, C–B, C–B♭, and diminished or augmented

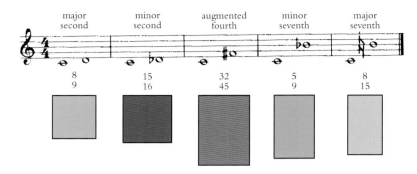

major second	minor second	augmented fourth	minor seventh	major seventh
8 9	15 16	32 45	5 9	8 15

Fig. 2.16. Five dissonant musical intervals, with their numerical ratios, and the rectangles based on those same ratios

intervals (e.g., C–F#; see fig. 2.16).[50] These can be associated with the rectangles printed below the music staff (and for which I have picked out an appropriately dissonant set of color codings).

Still another type of dissonance in music and architecture, Blondel says, lies in intervals that may be technically consonant but that are too extreme—for example, the octave and fifth, otherwise known as a twelfth, whose ratio is 3:1; or the double octave or disdiapason, 4:1; and other great leaps like these. Blondel remarks that in architecture this type of "dissonance" could even expand well beyond the normal musical range—even beyond human hearing—to infinity. But, he says, all this should be avoided. Instead, architectural intervals ought to be like those in an easily sung melody—in other words, with plenty of seconds and thirds, not many sevenths, and no thirteenths and fifteenths.[51]

Thus the twelfth, which is an octave and a fifth, 3:1, would in architecture be a triple square. It is "dissonant," as far as Blondel is concerned, even though it compounds two mutually consonant intervals. To be proper, he says, a twelfth needs an intermediate tone, say the intervening octave, between the two extremes. In short, the C–G' in figure 2.17 would not be acceptable, but the C–C'–G' on the right would be. It would be even better to add a G above middle C and an E above high C. That would bring the chord into line with the Blondel chords illustrated earlier.

Put into spatial and architectural terms, below in figure 2.18, the upper facade, with a height of 1 and a length of 3, which makes a musical twelfth, would in Blondel's terms be "dissonant." But the same facade with a frontispiece or jog that is 1:2, set into the 1:3 facade (C–C'–G'), would be acceptable. Obviously the more judiciously these longer intervals are filled in with

the proper intervening subdivisions—not only jogs and reen-
trant angles but pilasters, openings, frontispieces, and so on—the
richer and more harmonious will be the result. One could apply
the principle to a building's vertical composition as well.

Fig. 2.17. Dissonance re-
solved by an intermedi-
ate tone

And the same would apply to a plan, to an ornamental frieze or panel, to
a decorative motif, or to a town square—practically any piece of architectural design. Long unrelieved stretches are "dissonant" and should be filled
in with consonant intermediate tones, just the way two voices, one very
high and one very low, need intermediate voices to achieve a satisfactory
sonority. Blondel mentions a catalog of similar analyses, compiled by Ouvrard, of consonances, and of both good and bad dissonances, that he finds
in specific public squares, basilicas, treasuries, prisons, hôtels de ville, theaters,
baths, vestibules, cabinets, and peristyles.[52]

Can one extrapolate any of these ideas to other architects, other architecture? Yes. Aside from small-scale dissonances in moldings and room dimensions, one clear example of architectural dissonance, and this of a dis-
tinctly nonmusical type (at least at the scale of a whole building), would be
the plans and major volumes of Wren's City churches in London. These de-
lightful but very odd buildings were erected in the squeezed labyrinths of
streets left behind by the Great Fire of 1666. Sharply irregular plans were
often necessary. Yet, mathematician that he was, Wren would usually manage

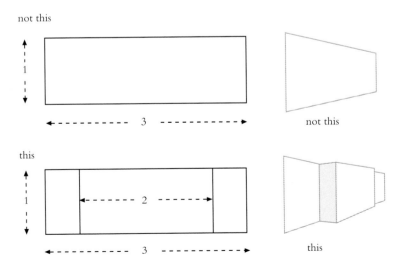

Fig. 2.18. *Above*, a dissonant architectural re-
lationship; *below*, a consonant architectural
relationship. Both sug-
gested by Blondel,
Cours.

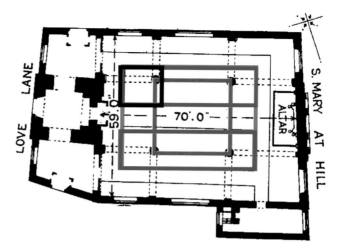

Fig. 2.19. Wren's plan of
St. Mary at Hill (London,
begun 1670; since re-
built). From J. Clayton,
*The Dimensions, Plans,
Elevations, and Sections
of the Parochial
Churches of Sir Christo-
pher Wren* (London,
1848–49). Colored rec-
tangles added.

to graft some geometrical goody onto a church's arbitrary footprint—an embedded regular decagon, a Greek cross, a hemisphere, or the like. The margin or frame of the church plan, then, may be exceedingly dissonant—not music at all, just noise. But the central interior space resolves that dissonant frame into a full-fledged consonance. Rather than a single note fusée resolving into a concord, with Wren you resolve into your concord from something more like one of Charles Ives's tone clusters.

Thus with St. Mary at Hill (fig. 2.19), the site dictated an irregular heptagon with a canted right-hand side, an irregular lower-left-hand jog, and a sloping base leading up to an equally lopsided trio of rooms along the Love Lane side of the site. Upon that irregular shape, however, Wren imposed a squarish nave or auditorium articulated by a tetrastyle—that is, a square of four central columns two by two, a device found in Vitruvius and Palladio. As its center the Greek cross formed by these columns and their entablatures has a perfect square (1:1, an octave, shown in red) superimposed on two rectangular sets of pews that, each in itself, is a double 3:4 rectangle (two perfect fourths, shown in blue); a rectangle that also, taking both sets of pews together, composes a minor sixth (5:6, shown in green).

The functional center of the church, in terms of square-based proportions, consists, then, of superpartiens tertias and superpartiens quartas shapes. And the basic small square that generates these rectangles, shown in black, is effably related to the Greek cross's square. That is, the main red crossing square is larger than the generating black square by a proportion of 5:7.

There is also one subsidiary room in Wren's church, the entrance vestibule in the base of the tower. In plan this is a perfect square, and is, once again, precisely equal to the generating square.

SPATIAL TRIADS

So far we have looked at architecture as it may be said to produce musical tones; but we have concentrated on intervals, like C–E, rather than chords proper, which must consist of at least three different notes. Such three-note chords are called triads. Blondel's Attic base, we saw, though we discussed it only as a set of intervals, actually combined those intervals into sonorous five-note chords. But the chords remained triads, though with some of their component notes doubled. If we can find musical intervals in plans and facades, is there a way to find musical triads in three-dimensional architectural spaces? Like music, architecture is strongly involved with the triad. In architecture's case the triad is length plus depth plus height. Given our geometrico-musical thinking, therefore, a musical triad should, would, or could express space in its three dimensions.

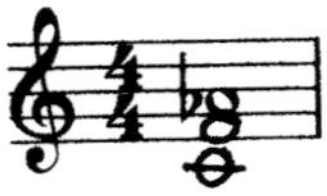

Fig. 2.20. An F minor tonic chord in its second inversion

Musical triads follow the architectural nature of the Baroque cosmos. Kepler, whose astronomical interests were deeply interwoven with music, wrote mostly about two-note intervals like thirds, fourths, and fifths, but he also allowed for celestial triads. Mercury, Earth, and Mars, he tells us, for example, often blend their voices at three different pitches. Even four-note harmony occasionally occurs.[53] He specifically likens this aspect of cosmic music to the traditional vocal chorus of earthly music with its sopranos, altos, tenors, and basses.[54]

Once one wishes to translate triads into spatial terms, however, a problem arises: let us take an F minor tonic chord in its second inversion—reading upward C, F, A♭ (fig. 2.20). Does one count the upper interval, F–A♭, as a minor third measured from F–C, which is a 5:6 ratio, or is it measured from the F, as a minor sixth, a 5:8 ratio? Musically we could do either—the same triad would sound in either case. On the other hand, a room with one wall at 3:4 (C–F) and another wall at 5:8 (a minor sixth, C–A♭) would be very different from a room in which that second wall was 5:6 (a minor third, F–A♭).

My mathematician colleague Michael Frame neatly solves the problem.

You have two sets of ratios. Multiply one set by the other. Or as he writes: "The ratio of lengths C to F is 3:4. The ratio of lengths A♭ to C is 4:5. Then the ratio of A♭ to C times the ratio of C to F is (4:5) × (3:4) = 3:5—exactly the ratio of A♭ to F."[55] (See fig. 2.21.)

THE MUSIC OF BERNINI'S BALDACCHINO

I will conclude this chapter by extrapolating triads, and even tunes, from perhaps the most famous construction in all of Baroque architecture— Bernini's baldacchino in St. Peter's. How does that masterpiece fit in with what we have been saying? Can we learn anything new about it, or about architecture generally, by investigating its "musical" content? Does its frozen music somehow help determine, or perhaps help us to understand, its visual magnificence?

I will begin by borrowing a term from Serlio: *corpo trasparente*, or the invisible rectilinear envelope within which the visible aspects of a building are inscribed. In the case of the baldacchino, the corpo trasparente is a set of parallelepipeds demarcating its main subdivisions.[56]

The photogrammetry drawings published by W. Chandler Kirwin (figs. 2.22, 2.23, and 2.24), which I will presume are the most accurate images of the baldacchino, show that, consciously or unconsciously, Bernini did in fact make use of ratios—all of which are musical. The largest rectangle within which the front of the baldacchino can be inscribed is 3:8, which is an octave and a fourth, or eleventh, C–F'. A major inner rectangle, measuring the width of the monument to the top of the ball at the summit, is 2:5, or an octave plus a major third—musically, a tenth. The rectangle from the base of the monument to the top of the main cornice is 9:6, a minor seventh. And the inner rectangle, rising from the base of the altar to the fringe of the lappets, is 3:5, a major sixth. The monument's side elevation has corresponding ratios, running from an outer double octave, through a twelfth, then to a minor sixth and, for the inner rectangle, 3:8—another eleventh (figs. 2.25 and 2.26).

If you play or sing either of these sets of notes they turn out to be perfectly musical, though they are clearly not what musicians of Bernini's period would have called proper melodies. The fact that the baldacchino is tall

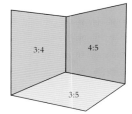

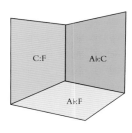

Fig. 2.21. *Top,* a room with 3:4 and 4:5 walls and a 3:5 floor; *bottom,* the same room with the geometric ratios transformed into musical notes, creating a triad

and thin makes for these spread-out intervals—which, by the way, also violate Blondel's taboo on large empty leaps.

Notwithstanding, the baldacchino's front elevation (always assuming our arbitrary platform of middle C) is a clear musical motif in the key of F major, with the repeated middle C as the second inversion of the tonic chord. In the side elevation, the sequence G'–C–A♭ is certainly, for the period of Lassus and Bach, unhappy—though, once again, we do have notes that compose a tune in the key of F. Both motifs, furthermore, could easily and suitably be harmonized in the style of the period.

Figs. 2.22 and 2.23. Bernini's baldacchino in St. Peter's (1624–33) (the side elevation is on the right). Photographs courtesy of W. Chandler Kirwin.

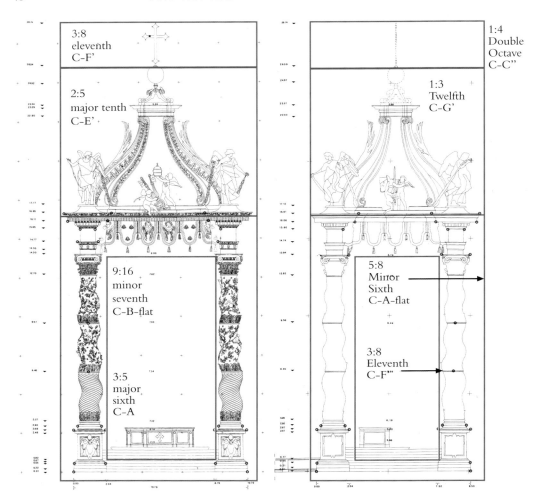

3:8
eleventh
C–F'

2:5
major tenth
C–E'

9:16
minor
seventh
C–B-flat

3:5
major
sixth
C–A

1:4
Double
Octave
C–C"

1:3
Twelfth
C–G'

5:8
Mirror
Sixth
C–A-flat

3:8
Eleventh
C–F'"

Fig. 2.24. The corpo trasparente of Bernini's baldacchino with overlays of component musical ratios.

In figure 2.25 I have rewritten the two tunes into a single melody. I'm cheating, I suppose. I make use of the entrenched and necessary musical tradition whereby a given note can be transposed an octave without overly damaging the musical sense (but which of course changes its number ratio since it changes its interval). But in this way we can make the baldacchino's original melodies more acceptable.[57] Anyway the old ratios and the new ones do remain linked, musically, even though the numbers change. This is because when we transpose a note up or down an octave, or even several octaves, it remains harmonically the same note.

Fig. 2.25. Intervals from the front elevation of Bernini's baldacchino.

Fig. 2.26. Intervals from the side elevation of Bernini's baldacchino (same order as fig. 2.24)

But to this we want to add our three-dimensional, "triadic" interpretation. Adapting Michael Frame's approach, we derive the third tone of the triad from the ratios of the two two-dimensional intervals, joining the main-front ratios to those of the side elevation. Thus if the principal rectangle for the front is 3:8 and that of the side elevation is 1:3, and we call the main rectangle's ratio C:F' and that of the side elevation C:G, then

3:8 × 1:3 = 3:24 or 1:8, a triple octave.

We thus have an eleventh, C–F'—that is, a triple octave C–C"—and a fifth, C–G, as the musical intervals of the outer shape of the baldacchino. Let's see what happens when we incorporate the other rectangles.

The major tenth rectangle is, on the front, C–E', 2:5. Its corresponding side rectangle is a minor sixth, C–Ab, 5:8.

2:5 :: 5:8 = 1:4, a double octave.

The rectangle on the baldacchino front is 9:16, a minor seventh—that is, C–Bb. The corresponding side rectangle is 5:8, a minor sixth, C–Ab. So:

5:9 :: 5:8 = 40:45 or 8:9, a whole tone

roundable to 3:1, a twelfth, C–G'.

The inner rectangles are respectively 3:5 and 3:8, a major sixth, C–E, and an eleventh, C–F'.

3:5 :: 3:8 = 15:24 or 5:8, a minor sixth.

Keeping our preference for a platform at middle C, then, we arrive at a ra-

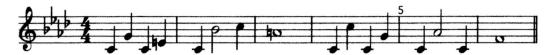

Fig. 2.27. The tune of
Bernini's baldacchino

tional set of musical intervals corresponding to the baldacchino's multiple, interpenetrating *corpi trasparenti* (fig. 2.27).

Bernini's masterpiece, we then note, is orthodoxly tonal. And we must keep in mind the literally hundreds of thousands of other, nonmusical intervals that he could have chosen for his ratios. Note too that here (as was not so in our analysis of the baldacchino's two-tone intervals) there was no need to monkey with the notes and ratios in order to bring them into musical form. The chords and/or melodies were directly produced by the four rectangles, as mathematically interrelated under the Frame system. Note also that the resulting tune makes use only of notes generated by the baldacchino. (Admittedly I have redone the meter by incorporating the two half-notes and two whole notes.)

Can I possibly think that Bernini consciously created the baldacchino thus, as a literal piece of frozen music? No, I cannot possibly think so. I have simply proposed a fresh but workable way of understanding what, most probably, he achieved by purely visual means (by eyeballing them with the right eyeballs). Bernini, like Piranesi but unlike Blondel, may be considered an unconscious practitioner whose designs turned out to be musically correct in a fairly exact visual analogy between the designer's sense of interval and the musician's perfect pitch.

We have looked at how music may be geometrically and architecturally mapped. One way of doing this was to examine Vincenzo Galilei's modular organ pipes. Another was the vision of a firmament filled with crystal domes and rings of angels, all making music—music that reflected, or generated, the rotations, size, shape, and spacing of the domes, just as earthly music was supposed to be the ape of heavenly music.

Another mode of frozen music, more earthbound, is architectural acoustics. As Kircher showed, buildings could be conceived as enormous sounding boxes, resonators designed for the scientific channeling and amplification of music and chant. Designed around the pulpit and the projection of the preacher's voice, some of Wren's City churches explore this idea.

An even closer intermarriage between music and architecture occurred in the 1670s in the theories of Blondel and Ouvrard. Blondel not only created a canon of architectural shapes that were supplied with musical intervals, he analyzed an Attic base as a set of intervals and chords. Borrowing Blondel's mantle, I then tried to show that his approach could be pushed further. If rectangles can be analyzed as musical intervals, three-dimensional spaces can be analyzed as triads. So I developed intervals, chords, and melodies out of the geometric envelope of Bernini's baldacchino.

THREE

THE LIGHT OF
UNSEEN WORLDS

P eople in the age of Gal-   N U M B E R ,   L I G H T ,
ileo, Kepler, Newton, and   A N D   M U S I C
Kircher believed that light
moved and functioned much like sound. And the two things
were otherwise interwoven. After all, frozen music could only be visible if
there was light to see it by. Moreover, like music, or like quintessence, ether,
and influence, light was considered a physical substance—a sort of fluid or
gas. As mentioned in chapter 1, Descartes in 1637 described light as "pressure" transmitted through a second cosmic substance that, as noted, he called
plenum.[1] Newton, disagreeing, thought light was an almost infinitely rare
"medium" (i.e., composed of widely separated particles) that permeated
every cranny of the universe.[2] Milton, meanwhile, equated light with both
quintessence and ether (*Paradise Lost* 7.220ff.).

One famous instance of the light/music analogy comes, indeed, with
Newton. In his *Opticks* (first published in 1704), he made a specific equation
between the colors into which a prism could divide sunlight, on the one
hand, and musical tones on the other (fig. 3.1). He showed that the resulting
bands of color corresponded precisely to the ideal interval ratios of a diatonic scale.

Newton's diagram resembles the monochord that in 1617 Robert Fludd
illustrates (fig. 3.2). Monochords were philosophical instruments, used to

Fig. 3.1. Isaac Newton, sunlight reflected through a prism onto paper, with the heights of the color bands equaling the intervals of the diatonic scale. From Newton, *Opticks; or, a Treatise of the Reflections, Refractions, Inflections & Colours of Light,* 1704. Reprint, London, 1730. Colors added.

Fig. 3.2. Robert Fludd, world-monochord with the elements coordinated to the intervals of the diatonic scale. From Fludd, *Utriusque cosmi maioris scilicet et minoris metaphysica* (Oppenheim: Typis Hieronymi Galleri, 1617).

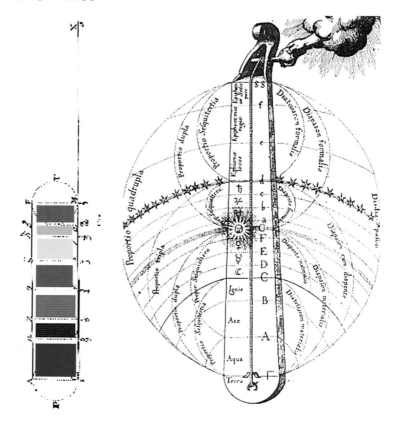

demonstrate the relationship of musical pitches to the physical distances between the instruments' stops—yet another instance, one could say, of tonal geometry or frozen music. Fludd's monochord consists of a string, its tuning peg, and the fretted neck against which the player's fingers stop the string to produce different pitches. The pitches on Fludd's monochord are the same as those in Newton's experiment with sunlight. That is, the widths of Newton's color bands are in the ratios 1:1, 8:9, 5:6, 3:4, 2:3, 8:5, 9:16, 1:2—in other words, major second, minor third, fourth, fifth, minor sixth, minor seventh, and octave. Like Fludd with his monochord, Newton marks the stops for these intervals on his diagram.[3]

But unlike Newton's colored band of musical stripes, Fludd's instrument is highly allegorical. It rises through a set of interpenetrating transparent spheres from Terra, at the bottom, to God's hand at the top. Emerging from a cloud, this hand tunes the great single string of the universe. The inter-penetrating spheres (which we mostly see in the forms of segments or quad-rants) represent, respectively, the four elements, the seven planets, and upper spiritual regions where the angels dwell. The spheres are arrayed in musico-geometric proportions and labeled as octaves, fourths, fifths, and with square-based ratios as well—sesquitertials, sesquialters, and the like.

But light, even Newton's purely physical kind, also interests Fludd. The monochord is emblazoned with stars, planets, and the Sun. The latter shines forth at G above middle C. The fixed stars shine down from the D above this. Each planet sheds its light from a note between middle C (Luna) to the C an octave higher (Saturn).

PROJECTING IMAGES

Light not only makes things visible, it projects images. In the previous chap-ter I noted that Corrado Giaquinto's painted heaven inside a dome is a sort of telescopic "view." The present chapter studies the way Baroque optical in-struments do something similar: they focus on scenes real and imaginary, and, more importantly, transmit them.

Few Baroque telescopists saw angels when they looked at the heavens. Yet, paradoxically, science had made discoveries that actually made the cosmos seem more, not less, inhabited than it had seemed earlier. At the beginning of the seventeenth century, for example, Galileo proved with his telescope that, far from being the smooth shining surface of a perfect sphere, as in tradition, the Moon was corrugated with mountains and valleys, and perhaps other Earthlike landscape features, possibly even rivers and seas (fig. 3.3).[4] Note in

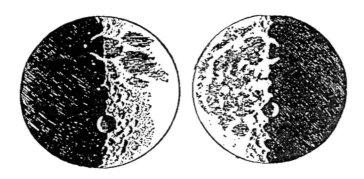

Fig. 3.3. Two views of the Moon's surface. From Galileo Galilei, *Sidereus Nuncius, or the Sidereal Messenger*, 1610.

Galileo's two images of the Moon what I can only call the powerful Caravaggesque modeling, the many craters and pockmarks suggesting volcanoes, and the contrast between these and the flatter areas of light and dark. What Galileo saw with his new instrument added to the Earthlike, indeed landscape, nature of the heavenly bodies.

Kircher, too, wrote almost ecstatically of an Earthlike lunar landscape.[5] He depicts the Moon as covered with oceans, continents, and islands. He describes the Moon's mountain ranges and even envisages possible forests and plantations: "We can only infer," he writes, "that the Moon is directly similar to our Earth, with many possibilities for propagating the seed that, blended by the Sun's rays, produces such a multitude of things on Earth that we daily admire." Needless to say, Kircher, a Jesuit, firmly believed that singing angels dwelt in these planetary landscapes. Meanwhile Kepler saw, or at least daydreamed that he saw, mighty architectural structures that had been erected by the Moon's inhabitants.[6]

THE EYE

Our primary knowledge of light comes from our eyes.[7] And the eye is quite a piece of architecture. It is a hollow sphere or spheroid with a lens at one pole and a concave interior surface, the retina, at the other. The retina repeats images transmitted to it by the lens. Like a very flexible optical instrument, the eye absorbs, refracts, and otherwise manipulates the light that forms these images (fig. 3.4).

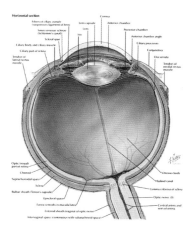

Fig. 3.4. Sagittal cross-section of a human eye. From Frank H. Netter, *Atlas of Human Anatomy* (Summit, N.J.: CIBA-Geigy, 1989).

In form and function the eye is a dome or sphere (light itself, of course, and especially projected light, radiates spherically). The eye-dome is framed by its retina (yellow in the picture), then successively by the choroid (pink; a vascular membrane containing large branched pigmented cells), then by the sclera (gray; a dense white fibrous outer coat).

At the dome's summit is the crystalline lens, an ellipsoidal solid, whose iris (pink) functions as a diaphragm, much as in a microscope. The lens is outwardly protected by its cornea (light gray). The cornea (a transparent coat on the eyeball covering iris and pupil) arches out over a void called the anterior chamber. We need not concern ourselves with the eye's other parts—the muscles that move it, the nerves along which its images travel, its vessels of communication, and its wrappings of tissue and biochemical coatings. I will say, however, that many of these other properties and functions have equivalents in optical instruments.

Optical instruments, in short, were often thought of as enlarged or extended eyes. Sometimes the enlargement could be to colossal—that is, to architectural—scale, as with the 70-foot telescopes made by Newton's contemporaries.[8] In his treatise on optics (1637), Descartes illustrates a huge human eye oriented upward, along with a man staring up into it (fig. 3.5). One purpose of the illustration is to show that exterior images (*V*, *X*, *Y*), when projected on the retina (*T*, *S*, *R*) are flipped. Thus the little triangle *V*, on the left outside the eye, turns into the little triangle *R*, inside the eye on the right. The diagram also shows that the lens, *L*, greatly refracts or condenses the outside image, reducing it to a tiny restatement of the exterior scene. Thus once again, by the way, we run into a phenomenon suggesting a self-similar graduated series. Note also, for future reference, that the visual rays are all of them cones—sources of the conic sections that will be so important in our study. But perhaps what is most important of all, at least for us, is that by changing its scale, Descartes makes his human eye into a dome or skylight. In Descartes's diagram, indeed, the eye is architectural in scale as well as design.[9]

Large or small, the human eye has always been a key element in symbolic iconography. Often its meanings have clustered around the notion of the di-

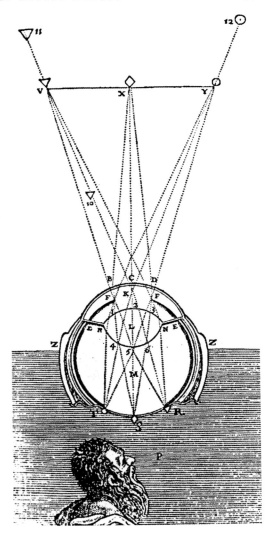

Fig. 3.5. An observer and a cross-section of an ox eye. From René Descartes, *Discours de la méthode plus la dioptrique, les météores et la géometrie*, 1637.

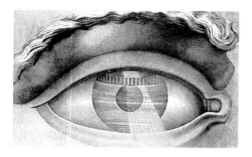

Fig. 3.6. Claude-Nicolas Ledoux, image of a theater for Besançon. From Ledoux, *L'Architecture considerée sous les rapports des moeurs, de la législation, et de l'art* (Paris, 1804).

vine all-seeing eye. In the 1780s Claude-Nicolas Ledoux was making real and allegorical designs for a proposed theater in Besançon (fig. 3.6). The theater is reflected in an eye looking out into an empty auditorium. What the eye sees, and what becomes its tiny inner projected image, is a circular theater all'antica, including a colonnaded seating area formed into a truncated cone, diminishing toward the stage.

Then, from an unseen source above, a conical beam of light shines down on the colonnade, streaming out from the pupil onto the lower eyelid and on outward onto the actor's face. Ledoux thus also illustrates the old classical notion that the eye projects beams of light outward like a lantern.[10] (It is still common to speak of eyes this way.) And the beam projected by the eye in Ledoux's design, moreover, is at the same time a stage light, a spotlight. It illuminates part of the colonnade and shines down on a section of the seating. (The theatrical spotlight, with its lens, reflector, and narrow concentrated beam, became possible with the introduction of Argand lamps at the end of the eighteenth century.[11]) Ledoux's notion of a theater as a gigantic eye, as an optical projection instrument, is full of meaning for what I am saying. In Greek, *theatron* means "thing seen." One also thinks of Roman amphitheaters, which are often compared to great eyes, embedded in the earth, staring up at the sky.

It is worth looking at the structure of Ledoux's design. Just as sound and acoustics were thought of in terms of cones and conic sections, so were light and light-projected images. Ledoux's eye is a confluence of interpenetrating cones—the cone that comes from the eye itself, the cone of the spotlight shining on the auditorium, and the wider, truncated cone of the auditorium proper. We will be looking at other conic interpenetrations later on, for example, in Wren's dome for St. Paul's—and indeed we will find these figures all through Baroque architecture.

LENSES AND REFLECTORS

The eye is the model for three significant Baroque light-projectors: the telescope, the microscope, and—last but not least—the magic lantern. Optical or artificial lenses are rigid versions of the eye's anatomical lens. The commonest type of artificial lens is the plano-convex, flat on one side and spherical on the other. Other lenses are convex or concave sections of two similar or dissimilar spherical segments. The fact that astronomers studied what were thought to be the crystalline heavenly spheres, and studied them through lenses that were themselves segments of crystalline or at least glass spheres, was by no means lost on Baroque astronomers. (Nor was the fact that the globe-shaped human eye includes a crystalline lens and is filled with what was known as a vitreous or crystalline humor.) Still other lenses were ground and polished into hyperboloids, paraboloids, and ellipsoids (i.e., hyperbolas, parabolas, and ellipses that were rotated into solids).

In mechanical light-projection, lenses are often used together with reflectors. The latter—usually polished metal mirrors—also make use of spheroidal shapes as well as of paraboloids and the like. If the mirrors Archimedes used at Syracuse to burn the Roman fleet were parabolic—that is, shaped like huge cups—their effect would have been greatly enhanced.[12] He would also have approximated the effect of a reflector in a magic lantern, which maintains its focus as its perimeters revolve to make a complete 180-degree curve. This enormously concentrates the light it reflects (figs. 3.7 and 3.10). As we shall see, the focus points used in drawing an ellipse or parabola, along with their three-dimensional forms, also constitute the focus point for light rays bounced into it.[13] We have already seen Kircher using these ideas in discussing acoustics.

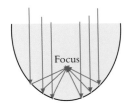

Fig. 3.7. Reflected light rays in a parabolic mirror

MICROSCOPES, TELESCOPES, AND MAGIC LANTERNS

The ancients, Seneca for one, knew that glass globes filled with water increased the apparent size of anything seen through them.[14] They also knew that similar devices could refract and condense rays of light. And, of course, it is this ability to bunch light rays into trajectories that leads on to the optical instrument proper.

But the true glass lens, like the eye's lens, not only condenses light but transmits images that are made out of light. It was apparently not until the thirteenth century that the image-transmitting lens came along, firstly in the form of eyeglasses. And not until Giovanni Battista della Porta, the sixteenth-century Neapolitan magician and philosopher, do we get descriptions of how lenses were shaped, ground, and polished—though he describes the technique itself as German.[15]

Then, early in the age of the Baroque, almost at one fell swoop, three optical instruments were invented: the telescope, the microscope, and the magic lantern. All three were virtuoso light-manipulators. They gathered it, filtered it, reflected it, condensed it, refracted it. And, more important, all three instruments projected images. With the microscope and the telescope, light gained new significance as the revealer of previously unsuspected worlds—with the microscope, worlds of unforeseen tininess; with the telescope, worlds unprecedentedly huge. Galileo reports in *The Starry Messenger* (1610) that through a telescope he had made for himself, "objects . . . appeared nearly one thousand times larger and over thirty times closer."[16]

The magic lantern, in turn, could import enlarged images from the microscope and telescope and then further reproduce, enlarge, shrink, and distort them. It could present them to audiences: put them in a theater (perhaps not unlike Ledoux's) so that many people—large crowds—could see the same image simultaneously.

The telescope seems to have been invented in Holland when in 1608 a certain Hans Lippershey applied for a patent.[17] More mystery surrounds the exact origin of microscopes, and they did not become prominent in scientific work for another half-century after they began to be built.[18] Thereafter, however, Anthoni van Leewenhoek and Robert Hooke made many important discoveries with microscopes.[19]

When lenses refract, bend, and concentrate light, the individual beams are gathered into cones and stellated or radiating bodies, like sunbursts. The individual beams are called "pencils," a term borrowed, appropriately, from projective geometry.

Lenses are mainly used in axial concentric groups, as in figure 3.8. They are mounted at set distances from one another, depending on their focal length (the distance from them at which the image is sharp). Lenses may enlarge and enhance detail, but all sorts of aberrations usually come into play that need to be counteracted, mostly with more lenses. The aberrations, which affect both the colors and forms of the images seen, can also be controlled with one or more diaphragms or adjustable apertures that act like the iris of the human eye. The diaphragms filter out stray pencils that diminish

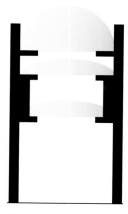

Fig. 3.8. Three plano-convex lenses set concentrically into a tube or stand

the image's brightness or otherwise distort it. It is the principle used in changing the f-stops on a camera.

Figure 3.9 shows a portable eighteenth-century wooden camera obscura (with a lens as opposed to a pinhole) with its foreground and rear walls removed. The lens is in the hutch on top and is mounted vertically, which condenses and projects the image from the exterior view reflected in the mirror.[20] The artist sits on the bench and draws on a screen mounted on the desk, the last surface onto which the image is projected. As Philippe Comar points out, it only remained for early experimenters such as Nièpce and Daguerre to replace the screen with an emulsion-coated plate, and photography was born.[21]

A magic lantern does all these things in reverse and inside out. Inside the box is a light-source such as a candle or, later, an Argand lamp. Behind it is a reflector. This forces as much light as possible into a single narrow cone. A slide with a translucent image on it is located at the focusing center of the system, at the point where the image is flipped, and a set of condensing and objective lenses then projects the slide's image onto a screen some distance from the projector. Because the lenses are adjustable, the projection can be either smaller or larger than the original. Thus the projected image travels along the cone of light from the magic lantern, continuously being enlarged. Once again, in short, a self-similar progressive series.

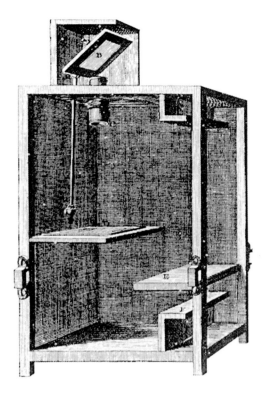

Fig. 3.9. A portable camera obscura illustrated in Diderot's *Encyclopédie*, 1751–72

We do not nowadays think of magic lanterns, those stalwarts of art-history lecturers, as scientific instruments. Figure 3.10 depicts a late-eighteenth-century specimen taken from J. G. Kruenitz's *Oikonomisch-Technologisch Enzyclopädie* of 1773. Indeed, in these early days magic lanterns tended to live up to their name. In the illustration, the slide (shown as a disk with an upside-down image inside the lantern at *F*), represents a heavily draped figure that is probably intended to be a ghost. Instead of a screen the image is projected onto a plume of smoke. As Gian Piero Brunetta makes clear in

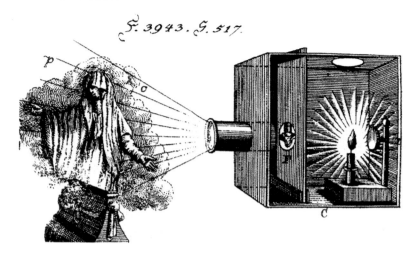

F. 3943. G. 517.

Fig. 3.10. A magic
lantern. From J. G. Kru-
enitz, *Oikonomisch-
Technologisch Enzyk-
lopädie* (Berlin, 1773).

his book on the history of this instrument, the earliest proprietors of the devices were wandering entertainers. Even in the age of the Baroque, those who worked seriously with magic lanterns complained about their use by charlatans and entertainers.[22] On the other hand, Kircher, in his treatise on optics, seems to relish precisely these "magical" aspects of the magic lantern.[23]

Anyway, magic lanterns were used in science. And for us what was (and is) really important about them is what is also important about the microscope and the telescope: All three devices use projective geometry to transmit images. And these transmitted images may be understood as self-similar progressive series—series that get bigger and bigger or smaller and smaller. And, further, by refracting, condensing, and reprojecting light, all three instruments can warp, wrench, and bend their images. Most of the improvements later made in the instruments sought to control or eliminate such distortions. But at the same time the possibilities of distortion itself, as an artistic goal, came to the fore. (We will take this point further in chapter 6.)

The magic lantern could have the same problems with spherical and chromatic distortion (turning straight lines into curves, or surrounding images with rainbow haloes) that telescopes and microscopes had. Yet the magic lantern, the slide projector, also came to be greatly improved.[24]

OPTICAL DOMES AND LANTERNS

Optics is more than a matter of lenses and diaphragms. It is the whole science of light—its creation, its transmission, its modification, and its use. So optics has always played a major role in architecture—which might be defined as the art of building adequately lit shelters. Windows, skylights, and the lanterns atop domes are optical devices. And, in architecture, light is not only propagated, directed, bounced, and diffused; it is used, almost as on the theater stage, to create emphases and special effects. In all these ways a building may be not only an acoustical but an optical instrument.

As noted (fig. 3.8), cross-sections of microscopes, telescopes, and magic lanterns show us sequences of lenses enclosed in cylinders or boxes. We look, that is, at a set of spherical segments that are light-conducting, light-enhancing, light-gathering, and usually arrayed along a single axis. We see much the same thing in Baroque architecture. The crossing bays, pendentives, drums, and sequences of domes in churches, for example, are arrayed like lenses and reflectors. Throughout this period, axial sequences of concentric sphere-segments (and, occasionally, conic sections) emerge more and more into ecclesiastical and other architecture, just as they were doing, in these same years, in microscopes, telescopes, and magic lanterns.[25]

ST. PETER'S

As a point of departure, let us look at what is probably the most famous of all domes: Michelangelo's at St. Peter's (figs. 3.11 and 3.12), 1546–64. Michelangelo created an inner hemispherical shell made of plaster- and marble-lined brick. Just outside this inner shell is the familiar outer shell, concentric with the inner one and merged to it at the shells' two bases. The outer shell is also brick, but marble-clad and provided with a perimeter of oculi and a clustered radiating set of pronounced, molded vertical ribs. Let us call them pencils.

Though he had contemplated making the outer shell a paraboloid, Michelangelo decided in the end that it was to be a hemisphere like the inner one. But then, after Michelangelo's death, his assistant Giacomo della Porta returned to the earlier profile, raising the dome's outer shell into the gentle paraboloid we see today.[26]

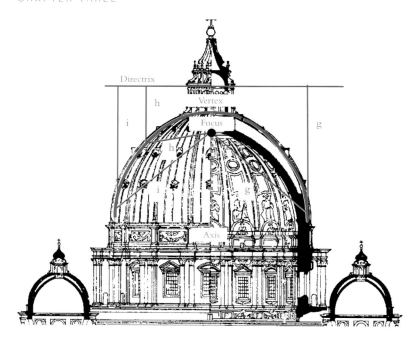

Fig. 3.11. Michelangelo and others, partial cross-section of St. Peter's dome, completed 1564. Courtesy Yale University Art and Architecture Library, Photograph Collection. The ellipse construction is shown in red.

In figure 3.11 I have superimposed, in red, the diagram of a parabola, which determines the profile of the outer dome. The parabola's axis is shown in a blue dotted line. The focus, the directrix, and the vertex are labeled. The point where the axis cuts the parabola is the vertex. The chords i, h, and g within the parabola must all equal in length the corresponding lines or tangents i, h, and g running from the outside of the parabola up to the directrix. When the parabola is rotated through 360 degrees, the result is a solid known as a paraboloid.

A long series of paraboloid domes came into existence after the completion of Michelangelo's. They reappear on the churches of Italy, France, and Britain, on the U.S. Capitol and its many architectural progeny among the state capitals; and, back in Europe, in Moscow's St. Isaac's Cathedral and Turin's Mole Antonelliana. In these domes the paraboloidal shape is usually more pronounced than at St. Peter's.

But we'll be talking further about domes as paraboloids in chapter 6. Here I want to speak of them as optical systems. Most are topped with lanterns or cupolas. The lantern is built on top of the dome's "eye," the opening at the center of the polar circle where the ribs join together around

Fig. 3.12. St. Peter's dome interior with mosaic figures by the Cavaliere d'Arpino, 1606. Photograph courtesy of Alinari/Art Resource, New York.

an oculus (note that word) or open ring. In geometry, this ring would be a torus. The lantern's weight helps keep the dome's ribs and curved plane forced into convex tension. (As far as I'm concerned "lantern" is a better word than cupola—"small tub"—for these features.) Dome-lanterns function like the iris of the eye or like an optical diaphragm. They let in a set amount of light and then shunt it, diffuse it, or otherwise transmit it throughout the dome interior—much as with the eye's lens, iris, and retina. Sometimes even the minidome that tops off a lantern can act as a reflector, much like the domical reflector in a magic lantern.

These are some of the ways in which an architectural lantern, functioning together with its dome, is an optical instrument. And, furthermore, it comprises shapes reminiscent of, or identical to, those used in lens systems: sections of spheres and paraboloids. Images (usually of Heaven), more often than not, appear on the dome's inner surface. These would be the scenes that the optical system looks at.

The interior of the dome of St. Peter's, for example (fig. 3.12), is just such a "telescoped" vision of Heaven and its chief inhabitants. Around the base are pendentive mosaics of the four Evangelists; above the drum, with its row of windows and paired pilasters, are further mosaics, all designed by the Cavaliere d'Arpino and executed in 1605 under Clement VIII. The lower tier of personages, in segmentally arched frames, presents busts of papal saints and Doctors of the Church. Then, higher, in free unframed space, comes a ring of large seated figures of the Redeemer, the Virgin, St. Paul, St. John the Baptist, and the Apostles. Higher still, a ring of angels carrying the instruments of the Passion; then come tondi filled with multiwinged cherubs and seraphs, then more angels with more attributes, and finally a tier of seraphs. At the center of everything, but also above everything, is the interior of the lantern. This is boldly set off with a ring of consoles and golden stars. Here, in this upper epidome, looking down upon us as though through an optical glass, is God the Father, blessing all who assemble below. One is reminded of Nicholas of Cusa, who, in his *De visione Dei* (1453), describes how God's eye, in a picture, sheds or projects its cone of "inaccessible Light" onto the viewer.[27]

And if God thus looks down at us through his lantern-spyglass, we look up at him through the vast eyeball of the dome and its upper lenses. Where, usually, we see him appropriately surrounded by his court, the chief citizens of Heaven, all basking in God's heavenly light. The contrast might have been intentional on the part of the designers. In St. Peter's this inner gilded globe is filled with an all-pervading luminousness very different from the light in the rest of the basilica. Note, too, that in many photographs of St. Peter's the drum windows act as spotlights, projecting pencils of brilliance onto parts of the molded annular entablature. These pencils would of course brighten, move, and dim throughout the day in accordance with the Sun's motions.

The divine optical system in St. Peter's is reinforced with inscriptions.

Around the entablature's frieze are Christ's words to St. Peter: *"Tu es Petrus et super hanc petram aedificabo ecclesiam meam; et tibi dabo claves regni caelorum"* (adapted from the Vulgate, Matthew 16:18, "You are Peter [which means 'cornerstone' as well as 'rock'] and on this cornerstone [rock] I will build my church; and to you I will give the keys of the kingdom of Heaven"). And it is Peter, whose body was thought to lie directly below this dome in its original Roman tomb, who opens the gates—the apertures—to the cosmic kingdom. [28] It is a kingdom matched, above, by the kingdom of Earth that is below. In the cross-section of the dome and its supports we see this lower crypt area, beneath the floor of the high altar, acting as a final "lens" or "objective" in the whole of the optical/visionary system. These ideas were taken over in several important subsequent dome-and-lantern systems, and in at least one other dome-lantern-tomb system.

Fig. 3.13. Jules Hardouin-Mansart's engraving of the lantern of the Invalides (Paris, 1687). Montréal, Canadian Centre for Architecture.

THE INVALIDES

But for all its qualities as an instrument for viewing Heaven, Michelangelo's dome is not the sort of optically complex configuration we find in later, more Baroque structures. I have in mind, particularly, the Invalides, St. Paul's, and the Paris Panthéon. In section, Michelangelo's dome has only a partial double shell. And two such shells, being nested, do not in this respect suggest a lens system. If we move forward in time from St. Peter's, however, we do see domes arranged concentrically in non-nested vertical configurations. In other words, we find domical structures that actually do resemble cross-sections of microscopes or telescopes.

Let's jump to 1687 and to Jules Hardouin-Mansart's great dome complex at the church of the Invalides, Paris (figs. 3.13 and 3.15). [29] Here, supported by a ring of consoles, the lantern complex, formed into a tempietto, rises from the tall molded rim of the great dome's eye. The plan of the complex maps the way the lantern's light floods down through a forest of wooden framing, and through successive lower diaphragms or irises, to fill the global volumes of the dome proper.

Fig. 3.14. A solar microscope (c. 1750). From Hankins and Silverman, *Instruments and the Imagination* (Berlin: Springer, 1995). The image has been rotated 90 degrees to the left.

Note here the similarity between Mansart's lantern and a solar microscope—that is, one that uses a mirror to reflect sunlight through the slide (fig. 3.14). It is true that this particular instrument dates from sixty years or more after Hardouin-Mansart's dome. But opticians had been making just

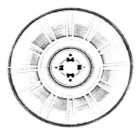

Fig. 3.15. Plan of lantern stage for the Invalides (completed version of original half-plan).

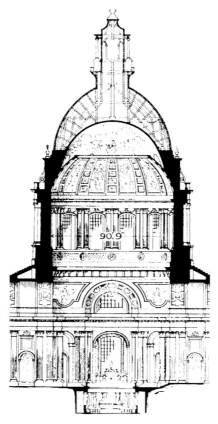

Fig. 3.16. Hardouin-Mansart's engraving of the dome system of the Invalides (Paris, 1687). Montréal, Canadian Centre for Architecture.

such complexes of ribbed and molded cylindrical containers for decades, with the outer cylinders filled with linear series of lenses that were almost always segments of spheres or paraboloids.

By 1687 there was no longer anything new about all this. So let us look at something more interesting: In the Invalides, the entire system of domes expands, in section (fig. 3.16), into a latticed paraboloid to form the church's main outer dome. Down through that lattice, moreover, there descends a central cylinder of open space. This cylinder ends up against the plane of a sphere-segment—a segment that like many plano-convex lenses is less than a full hemisphere.

Then—and this is the novelty—that dome-segment is fronted by another such segment, of even flatter profile. This consists of an enormous oculus, three times the diameter of the upper one. In other words, we view the church's painted Heaven, quite literally, through an iris or pierced lens. Using bounced and diffused sunlight or skylight, rather than artificial light, we see, through this aperture, a scene set in Heaven—Charles de Lafosse's dome painting, *St.-Louis Giving Up His Sword to Jesus Christ.* The whole setup is strongly comparable to that of the magic lantern or camera obscura.

The dome system at the Invalides received a final "optical" element when Napoleon I's body was returned to France. For it in 1841 Ludovico Visconti designed a new crypt. This is a vertical cylinder open to the floor above and directly on axis with the center of the dome above it. The crypt became the outer "objective" lens for the system. The tomb of the hero became the final image that God, gazing down through the lantern, sees—much as, at St. Peter's, he looks down on the apostle's tomb. Of course it is equally easy to imagine Napoleon's earthly remains looking up to God from below. These systems, as with other optical systems like microscopes and telescopes, can work in both directions.

ST. PAUL'S

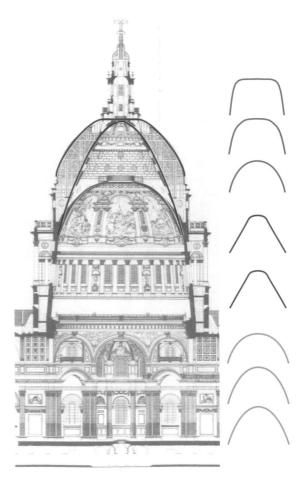

As noted, paraboloid domes appeared all throughout Europe and on just about every continent visited by Catholic missionaries. And there are Protestant paraboloids—or, rather, paraboloid variants. Across the Channel is St. Paul's, the masterpiece of Sir Christopher Wren (1675–1710; fig. 3.17).[30] There, however, one finds not a true paraboloid but a set of three domes. The outer dome is a flattened hemisphere—half an oblate spheroid, one might say, perhaps as a bow to Wren's colleague Newton. Then, within, are catenoids. These form the two inner domes supporting the outer. A catenary is the type of plane curve formed by a chain hanging from two points. A catenoid is a catenary curve revolved through 360 degrees. Cubical catenoids and paraboloids have flattened apices. When Wren was designing the dome of St. Paul's, catenaries had just recently been distinguished from parabolas (they have different formulas), notably by Jacobus Bernoulli in 1691.[31] Wren's dome in its definitive form was begun some time after 1702.[32] In the illustration (fig. 3.17) I show the outer dome as a cubical catenoid (in green), the middle dome as a paraboloid (in red), and the inner dome as a cubical catenoid (in blue). Next to the cross-section of the cathedral are other catenaries (blue), a cubical parabola and a truncated cone (both red), and more catenaries (green), the

Fig. 3.17. Cross-section of the dome of St. Paul's (Christopher Wren, London, 1675–1710). From Arthur F. E. Poley, *St. Paul's Cathedral, London, Measured, Drawn, and Described by Arthur F. E. Poley* (London: the Author, 1878).

latter three not being cubical. All these shapes were generated mathematically, for which I thank Michael Frame. They provide a wider picture of the geometrical possibilities Wren was working with. The formula for a catenary, by the way, is

$$x = (a/2) \ (e^{x/a} + e^{x/a}).$$

Both of Wren's inner catenoids are exactly 100 feet wide across their narrow axis and 120 feet long.[33] The inner catenoid cants the interior wall of the drum inward. This establishes the bottom section of the second catenoid, which has about a 10-degree slope. The effect is to build a theatrical forced perspective structure into the drum interior—making it seem higher than it is. In other words, Wren is achieving greater majesty through optical distortion. These same anamorphic projections are followed in the painted scene on the inner dome, which represents an arcaded rotunda through whose arches heroic scenes are glimpsed.[34]

Down through the centers of Wren's system is the by-now-expected cylinder of oculi or diaphragms. These form the main course of the system's vertical illumination. The vertical cylinder is supplemented by the horizontal illumination coming in from the windows of the drum. Here the analogy would be not with the lenses but with an optical projector's canted reflectors. Wren had in fact designed a double reflector-telescope that exploited just this principle.[35] So far as I know, St. Paul's has the only catenoid domes erected in this period.

THE PARIS PANTHÉON

By 1715 Wren's dome was in place. In the years afterward the optical, and specifically telescopic/microscopic, character of these structures in domed churches only increased. Look at Jacques Soufflot's dome of the Paris Panthéon, completed in 1790 (fig. 3.18).[36] Here, lantern, dome(s), and even the church's aisle vaults make for a setup that is extraordinarily "optical," complete with auxiliary "lenses" and "reflectors." Moreover, the section of each of Soufflot's lens-domes—those of the lantern and those served by it, including outer shell, middle shell, and inner shell—all have different paraboloidal or spherical sections.

For comparison I illustrate a microscope (fig. 3.19) taken from the trade

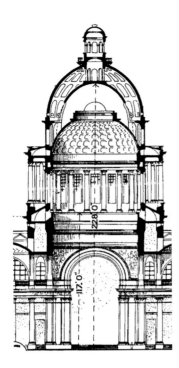 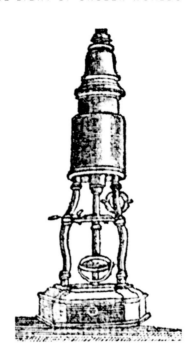

card of the British optician John Cuff (who also supplied the solar micro-scope we looked at earlier). Seen as a model dome system, Cuff's micro-scope, starting at the top and descending, consists of eyepiece (lantern), dome, oculus moldings, and drum. There, as in Soufflot's church, the struc-ture separates into a set of legs around an opening. In the church we get the four crossing piers, in the microscope the three cabriole legs. Meantime, re-placing the human observer who would stand at the church's crossing, the microscope has an adjustable mirror that bounces light upward through the slide and into the eyepiece. Here again is an equivalent in function (not po-sition) to the sidelighting furnished by drum windows. The "lantern slide," meanwhile, is a painting by Baron Gros, *The Apotheosis of St. Généviève*. One gazes up to Heaven, with all this optico-architectural assistance, to watch the saint being welcomed there.

Many other such domes were built in the Baroque era. Thus, in 1653–57, Borromini designed a paraboloid dome for Sant'Agnese in Agone. Some other Roman churches with such domes are Domenico Fontana's Cappella Sistina at Santa Maria Maggiore (begun in 1585)—like the St. Peter's dome

Fig. 3.18. Partial cross-section of the Panthéon (Jacques Soufflot, Paris, 1764–90). From Fletcher, *History of Architecture on the Comparative Method* (1892; reprint, New York: Scribner's, 1950).

Fig. 3.19. Detail from John Cuff's trade card (c. 1750?). From Hankins and Silverman, *Instru-ments and the Imagina-tion* (Princeton, N.J.: Princeton University Press, 1995).

a Renaissance predecessor of the Baroque paraboloids; Carlo Maderno's dome for Sant'Andrea della Valle (1622–25); Rosato Rosati's for San Carlo ai Catinari (1612–20); and the dome of Sant'Ignazio (begun in 1626) by Orazio Grassi, Carlo Maderno, and others. These paraboloids then led to others, including, as noted, the dome of the U.S. Capitol.

It is completely appropriate, optically, cosmically, and terrestrially, that Baroque domes should have these properties. The whole complex of ideas and forms, of lenses and lenslike devices, of reflectors and mirrors, and of seen and unseen worlds goes back to the concept of the sphere. We are returned to spherical segments, to spheres' behavior, and to the various luminous substances of which the planets, the planetary spheres, and perhaps even the planetary beings were supposedly made.

ARMILLARY SPHERES AND ORRERIES

So much for lenses and scopes—scientific and architectural. Now let's look briefly at two other devices in the Baroque scientist's instrumentarium— armillary spheres and orreries. These too can have important architectural reflections; these too are involved, in different ways, with projecting the light of unseen worlds.

Armillary spheres (*armilla* = bracelet, hoop) have been known and used since antiquity. They take the form of round, overlapping concentric rings, each at a set angle. The rings are often marked with degrees (usually musico-geometric intervals such as diapasons, diapentes, and the like). The spheres display the great circles of the heavens including their equators, ecliptics (the path of the Sun around Earth or, alternatively, Earth's path as seen from the Sun), the tropics of Capricorn and Cancer, and the meridians of longitude. They show Earth's poles and polar circles.

In their way, armillary spheres also analyze light: They represent (albeit in a stylized manner) the unseen geometric framework, and the motions, through that framework, of the universe's many luminous bodies.

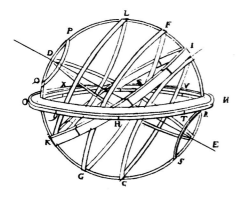

Fig. 3.20. Guarino Guarini, an armillary sphere. From his *Architettura Civile*, 1686.

Armillary spheres demonstrate the tracks along which these glowing globes travel, interweave, approach each other, and withdraw (fig. 3.20).

And these forms and ideas are reflected, or projected, in Baroque architecture. One example is Guarino Guarini's dome of San Lorenzo, Turin (1668–80; fig. 3.21). Note that both the armillary sphere in fig. 3.20 and Guarini's dome consist of continuously rotated armatures creating a stack of arcs, ribs that are segments of rings or armillae.[37] In other words, looking up into Guarini's dome we are being put, as it were, inside an armillary sphere.

Note, too, that Guarini uses his armillary setup as a lattice through which to project light. The Sun moves around the windowed drum and the windows map the dome interior with their moving beams. If we think of this interior as a set of tropics, poles, equators, and ecliptics, as a skeleton spheroid whose ribs are the orbits of light-sources, then Guarini's dome, despite the absence of a painted scene of Heaven and its dwellers, is a heavenly image.

Orreries are a much more recent invention. Named after Charles Boyle, the fourth Earl of Orrery (d. 1731), these wind-up machines demonstrate the relative movements of model planets—for example, Earth, the Moon, and the Sun—made at some arbitrary but consistent scale so as to swivel on

Fig. 3.21. Guarini, interior of the dome of San Lorenzo (Turin, 1668–80). Photograph courtesy of Erich Lessing/Art Resource, New York.

Fig. 3.22. A Copernican
orrery with Earth, the
Moon, and the Sun

their own axes and also, sometimes, to circle around one another in their orbits, approaching and withdrawing according to their proper laws. The more
elaborate orreries can contain two kinds of spheres—the old-fashioned
Ptolemaic kind in which a planet is embedded, and/or the sphere that is the
planet itself. In some orreries, on the other hand, a planet's larger orbit is de-
lineated only by its movement through the air; its "sphere," so to speak,
being invisible. Normally, orreries can be either heliocentric or geocentric,
but they do generally involve circular orbits, while the planets themselves
are perfect spheres—though, of course, by this time it was well-known that
planets were spheroids and their orbits elliptical.

In the orrery depicted in figure 3.22, a clockwork belt drive extends outward from the orrery's stanchion, which supports a many-times-too-small,
many-times-too-near Sun (the Sun is 372 times as far from Earth as the
Moon is). The belt rotates Earth and its nearby Moon (whose scale is about
right with respect to Earth). Note the slight hook in the Moon's axle, which
furnishes it with its characteristic wobble or libration. The belt drive also
swivels Earth and the Moon around the Sun while at the same time revolving the Sun on its own axis.

One might say that armillary spheres solidify the tracks of heavenly bodies, these latter being omitted and therefore invisible in most such devices.
And orreries do just the reverse: They portray the actual bodies, but their
movements are not turned into visible tracks.

BOULLÉE'S NEWTON TOMB

Another name for an orrery is planetarium; and in architecture the most famous planetarium is undoubtedly Etienne-Louis Boullée's project for a
cenotaph to Isaac Newton.[38] This was to have been a huge hollow masonry
sphere set into an annular pedestal ringed by groves of cypresses, as in a Hel-
lenistic or Roman tomb. But of course this image, a sphere set into a ring,
also evokes an orrery—and, for that matter, the rings of angels and saints we
see in the spheres and spheroids of domes. A basement orifice, also circular,
was to form the entrance to the Newton monument. Inside, the movements
of the planets were to be projected by the moving Sun shining through
carefully mapped holes in the dome, throwing the shapes of luminous mov-

ing bodies onto the dome's interior. Paradoxically, therefore, the Sun would produce a map of the nighttime sky. The whole setup, once again, recalls the camera obscura and the magic lantern.

In another version of Boullée's project (fig. 3.23), representing the daytime cosmos, a giant armillary sphere hangs in the center. Artificial light, probably from an Argand lamp, would represent the Sun at the center of the armillary sphere. A lot of the Newton propaganda in Boullée's period invoked Newton as "our Sun." In a comparable mode, Pope's famous epigram equates Newton with light itself.[39] So far, Boullée's project couldn't be more appropriate.

Fig. 3.23. Monument to Isaac Newton (Etienne-Louis Boullée, 1784). Interior with armillary sphere. Bibliothèque Nationale, Paris.

At the same time it does have an oddly retardataire character that I have not seen pointed out. Boullée is usually billed as a "revolutionary architect," a child of the Enlightenment, even a herald of the International Style. His interest in science is demonstrated by his library's history of astronomy.[40] Yet that history would have taught him that it had been accepted, for decades, that there were no planetary spheres and no sphere of fixed stars. The same goes for circular orbits. Yet the inside surface of Boullée's sphere is precisely a sphere of fixed stars. And his armillary sphere has circular orbits. Actually, everything physical and visual about Boullée's Newton monument is pre-Newtonian. It displays the notions that Newton's Laws replaced.

Fig. 3.24. Boullée's Newton tomb as an oblate spheroid, in conformity with Newton's discovery

So, as well, does what Boullée writes in homage to Newton the man: "O Newton, as by the extent of your wisdom and the sublimity of your genius you determined the shape of the Earth, I have conceived the idea of enveloping you in your own discovery." What is Boullée saying? Newton had proposed that Earth wasn't a sphere, offering evidence that our planet is an oblate spheroid, a squeezed ball with flattened poles.[41] As early as 1736 the astronomer P. L. M. de Maupertuis proved Newton right.[42]

In figure 3.24, therefore, I amend Boullée's homage with a Newton tomb that I have reconfigured as a proper oblate spheroid. And the armillary sphere now properly becomes an ellipsoid.

ST. BRIDE'S, FLEET STREET

Even when no particular cosmic theme was intended, the new optics of our period could come into play in church design. I return for a moment to Wren. We have noted how he infused geometrical regularity into the odd-shaped perimeters of his City churches.[43] Wren felt that his main model for several of these, ancient Rome's so-called Temple of Peace (Basilica of Constantine and Maxentius, as published by Palladio), was "very lightsome whereas the consecrated [Roman] Temples were generally very obscure."[44] Wren was undoubtedly attracted to the basilica's tetrastyle—four supporting columns in the center of a vaulted space, with aisles, apses, and other subsidiary spaces framing a central raised core. This arrangement created wide interior spaces that did little or nothing to block sight lines from all parts of the interior. Even more appropriately to Wren's purposes, Palladio includes giant thermal windows in a clerestory running along the building's sides (fig. 3.25).

St. Bride's, Fleet Street (fig. 3.26), has a basilican plan (though no tetrastyle), with the addition of galleries. But its main innovation, at least in the context of Rome-derived Baroque British church architecture, is surely its enormous provision for light, achieved with walls of arched windows similar to those in the Temple of Peace. The preacher, elevated and elegantly framed in his thrusting pulpit, will be bathed in light, and bathed at three levels—below the galleries, above them, and by light from a clerestory on top with broad oval windows. Wren's windows, based on his conception of a Roman precedent, constituted a battery of light-projectors.

The plans of St. Mary-le-Bow, St. Dionis Backchurch, St. Anne and St. Agnes, St. Martin Ludgate, and other City churches

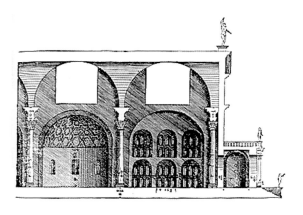

Fig. 3.25. The "Temple of Peace." From Andrea Palladio, *Quattro Libri* (Venice: De'Franceschi, 1570).

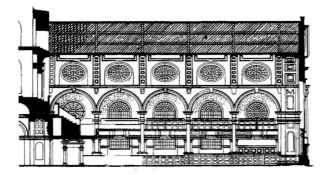

also reflect this notion of a central cluster of columns supporting a higher clerestoried space, sometimes with galleries, and then lower framing spaces. As noted, Wren showed enormous facility in adapting the system to the odd-shaped lots he was often given. Sometimes the tetrastyle is a hexastyle or even an octastyle, and the enclosing frame, when it is not irregular, can be a hexagon, an octagon, a truncated triangle, or something similar.[45] Everything in these buildings is thus open for uninterrupted seeing and hearing, and for new optical levels of "lightsomeness," often achieved via the play of geometry.

Fig. 3.26. Interior side elevation of St. Bride's, Fleet Street (Wren, London, 1680). From J. Clayton, *The Dimensions, Plans, Elevations, and Sections of the Parochial Churches of Sir Christopher Wren* (London, 1848–49).

In the age of the Baroque, number, music, and light were more tightly interwoven than nowadays. In a way, if the late-eighteenth-century "revolutionary" architects with their massive masonry Platonic solids seemed genuinely new, earlier architects of the Establishment such as Wren, Hardouin-Mansart, and Soufflot seemed equally, if differently, so. Light in the Baroque world, like music, was a matter of movement—a parallel to sound with its reflections, transmissions, concentrations, and amplifications. Light was particularly bound up with pencils or individual rays, with their bending, gathering, and focusing, and with the projection of images. These latter, whether they were microscopic, telescopic, or even painted views of the Heavens, constituted the new and previously unseen worlds this chapter has dealt with.

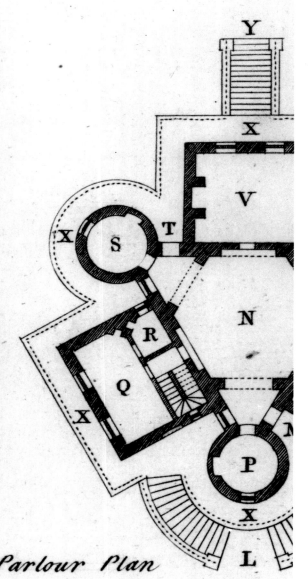

Parlour Plan

Scale

FOUR

CUBICES
RATIONES

T his chapter is mostly about fitting regular straight-sided shapes together, both in two and then in three dimensions. The cube presides over this process. Why the cube? We have looked at square-based proportional systems; and, of course, the cube is the solid that is born of the square. The greatest Renaissance architectural theorist, Leone Battista Alberti, claimed that the cube was in fact the parent of all forms. To him it was also by far the most beautiful.[1] Other shapes, and their associated number sequences, he ranked according to their genetic closeness to the cube. The age of the Baroque felt pretty much the same way.

The doctrine that I am calling *cubices rationes* stems from this set of beliefs.[2] It also embraces the world of sesquialters and superbipartientes discussed in chapter 1. For, more than any other, this system derives everything from this square-faced, square-based cubic mother. As to other forms that were considered close to the cube, much was made of cubes inhabiting spheres, while tetrahedrons, octahedrons, and the other Platonic solids were presented as the cube's direct offspring. They too can inhabit spheres. And thus, too, in one of Kepler's schemes for the cosmos, do all five Platonic solids nest one inside the other, and each also inside a sphere, to create the edifice of the heavens. The "mother" of Kepler's edifice is a vast outer cube holding everything else inside it (fig. 4.15).

ENGENDERING GEOMETRY

Kepler made a good deal of his notion of the sexual production, and reproduction, of geometric shapes and, in particular, of the Platonic solids. These
ideas I will also place under the rubric of cubices rationes. Why? First of all,
the word *cubices* has curiously consistent associations. I would link the root
of *cubus* to a basic measure, the cubit, from the Latin *cubitum*, meaning elbow
or forearm (1 cubit = approximately 18 inches); also with the word *cubicu-
lum*, bedroom; with *cubo*, "I lie down"; and with *cubile*, bed. These associations suggest recumbency (also related, from *cumbus = cubus*). (The cubit has
to do with lying down, say the dictionaries, because your elbow supports
you when you recline.) And you lie down in your bedroom, your cubicu-
lum. Lying down in a bedroom, in turn, suggests, among other things, sex.
And that association becomes stronger, even demonic, when we think of
other cube-related words, one being *incubus*, the evil spirit that lies on top of
you when you're asleep. If you're a woman the incubus may give you an un-
wanted pregnancy. *Succubi*, meanwhile, are demonic female bed-haunters
who lie beneath sleeping men. They too can be bad news.

     If these thoughts all cluster around images of the recumbent human
body, it is also a recumbent body that Vitruvius, discussing what he refers
to as *cybicae rationes*, uses as his measure of square and circle (*De architectura*
3.1.2). This is indeed a main ancient source of the idea that the cube (and
its side the square) are the begetters of all other forms. These parent-
shapes, in turn, receive their beauty, as Vitruvius famously says, from their
relationship to the human body. If a well-shaped man lies down and spreads
his arms out straight, Vitruvius explains, you can inscribe a square around
him. And if he spreads his legs into an equilateral triangle, raising his arms
a few degrees, the square turns into a circle. Thus (say Renaissance theorists) does the square "generate" the circle. Vitruvius adds that the center,
the origin-point, of the circle will be the navel. (Leonardo's famous drawing, illustrating this passage, proves that while the circle originates at the
navel, the square will have its origin at the penis. As an origin-point or
generator, however, a penis is just as appropriate as a navel, perhaps more
so.) Anyway, throughout the Renaissance and Baroque periods, the male
body was thus seen as an aspect of cubices rationes, fathering geometric
and architectural forms.[3]

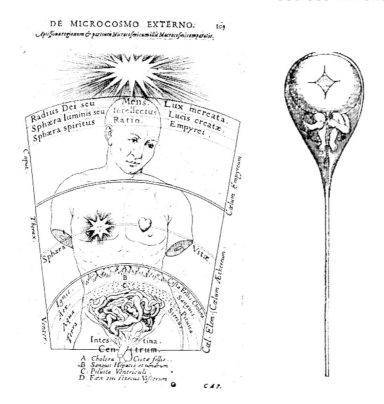

Fig. 4.1. Correspon-
dences between macro-
cosm and microcosm.
From Robert Fludd,
Utriusque cosmi, 1619.

Fig. 4.2. A homunculus
within a human sperm
cell, as seen and drawn
by Nicolas Hartsoeker in
his *Essai de dioptrique*,
1694

Robert Fludd loved these games. Indeed his book of 1619, *Utriusque cosmi*, takes over Vitruvius's discussion of the number of vertices, faces, edges, and so on in the Platonic solids and links those numbers to musical intervals, to optics, and to cosmic beauty generally.[4] Going further, he superimposes the image of the microcosm, a man's body, on it all. That body becomes a microcosmic monochord (fig. 4.1). And it generates geometry. It engenders—begets—sesquialter and related ratios and, as well, miniatures of the planetary spheres, transparent globes that envelop the man like large seethrough bubbles.[5] These crystalline spheres rise through the four elements, through ether, life, and the *mens*, culminating up above in an upper sunburst of God's uncreated light—the light that preexisted Creation and is both the light of physics and of theology.

Notice that Fludd labels the penis as the *centrum*, by which he means it is the origin of the whole setup. The compasses that drew the arcs of all these Worlds and elements were anchored on this centrum—at this point in the

form-and-number-generating male body. Note that the man's heart revolves around it in a great circle. And the Sun is on the same circuit, being
for the macrocosmic man what the heart is for the microcosmos. In this and
other drawings in the book the centrum emerges, also, at the juncture, the
horizon, of day and night, controlling their rise and fall. Even the man's head
proceeds from this penis, as one of a series of epicycles erected, or reproduced upward from the centrum. This is appropriate, since in Greek a κέντ-
τρον is first and foremost a sting, or prick, and the same goes for *centrum* in
Latin. Only secondarily is the centrum a center (the place where you prick
the paper with the compass's point).

Next to Fludd's microcosm I illustrate a human sperm cell as seen and
drawn by an early Baroque microscopist, Nicolas Hartsoeker (fig. 4.2). Paradoxically, the advent of the microscope gave new ammunition to those who
believed the old fable about each male seed containing a microimage, a tiny
portrait correct in every detail, of the adult that would grow from this seed.
Hartsoeker claimed actually to have seen these homunculi, as these tiny beings were called, in his microscope. The one he drew, seated, gripping its
knees, peers out from a spherical cloud. He is enveloped in a globe—a
dome—of semen. Thus we might speak once again, and now at this tiny
scale, of the man inscribed within the circle, though that now becomes a
sphere, and the man is hunched together rather than spread-eagled.[6] We
might also speak of the self-similar sequences of images caused by optical
projection. And since the globe or planet that the homunculus occupies is
in fact made of sperm, he's reproductive just like a transmitted optical image.
So, in the age we study, geometry and reproduction, square and circle, and
the human body and the sphere lie down together, recumbent in their cu-
biculum, and bring forth new life.

"CONGRUENCE" OR TILING

Cubes are solids—three-dimensional. But any such solid is of course
bounded by two-dimensional planes—its faces. Kepler, in book 2 of the
Harmonices mundi (which book, by the way, he calls the *Liber architectonicus*),
prints a number of these cube-derived plane figures.[7] They consist of one or
more shapes, such as squares or triangles, laid out so that all edges meet the
edges of their neighbors with no overlaps and no gaps. Kepler's diagrams

look like designs for fancy tile floors. He called the forms that could be laid out in this manner congruent. Nowadays mathematicians call Kepler's procedure *tiling*.[8]

Kepler's tileable polygons are either regular (with sides that are straight lines) or stellated (each side is lengthened into a triangular ray as with a star). He states that there is a total of twelve regular polygons, eight flat-sided and four stellate—no more and no less—that are "congruent" in his sense.[9] The flat-sided polygons are the triangle, the tetragon, the pentagon, the hexagon, the octagon, the decagon, the dodecagon, and the icosagon. (Actually Kepler is mistaken. If one is tiling with single shapes, only the triangle, the square, and the hexagon work.[10]) Meanwhile Kepler's four tileable stellated shapes are the pentagon, the octagon, the decagon, and the dodecagon.[11] Because of their limited number and many regularities of edge-length, angle, and so on, he considers such polygons to be fully effable.

But there are really two kinds of tiling. There are patterns that use only one shape and those with two or more. Multiple tiling offers other possibilities than tiling with single shapes. This is so, especially, if you can combine large and small shapes—but always with the arrangement around each vertex or corner the same.[12]

Tilings that use more than one shape are known as Archimedean tilings. When three different shapes are used, there is a total of eleven possibilities. I hope the diagrams in figures 4.3 and 4.4 will clarify these points.

But how does architecture come into it? My answer is that Kepler's patterns (fig. 4.4) show that the *Liber architectonicus* was well named. Many of the diagrams look like Baroque and Rococo church plans, or like the polygonal palace plans one sees in the mathematically minded architectural

can't be tiled

can be tiled

can be tiled with supplementary shapes

Fig. 4.3. Tileable and untileable polygons: stellate pentagons, plane pentagons, hexagons, and decagons

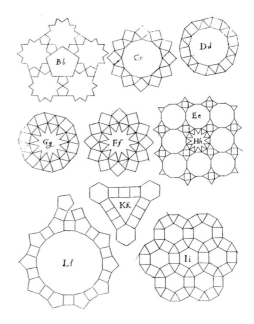

Fig. 4.4. Patterns of "congruence" or tiling among regular polygons. From Johannes Kepler, *Harmonices mundi*, book 5 (Linz: Gottfried Tampach, 1619).

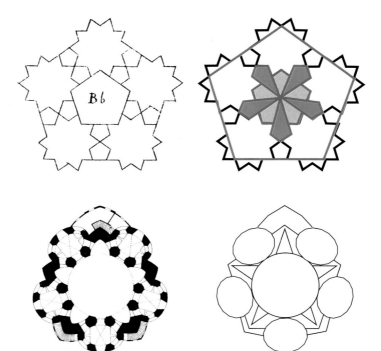

Fig. 4.5. Kepler, "Harmonic Figure." From his *Harmonices mundi*.

Fig. 4.6. Color analysis of Kepler's "Harmonic Figure"

Fig. 4.7. Plan of St. John Nepomuk (Johann Santin-Aichel, Saar, Czech Republic, 1719–21). From Bottineau, *L'Art Baroque*.

Fig. 4.8. Santin-Aichel's plan redrawn as a piece of Kepler tiling or "congruence"

treatises such as Juan Caramuel Lobkowitz's *Arquitectura civil, recta y obliqua* and Guarini's book.

To illustrate: In figures 4.5 and 4.6, first, is another of Kepler's tilings, a set of five stellated decagons arranged in a pentagonal footprint, with a central smaller pentagon serving as the centerpiece. The little spaces between the rays of the decagonal stars are also pentagons. Already this could almost be a church plan, with five chapels and a central pentagonal nave. Specifically, it could be compared with Johann Santin-Aichel's plan of St. John Nepomuk, near Saar in Slovakia, dating from 1719–21 (figs. 4.7 and 4.8). That too has a pentagonal footprint with a central nave—though in this case the chapels are ellipses rather than stellate decagons, and the central nave is circular instead of pentagonal. But these differences are trivial. The chief point remains that the tiling and the plan are instances of Kepler's "congruent" conjunctions of polygons—his tilings.

Yet there is one other difference, and it's not so trivial. Kepler's pentagonal setup, despite its unlike components, tiles perfectly within its pentagonal border (though it cannot be extended to infinity, so it is not truly a piece of mathematical tiling). Santin-Aichel's components, on the other hand, often overlap or else do not join edge-to-edge. Spatially, Santin-Aichel's plan comprises a convex or spherical triangle, a pentagon, a stellate pentagon or star, and a circle. There are also five nonoverlapping but also (seemingly) nontiling elements: namely, the three elliptical chapels, each rotated 72 degrees with respect to its neighbor.

In order to tile these separated, unlike shapes, the architect has filled the spaces between them with areas of "wall." I use quotes because the black areas on Santin-Aichel's plan are not really walls in the traditional sense. That is, they are not thin continuous vertical planes but, rather, thick vermicular fragments—like pieces of a chopped-up earthworm. "Walls" of this type had been in existence at least since Bramante's 1506 plan for St. Peter's.[13] Their purpose is not, as with a traditional wall, to wrap space. Instead, each "wall" is an independent or semi-independent shaped solid, not unlike (but more irregular than) the solids we have been discussing. In plan they are polyhedrons; in three dimensions, they are irregular solids. In figure 4.9 I illustrate, in solid gray, and with linear profiles of the actual built shapes superimposed on them, the orthodox polygons from which the distorted shapes of some of the piers in the Saar church derive. Keep in mind that the regular polygons are the invisible "inhabitants" of the irregular ones.

Tiling with irregular tiles—tiles comparable to those taken from the church plan in figure 4.7—is a well-established mathematical procedure, so the irregular polygons we see in the solids and voids of Baroque architecture are no bar to an alliance between mathematical tiling and the building art. I am illustrating what Grünbaum and Shephard call "monohedral tilings by anisohedral convex pentagons."[14] This means that each tile is of the same size and shape (monohedral) but that in a given tile each of the five faces is a different length (anisohedral; fig. 4.10). The only thing that happens to each pentagon is that it is rotated to fit into its place.

I haven't been able to do quite this with any of Santin-Aichel's "tiles," but in principle one should be able to find plans that offer the possibility—a construct that would consist, for example, of columns, rooms, porches, or staircases packed together as tiling elements. So considered, tiling, with some of the "tiles" remaining as flat floor but with others turning into towering piers, may now have little likeness to a tiled floor. But it does, with this

Pentagon Pier

Heptagon Pier

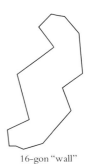

16-gon "wall"

Fig. 4.9. Sections of two piers and a wall-segment from St. John Nepomuk, shown as distorted regular polygons

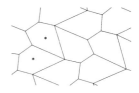

Fig. 4.10. The tiling of irregular pentagons. From Branko Grünbaum and G. C. Shephard, *Tilings and Patterns* (New York: W. H. Freeman, 1986).

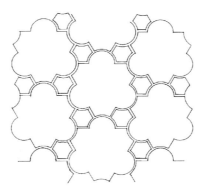

change, have more of a likeness to more ambitious architecture such as hypostyle halls—or for that matter, as we have just seen, entire churches.

Indeed Martin Raspe has discovered that with the aid of a repeated small hexagon that has alternating concave and straight sides, the perimeter of Borromini's plan for San Carlo alle Quattro Fontane, Rome (San Carlino), tiles perfectly into a truly infinite Archimedean arrangement (fig. 4.11).[15] Here again we see monohedral tilings by anisohedral tiles, regular convex-concave dodecagons.

Again and again, when it comes to tiling, Baroque architecture matches up with Kepler. His equilateral triangle, with hexagon corners and faces consisting of three tetragons each (fig. 4.12), almost directly anticipates work by one of the more geometric French architects of the later Baroque, Jean-François de Neufforge, a pupil of Blondel. Neufforge's scheme for a temple (fig. 4.13) involves exactly Kepler's equilateral triangle and exactly Kepler's faces, each broken into strings of three tetragons—though, in Neufforge, Kepler's corner hexagons become little circular rotundas, matching and framing the larger rotunda in the triangle's center. Kepler will be developing the idea that effable shapes "beget" one another. Neufforge's

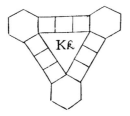

Fig. 4.12. An equilateral triangle formed of hexagonal corners and faces formed of tetragons. From Kepler, *Harmonices mundi.*

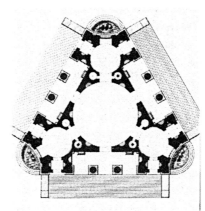

Fig. 4.13. Jean-François de Neufforge, plan of a temple. From Neufforge, *Receuil élémentaire d'architecture* (Paris: Chez l'auteur, 1757–77).

forms do this too. Thus the central rotunda's diameter is precisely double that of the corner rotundas; and that same diameter, the central rotunda's, also establishes the lengths of the outer triangle's faces. Finally, if those faces are extended to meet one another, forming a triangle, the distance along each side is precisely three times the inner rotunda's diameter: in short, an intensely geometric and, in every sense suggested above, tiled plan; and a plan, also, in which the geometric shapes are related by simple dimensional repetitions that establish "genetic" bondings.[16]

THE CUBE AND ITS PROGENY

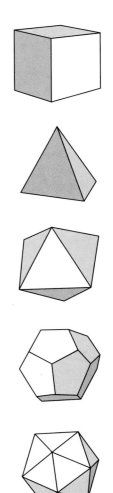

In Vitruvius and among later thinkers in the field of cubices rationes, the words "cube" and "cubic," in addition to their reproductive associations cited earlier, suggest both the geometric shape and its arithmetical equivalents. The cubic power 3, and 8 the first of cubes (2^3), are in this sense "cubic." And so are the numbers generated by the geometrical cube (4 edges per face, 6 faces, 8 vertices or points [where 3 faces meet in a corner], 12 edges, 12 dihedral angles, 24 edge angles). When made into a clustered series all these numbers are therefore linked to the three-dimensionality, to the solid state, that is natural to architecture.

Also, a cube is a polyhedron. This is one more way in which it joins a select company. The faces of the regular or Platonic polyhedrons are all regular polygons—that is, squares, triangles, and pentagons with all edges straight, all edges the same length, and all angles the same (fig. 4.14). The number sequence generated by the cube—3, 6, 8, 12, 24—gains additional status from its participation in this stringently limited group.

The same goes for the other Platonic solids in figure 4.14. The tetrahedron (top row, right) has 4 faces, 4 vertices, and 6 edges. Its base is an equilateral triangle. The octahedron (bottom row, left) has 6 vertices, 8 faces, 12 edges, and 12 plane angles (a plane angle is the angle between two faces sharing an edge). The dodecahedron (bottom row, center), with 12 faces, all of them identical regular pentagons, has 20 vertices and 30 plane angles. The icosahedron (bottom row, right) is made of 20 equilateral triangles and has 12 vertices and 30 plane angles. In the age of the Baroque, as in antiquity, these facts—the numbers and their corresponding shapes—had transcendent importance.

Euclid had discussed the five Platonic solids, much in these terms, in book 13 of the *Elements*.[17] There he actually proved their special status mathematically. Not only do they have all the consistencies named, they are a finite group—no other such bodies are possible. Euclid also showed how all five polyhedrons are inscribable into spheres, which may be what led Ke-

Fig. 4.14. The five regular or Platonic solids: cube or hexahedron (6 faces) and tetrahedron (4 faces); and octahedron (8 faces), dodecahedron (12 faces), and icosahedron (20 faces)

pler in turn to inscribe them, along with their inscribed spheres, into the heavens.

There is another aspect to this sort of geometric nobility—the ease with which the forms can be drawn out. In the tenth century the Islamic philosopher Abul Wefa was able to perform the feat of drawing all five Platonic solids using only a straightedge and a pair of compasses at a fixed setting. Such fixed compasses (known as "rusty" compasses) have been the tools of virtuoso geometrical draftsmanship in many periods.[18]

In the age of the Baroque the five Platonic solids only increased the nobility of their natures. Further uniquenesses were pointed out by the mathematicians Leonhard Euler and Johann Elert Bode. Euler showed that a single equation is valid for all five forms: The number of vertices (v) minus the number of edges (e) plus the number of faces (f) always equals 2:

$$v - e + f = 2.$$

This remains true even if you put a vertex onto a face—changing it from a flat plane into the three upper faces of a tetrahedron (this is the polyhedron's stellate form). Nor is there any change in the principle if you do the same with an edge. Even if you convert your polyhedron to spherical form—essentially swelling it into a ball but retaining all edges, vertices, and so on, a bit like the seams on a soccer ball—even then the equation never changes.

If Kepler ultimately abandoned his idea that giant versions of these solids filled the heavens,[19] his concern with the solids themselves continued. Indeed it increased.[20] But let us go back to his cosmic scheme, eventually rejected though it was, before turning to his later work. Figure 4.15 shows the setup he had in mind for the planets along with their accompanying polyhedrons and spheres.

The illustration depicts a model—a sort of updated armillary sphere. You have to imagine each sphere revolving at a different rate, depending on its planet's period. The outermost sphere is that of Saturn. Just inside Saturn's sphere is the first of Kepler's Platonic solids—a cube that is imaginary or invisible, a fact symbolized in the print by its skeletonized form. Just within that, in turn, is the sphere with Jupiter embedded in it. Just inside that, in turn, is a skeletal tetrahedron. Next, further inside, and of course at smaller scale, comes Mars. And so on, downward in scale and always going inward to the center, through a skeletal dodecahedron (in which Earth is inscribed) and a skeletal icosahedron for Venus, and a skeletal octahedron for Mercury. At the very center, hardly moving at all (and absolutely tiny) is the Sun. (The Sun is actually by far the largest of any of these bodies, though it has a relatively small orbit.)

Kepler's arrangement does indeed account, fairly neatly, for all five polyhedra and for all six planets as their mutual distances were then known. While all the spheres are curved continuous surfaces (Kepler shows them cut in half for illustration's sake), the five solids, as noted, are skeletons. Only their edges and angles, not their faces, are preserved. This too is for illustrational purposes—to reveal what's inside them. The skeletonizing also abets Kepler's idea that the Platonic solids are invisible, at least to mortal eyes. The skeletal polyhedrons are therefore a bit like the corpo trasparente, the crystalline geometrical envelopes that Serlio had imagined around architectural compositions.[21] Or like the similar three-dimensional lattices that crystallographers create around crystals.

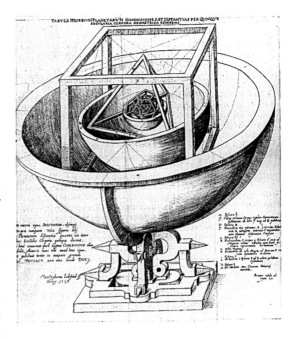

Fig. 4.15. Kepler's scheme of the planetary spheres and their intervening Platonic solids. From Kepler, *Mysterium Cosmographicum*, 1596.

Let us note finally that Kepler's huge cosmic contraption has far more to it, more shapes, more spaces, more angles and surfaces, than the old Aristotelian-Ptolemaic cosmos with its rotating concentric globes. There, everything circulated inside or outside domes. Kepler's scheme is much more variedly architectural, and it reflects Baroque architects' love for varieties of geometric form.

PREGNANT PLATONIC SOLIDS

But, as I say, Kepler gave up on this great cosmic temple. But not on Platonic and Archimedean solids. Far from it. In the *Harmonices mundi* (1619) he studied these solids simply in terms of their own inherent fascinations, with emphasis, once again, on their reproductive abilities. He divided the Platonic group into three primary forms (cube, tetrahedron, and dodecahedron) and

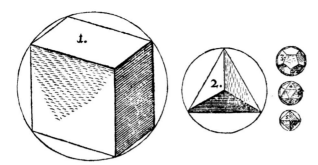

two secondary forms (icosahedron and octahedron). He then inscribed all five shapes, as in the astronomical version of his scheme, in spheres. Then, also as in the cosmos model, they were scaled to different sizes so that they fitted one inside the other (fig. 4.16).

To expound this procedure further, Kepler develops an old idea—that the five forms couple with one another in order to generate offspring.[22] He writes: "The cube (1) is the outermost and most spacious [of the five solids], because it is the firstborn and, in the very form of its generation, embodies the principle of all the others":

Fig. 4.16. Kepler, cube transformed into other Platonic solids. From *Harmonices mundi*, 1619.

> These shapes join together in two noteworthy types of matings [*coniugia*], because they have different sexes. For among the first group of three, the cube and the dodecahedron are male, and among the second group the octahedron and the icosahedron are female. To this is added the bachelor or androgyne, the tetrahedron, because this [form] is inscribed in itself [i.e., it mates with itself]. The female solids are inscribed inside the males and are as it were subject to them, and have the characteristics of the feminine as opposed to the masculine sex, namely, that [when they are nested inside male shapes] their angles are opposite the [male] faces. [23]

By this last phrase he is referring to the faces of the outer forms; for example, in figure 4.16, the tetrahedron inside another tetrahedron, or a tetrahedron inside a cube, or an icosahedron inside an octahedron.

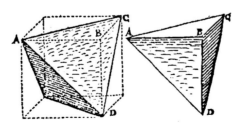

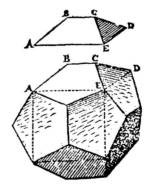

Fig. 4.17. Kepler, illustrations for *Harmonices mundi* (1619): a tetrahedron carved from a cube, all vertices touching; and a cube (dotted lines) inscribed in a dodecahedron with one of the four pentahedrons (the roof shape, *above*) that will be left over.

This notion that the Platonic solids reproduce sexually is key. Indeed Kepler's discussion of this serves to introduce his distinction between effable and ineffable shapes—the distinction that pervades his entire concept of geometry. The male forms, he adds, are *effabiles* and the females *ineffabiles*—inexpressible or irrational. To me, I have to admit, the consequences of this distinction

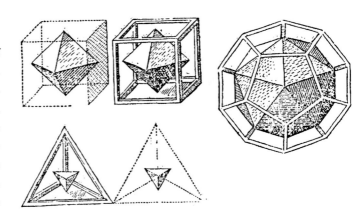

are not completely clear, since the female number sequences and ratios are in fact all in modern terms rational. Maybe it's just the purblind sexism of Kepler's age. In any event, he adds more gallantly, these same female forms, because of the male solids' dependence on them for reproduction, are divine.[24]

Kepler gives further graphic explanations. On the left of figure 4.17 we see the two tetrahedrons as they are being sectioned out of, or born from, their enclosing cube. On the right we see another cube (dotted lines) buried inside an octahedron. This latter, in turn, had been produced by truncating the cube's vertices. If, having done that, you then remove the octahedron's hip-roof-shaped outer surfaces, you reveal the inner cube. This, says Kepler, is the fetus in the mother's belly. Thus do the Platonic solids beget one another in unexpected sequences, perhaps in the way, in genetics, that a family trait will skip a generation or two and then turn up again.

The drawings in figure 4.18 illustrate more of this. After it is born, the tetrahedron's cube-mother, who had been carrying the tetrahedron around in her womb, doesn't disappear. On the left Kepler shows her, first, as a *corpo trasparente* for her octahedral fetus, and then as a skeleton like those he had used for the cosmic shapes in the *Mysterium cosmographicum*. But he doesn't forget the sex angle. Inside this frame the two pyramids sit, as Kepler puts it, "mouth to mouth" (*hiulcos*). The androgynes are kissing! Just below is an octahedron inside a larger, skeletal tetrahedron. On the right, an icosahedron floats inside a dodecahedral skeleton. Indeed any Platonic solid can be pregnant with any other Platonic solid. And though they look different

Fig. 4.18. *Left,* two tetrahedrons, mouth to mouth, inscribed in an invisible cube and then in a skeletal cube; *below left,* ditto for two tetrahedra; *right,* a skeletal dodecahedron pregnant with a solid icosahedron. From Kepler, *Harmonices mundi.*

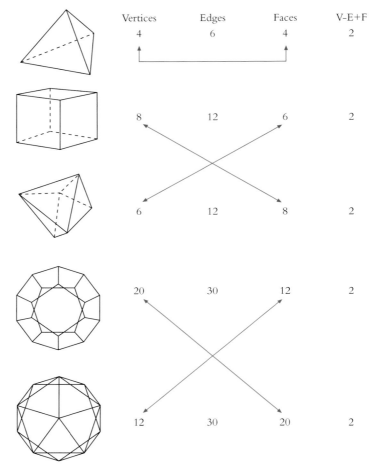

	Vertices	Edges	Faces	V–E+F
	4	6	4	2
	8	12	6	2
	6	12	8	2
	20	30	12	2
	12	30	20	2

Fig. 4.19. The duality of the five Platonic solids. After a drawing by Michael Frame.

from one another, says Kepler, the five shapes are really all the same. We might even, at a stretch, think of Kepler's series as progressively self-similar.

And that self-similarity could progress, downward, to almost infinite smallness. If Kepler gave up on his huge cosmic versions of the Platonic solids, he had plenty of attention left over for minisolids. Indeed it had for centuries been established that versions of these solids existed at the tiniest scales. Plato claimed that they in fact composed all matter.[25] Nor, by our lights today, is this notion so misguided. Matthias Brack writes: "When a large number of metal atoms (about 1,000 or more) aggregate slowly at relatively low temperatures, they form tiny solids in which the atoms pack themselves tightly, like oranges in a grocer's pile, to form regular geometric shapes."[26] These shapes are none other than the cube, the tetrahedron, the octahedron, and the icosahedron—one of Kepler's effable male solids, his androgyne, and his two female ineffable solids. Furthermore, and yet more appropriately to our purposes, even with an electron microscope these Platonic microsolids are invisible. We know they're there but we can't see them. So the Baroque concern with invisible geometric solids is not peculiar to that period.

Figure 4.19 lays out the modern version of these ideas, which is known as duality—a contemporary term for Kepler's sexual reproduction of shapes. The drawing emphasizes the interrelationships between the five solids as shapes, and their different but related counts of vertices, faces, and edges.

As to how the Platonic solids play out in architecture, one hardly has to urge the cube itself as an inspiration for built buildings. Kepler's visions of nested solids, seen dead on, have a more specific architectural relative in that typical Baroque artifact, the steeple. In plan, steeples usually begin with a surrounding base or tower, square in plan. Inscribed within that, and rising upward in successions, will be stellate octagons, tetrahedrons, or more rarely hexagons or other regular polygons. In plan, the steeple's solids nest one inside the other, like Kepler's, and are extruded (or born) one from the other as each new stage grows out of its predecessor. A good example is the top view of the steeple and bell tower of Wren's St. Bride's (figs. 4.20 and 4.21), which is a parallelepiped base with a set of concentric self-similar progressively shrinking octagons set one on top of the other, at recursive scale with approximately 85 percent reduction each time. The upper steeple itself is then a recursively reduced stellated octagon—a stellated octagon that is itself inscribed on a tall slender cone.[27]

A steeple is thus like that other Baroque artifact, the telescope, which also opens up into a set of contiguous cylinders. In the closed position—that is, in plan—the cylinders are nested or framed one inside the other. When the telescope is opened, the nested tubes extend themselves axially. With a steeple, a nested set of regular polygons turns into a nested set of architectural stories. Indeed, when they are made of wood, that is how steeples are built. Each new, narrower stage is hauled up through the preexisting wider lower stages. Then comes the final stage, the pinnacle, which is usually a cone, a tall narrow tetrahedron or, as in St. Bride's, a stellated octagon. So you might call a wooden steeple a conical telescope.

Fig. 4.20. Elevation of steeple and bell tower, St. Bride's, Fleet Street (Wren, London, 1680). From J. Clayton, *The Dimensions, Plans, Elevations, and Sections of the Parochial Churches of Sir Christopher Wren* (London, 1848–49).

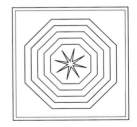

Fig. 4.21. Simplified top view of St. Bride's steeple and tower

RHOMBIC AND ARCHIMEDEAN SOLIDS

All the faces on a Platonic solid must be the same size and shape. But there are other solids, equally regular, equally symmetrical, that mix different kinds of faces. Kepler addresses these when, in the *Harmonices mundi*, he speaks of rhombic and Archimedean solids. Archimedean solids may have two or more kinds of faces, though all of them must be same-size regular polygons such as squares, equilateral triangles, pentagons, and the like. In other words, the angles of each face on an Archimedean solid are uniform. On the other hand, rhombic solids have some faces that are diamond shaped—rhombs— and with these, of course, every angle is not the same.

In figure 4.22 we have six Archimedean solids, ranging from one with 14 faces to one with 80. Kepler calls no. 8 a cubo-octahedron with triangular and square faces. No. 9 is made up of pentagons and triangles. No. 10 consists of 8 triangles and 18 squares: a hexakaiicosahedron. If you like these Greek names, no. 13 is an enneankontakaidihedron—that is, a 92-sided shape, in this case made up of 80 triangles and 12 pentagons. Like the Platonic solids, the Archimedeans have a strictly limited membership: there is a grand total, says Kepler, of only 13.[28] The best-known Archimedean solid

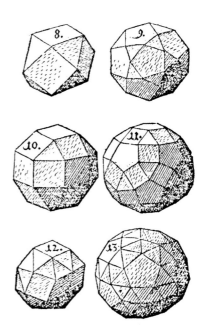

Fig. 4.22. Kepler, Archimedean solids. From *Harmonices mundi*.

nowadays is the soccer ball. This is 34-sided and made of 20 hexagons and 14 pentagons. It is inscribed onto a sphere, of course. (Anyone care to go out and kick around the spherical tettariskaitriakontahedron?)

In figure 4.23 we see two rhombic solids—a dodecahedron with square and rhombic faces, and next to it an icosahedron made up of two types of rhombs.[29] So far as I know the possible number of rhombic solids has not been determined. It is certainly high. So these forms, though we find them all over the place in Baroque architecture, are a lot less effable than their Platonic and Archimedean cousins.

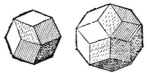

Fig. 4.23. Kepler, rhombic solids. From *Harmonices mundi*.

Rhombic and Archimedean patterns of just these types, and variant forms of them, frequently appear in the coffers and ribs of Baroque domes. Guarini's dome at San Lorenzo, Turin (1668–80; fig. 4.24), while it is not one of the 13 classic Archimedean solids, is a set of repeated tiled geometric faces formed into a sphere segment. The faces are equilateral triangles (around the lower windows), elongated pentagons (rising to the upper level of windows), tiny triangles formed by the superimposed ribs, and 45-degree-rotated squares that create a central octagon. So, of the forms we have discussed, Guarini's dome relates most strongly to the rhombic solids, as in fig. 4.23.

More simply, one can also see the dome as a circle, as shown in red in figure 4.25, inscribed around a stellate octagon and, inscribed inside the inner points of that octagon, in brown, and another octagon, but with plane sides, in green. In either case we have the upper hemisphere of a triakaihexagon—a 36-sided figure made up of two slightly different triangles. There is also an octagon on the top and (in the complete sphere of which this dome is a segment) on the bottom and in the center of each side. A dome like this could only be the work of someone, like Guarini, who had studied rhombic solids.[30]

Fig. 4.24. Interior of the dome of San Lorenzo (Guarino Guarini, Turin, 1668–87). Courtesy Yale University Art and Architecture Library, Photograph Collection.

The faces of the solids we have looked at tile into spheroidal shapes. But the same forms can be regarded as flat planes, especially since, when printed on a page, that is literally what they are. Which also happens

Fig. 4.25. Guarini's San Lorenzo dome diagrammed as half of an Archimedean solid

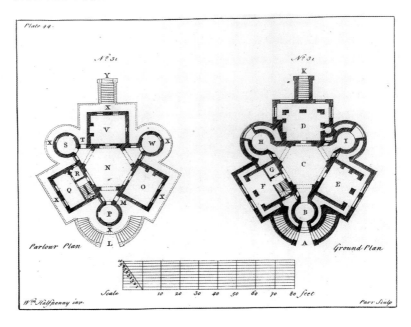

Fig. 4.26. William Half-
penny's plan of a house.
From Halfpenny, *A New
and Compleat System of
Architecture*, 1749.
Photo courtesy of Yale
Center for British Art.

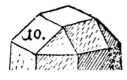

Fig. 4.27. Detail from Fig.
4.22

in the plans of buildings. Such plans can make use of the faces of
Archimedean and rhombic solids.

Let us look at the work of a late Baroque architect who did this (though
he dressed his Baroque bodies in neoclassic trimmings): William Halfpenny.
Halfpenny was the author of numerous villa books, including *A New and
Compleat System of Architecture* (1749). In that book, the plan of house no. 31
(fig. 4.26) consists of a central equilateral triangle with, on each side, a 4:3
rectangle (the latter are not all exactly the same size, but never mind). For
simplicity's sake I will ignore the three circular rooms at each corner of the
triangle.

This cluster maps what we saw in Kepler's Archimedean solid no. 10,
and, as well, what we see in any other such solid where squares and triangles
abut (fig. 4.27). It is true that Halfpenny's shapes do not turn spherical; the
house remains flat-floored throughout. But, I will also note, if Halfpenny's
"faces" were to be extended—that is, if other clusters of the same shapes
were added—it would then fold into a hexakaiicosohedron, a 20-sided
Archimedean solid with 8 equilateral triangles and 18 squares. The result

would look just like Kepler's solid except that the edges would all be con-
figured as walls with doors and windows in them.

Cubices rationes—what might also be called the doctrine of architectural cubics—assumes that certain gendered geometric entities have
sexual intercourse and reproduce. Into this scenario we also have to fit Kepler's ideas about the tiling of regular planar shapes and about Platonic,
Archimedean, and rhombic solids. Any sort of "congruence," whether two-
or three-dimensional, evokes the ideas of reproduction that are to be associated with the notion of the cube and its Platonic, Archimedean, and rhombic offspring, and hence with much of Baroque architectural geometry. We
have glimpsed some of the ways in which these things happen in Guarini,
Halfpenny, Neufforge, and others. These examples should be sufficient to
make the proper points, and to suggest how each point could be elaborated—much like a self-similar progressive series or sequence of its own.

SYMMETRIES

ere's a quick and dirty answer: something that was very
different in the seventeenth
century from what it is today. And in fact one of the achievements of the Baroque age was to start replacing older concepts of symmetry with meanings closer to the deeper, more diverse mathematical ones the
word has now. This changed the way Baroque architects thought about crucial procedures in their design techniques—among them mirror reflection,
repetition, inversion, lattices, and rotation.

WHAT IS
SYMMETRY?

From its beginnings, modern mathematical symmetry has been architec-
ture-minded. One of the fathers of modern symmetry studies, Hermann
Weyl, in his classic 1952 book, illustrates his points with the Alhambra,
Chartres Cathedral, San Marco at Venice, and many other masterpieces.[1]
Other modern-day symmetricians write about architecture and architectural ornament. On the other hand, unfortunately, architectural historians
and critics almost never write about symmetry, except in the obvious and
primitive senses that this chapter will seek to supplement.

What advantage might we enjoy, looking at architecture in this way?
Here's an example. One of the earliest of all modern symmetry studies is
Edith Müller's 1944 thesis on the decorative panels of the Alhambra at
Granada. A student of group theory, which is a form of mathematics

closely tied in with symmetry, Müller showed that of the total of seven-
teen possible symmetry groups involving one-color plane patterns, the Alhambra artists used eleven. Later experts have shown that the remaining
six groups are also present in the mosaics.[2] In other words, these four-
teenth-century Islamic artisans, perhaps in contact with court mathematicians, worked out a practical symmetry mathematics that was not to be
formulated analytically until centuries later.[3] Yet most writers on the Alhambra, and on Islamic pattern, have paid Müller no mind. They have certainly not looked at the possibilities for architectural analysis elsewhere
that her work encourages.

In part this is because symmetry has really blossomed, as a subject, only in
recent decades. One index of its growth is that the 1929 *Encyclopedia Britannica* prints only a few lines next to the word. The current editions have a
major article. By now, any number of books, congresses, and exhibitions have
been devoted to symmetry. Studies range all through the arts and through
physics, mathematics, and biology. For example, literary symmetry is studied
by Mitchell Greenberg in *Corneille, Classicism, and the Ruses of Symmetry,*
which looks at the balancing-off between bloodshed and friendship, perse-
cutor and the persecuted, and so on, in French classic tragedy.[4] Michael Layton has investigated the subject more mathematically. He thus includes group
theory and then extends it to artistic, linguistic, and political symmetry.[5]
There are now historians of the subject, as witnessed by Dorothy K. Washburn and Donald W. Crowe, authors of *Symmetries of Culture: Theory and Practice of Plane Pattern Design* (1988).[6] Yet, curiously enough, in all these writings,
even those on the visual arts, architecture has so far played little or no role.

WHAT HAS SYMMETRY BEEN?

But we have to begin with the most basic meanings of the word. In everyday speech a thing is symmetrical when it is reflected on two sides of a central axis. Human (and most other animal) bodies are examples. Symmetricians call this bilaterally reflective, or mirror, symmetry. Another word is
dihedral (two-sided) reflection. But all this, with its axial mirror and what I
will call its two sides or hedrons, one reflecting the other, is really only one
of many types of symmetry.

Anyway, the word itself, which is Greek in origin, did not at first mean

reflective symmetry at all. Or, at least, no dictionary of ancient Greek quotes a passage that clearly
uses the word this way. In Greek, and also in classical Latin, which borrowed the word and transmitted it to us, "symmetry" simply meant "measuring together" or "measured together"; in other
words, something like our "commensurate." Vitruvius uses the word *symmetria* 84 times (and the
adjective *symmetros* once). Mostly, for him, it
means rules for design, good proportions, or even
simply style. Or it can mean "of the same size and
shape." Thus we read that the Corinthian column

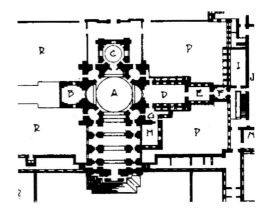

Fig. 5.1. Plan of the
church of Val-de-Grâce
(François Mansart, Paris,
1645–50). Courtesy Yale
University Art and Archi-
tecture Library, Photo-
graph Collection.

shaft is "symmetrical" with the Ionic (*De architectura* 4.1.1). These meanings
stayed with the word for centuries.

Where did our modern notion, that symmetry referred mainly to axially
mirrored elements, come from? I can only begin to suggest an answer. Walter Kambartel points out that in the mid-1660s there is a recorded instance
in which "symmetry" seems for the first time to have received something
like this meaning. This was in 1665, when Gian Lorenzo Bernini was sum-
moned to Paris by Louis XIV. During his stay Bernini was asked to design,
for the Queen Mother, Anne de Bretagne, a high altar for the church of Val-
de-Grâce (fig. 5.1).[7] At one point Bernini planned to situate his altar so as
to make it impossible for a visitor standing in the church's crossing (point *A*
in fig. 5.1) to see both into the church's left and right transepts (points *B* and
D). Bernini wanted to do this because the two transepts did not match. They
had, he said, a "*défaut de symmétrie.*"[8]

Of course in one sense Bernini's phrase only meant that the two
transepts were of different sizes, just as, 1600 years earlier, Vitruvius had implied that two column shafts of different sizes were not "symmetrical." He
could have called this a *défaut de symmetrie.* But Bernini's use of *défaut,* which
can mean absence or default in the bad sense, also implies, and more than
implies, that these nonmatching transepts were a solecism. It has been
claimed, accordingly, that this is the first recorded instance in which "symmetry" meant mirror reflection rather than commensurability.[9]

Quite possibly so. More definitively, some years later, in 1673, Claude
Perrault published his *Ordonnance des cinq espèces de colonnes.* He too uses the

Fig. 5.2. Colonnade of the Louvre (Claude Perrault, assisted by Louis Le Vau and Charles Le Brun, Paris, 1667–71). Photograph courtesy of Erich Lessing/Art Resource, New York.

word symmetry, "which," he says, "in French signifies the kind of proportion that produces . . . the relationship the parts have, collectively, as a result of the balanced correspondence of their size, number, disposition, and order." And again: "symmetry. . . is a balanced and fitting correspondence of parts that maintain the same arrangement and position."[10] I will suggest that by speaking of a same arrangement and position, one that is "balanced," Perrault meant reflective symmetry. The word *balancé*, in the seventeenth century, even suggests a beam balance—known in France precisely as a *balance*—that is, a weighing machine that puts two equal weights on either end of a horizontal beam propped on a central fulcrum. (It is the kind of weighing machine that figures of Justice hold.) A beam balance, in short, has reflective symmetry. You might even say that it makes use of reflective symmetry in order to perform its work, its "mirror" being the central fulcrum. As the recipient of a medical education and author of a treatise on mechanics, Perrault would have been thoroughly familiar with beam balances.[11]

To us, then, Perrault's special definition of "symmetry," which he carefully differentiates as being French (i.e., neither Italian nor Latin), refers to an architectural composition that would reflect the principle of a beam balance. So one cannot really claim that here, by the word "symmetry," Perrault simply means same size, commensurability, or rules for composition—symmetry in Vitruvius's senses. Perrault's definition of "symmetry" seems to be new (to writings on architecture, though perhaps not to the spoken languages of the time). Perrault does not completely express the modern definition of reflective symmetry, but he does come a lot closer than did people before him. His usage is more unquestionably new even than Bernini's.

As to how such a version of "symmetry" might occur in architecture, we need look no further than Perrault himself and his celebrated Louvre Colonnade, dating from the very years in which he was redefining the word (fig. 5.2). The facade is a monumental expression of a beam balance. And here we note that a beam balance is not simply an axis with self-similar reflected flanking elements. In that sense a square with a line down its middle is a piece of mirror symmetry. A beam balance, in contrast, differentiates three types of components within its mirror symmetry. There is the central axis—the mirror or fulcrum or other reflecting device. And there are two arms, centered on that fulcrum, going out from it to the left and to the right. Then there is a pair of identical (in weight at any rate) pans or holders at either end of the arms. In the Louvre Colonnade, the central gabled temple front with its entrance is the fulcrum, the double expanses of eight pairs of columns are the beam's left-hand and right-hand arms, and the terminal pavilions with their triumphal-arch motifs are the pans.

But of course this type of facade is practically as old as architecture itself. Egypt, Greece, and Rome built many a "beam-balance" structure, though the word "symmetrical" seems never to have been used to describe them. Such symmetry had always existed, throughout nature and in the bodies of the human beings who designed these structures. The point is that the traditional arrangement now had this new name. And that name, once it was applied to the old principle, brought new ideas into being.

REFLECTIVE SYMMETRY

Bilateral reflection is only one of many kinds of reflection. As soon as we think of a central "mirror" axis with left-hand and right-hand sides or

Fig. 5.3. North front of
Kedleston Hall, Der-
byshire (James Paine,
1761).

Fig. 5.4. Central block,
south front of Kedleston
Hall, Derbyshire (Robert
Adam, 1760–64).

hedrons, we realize that there could be further hedrons—trilateral, or multilateral. And there could be up/down reflection as well as left/right—or
both kinds together, not to mention reflection at other angles. To put it differently, a mirror axis could have several faces.

And, in complex things like buildings, different kinds of reflective symmetry can mingle and mate. Let's take Kedleston Hall, Derbyshire (fig.
5.3).[12] It has multilateral, multi-axial reflection. On the north front there is
certainly dihedral symmetry with left-handed and right-handed hedrons
flanking a center. But this center, the mirror element, is bilaterally symmetrical within itself, with a hexastyle portico flanked by three identical windows on each side, all of it fronted by an equally symmetrical dogleg staircase. Then, flanking this mirroring element, are reflected but otherwise
identical arms and terminals. So you can say that this facade has two dihedral reflective symmetries, one nested inside the other.

The south front of the main block of Kedleston (fig. 5.4), by Robert
Adam, is bilaterally symmetrical in this same double way: a dihedral center
block—dihedral triumphal arch, dihedral wings, dihedral staircase, all of
them left- or right-handed. And this whole "mirror" is set into equally dihedral, reflected pairs of arms and terminals. The composition is once again

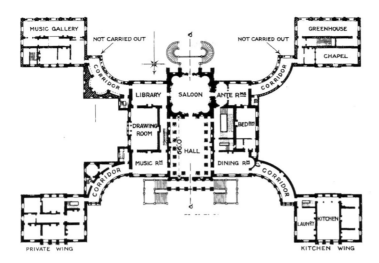

composed of highly differentiated elements—a central saloon, flanking library and anterooms, quadrants leading left and right, and, as one terminal,
the music gallery and as the other the greenhouse (these latter shown only
on the plan, fig. 5.5). It is the bilateral symmetry, the fact of reflection, that
unifies these heterogeneous things.

But at Kedleston it is the symmetry of the plan that really sings (fig. 5.5).
The main vertical axis divides into identical left- and right-hand hedrons,
with the mirror element once again as the main block. Nor is this all. From
the corners of the main block four "arms" or quadrants lead left and right,
up and down, NE, SE, SW, and NW, to pavilions that are miniature versions
of the main north-front block—tetrastyle rather than hexastyle, and with
only one flanking window on each side.

If you draw a horizontal axis through the middle of this plan you get
more bilateral symmetries, formed by these same arms and pavilions. On
the right-hand side, the rear greenhouse and front kitchen wing balance
each other; while the central block, tight-packed with dining room, bedroom, anterooms, and so on (not among themselves symmetrical), forms
the fulcrum. A corresponding effect appears on the other side. So, then, in
terms of our beam-balance principle, there are altogether at Kedleston four
different mirroring fulcrums, four different pairs of arms, and four different
pairs of terminals.

The Louvre Colonnade, our initial example of reflective dihedralism,

Fig. 5.5. Plan of Kedle-
ston Hall, Derbyshire
(Robert Adam and
James Paine).

had bilateral reflective symmetry in and of itself, but no symmetries vis-à-vis the rest of the building, to which the Colonnade is in fact entirely unrelated. Kedleston, in contrast, has nothing less than four-way reflective symmetry, a symmetry that works through, binds together, and unifies a structure formed of diverse components.

TRANSLATORY SYMMETRY

There are many other kinds of symmetry. Let us stay for the moment with the British Baroque and look, as symmetricians, at the main facade of Vanbrugh's Blenheim Palace (fig. 5.6). Like any number of other buildings in the period, Blenheim is composed of end pavilions, various frontispieces, and a central temple front. An ordinary person would call the result symmetrical. And, expounding this insight, a symmetrician would agree that on being reflected in a mirror, the total combination would not change in appearance. Yet when we take the facade apart and look at its individual elements, it of course loses all this symmetry—paradoxically because those elements are variously left- and right-handed.

There is asymmetry between the left-hand and right-hand sides as they extend from the central temple. Think of this central portico as a mirror seen on edge. If we label the outer, lower end-pavilion A; its taller neighbor, the frontispiece toward the center, B; the recession with its colonnade, C; and the taller section with pilasters flanking the central temple, D; the composition as it exists is:

$$ABCD \Leftarrow \text{Mirror Element} \Rightarrow DCBA$$

And the type of symmetry I have in mind at this point, which is not mirror symmetry but translatory, would require the following instead:

$$ABCD \Longleftrightarrow ABCD$$

In other words, exact repetition of one side on the other, with no handedness, no reflection, and in the original order. To achieve this sort of symmetry we would have to rebuild Blenheim as in figure 5.7. (I have preserved the mirror element, the portico, but maybe it shouldn't be there.) Translatory symmetry would make Blenheim Palace pretty weird, though no doubt buildable.

Fig. 5.6. Elevation of Blenheim Palace (John Vanbrugh, 1705–24). Photo courtesy of Bildarchiv Foto Marburg/Art Resource, New York.

Despite that weirdness, strict translatory symmetry of this type is probably more common, in architecture, than any other kind. This is because it is what you get in moldings, friezes, string courses, and the like, which are found in just about every period and culture. (The very word "frieze" implies repeated motifs. It comes from the Latin *phrygium*, "embroiderer," meaning a person who makes lots of repeated stitches.)

Fig. 5.7. Blenheim's main facade, redone in sequences of translatory symmetry flanking the central "mirror" or temple front.

The upper part of the frieze in figure 5.8, which became part of classicism's common patrimony, consists of a row of palmettes supported by confronted curled tendrils, these latter being linked curl to curl. Individually these objects have reflective symmetry. But, in being repeated, unchanged, along their horizontal axis, and with no reflection in those repetitions, their symmetry turns translatory.

Fig. 5.8. Adapted detail of an ancient Roman molding frieze drawn by Léon Vaudoyer, 1812. From Eve Blau and Edward Kaufman, eds., *Architecture and Its Image* (Montreal: Canadian Centre for Architecture, 1989).

The lower molding in the frieze is an egg-and-dart sequence at much smaller scale (there are eight eggs-and-darts to each palmette). These too have simple translatory symmetry. The constant difference in scale between the two, their countable ratios, emphasize their symmetry's translatory nature. If we call the curls *A* and the palmettes *B*, the order is: *ABABAB*, and so on, and the darts and eggs are similarly organized. Mathematically the frieze could go on forever. There are no beginnings, endings, subdivisions, or the like. It's like a number sequence as opposed to a number series.

GLIDE SYMMETRY

I have been distinguishing translatory from mirror symmetry. A third type combines the two. A motif will be repeated on alternating sides of an axis in such a way that it is reflected or mirrored each time. Glide symmetry, and therefore ornament of this type, is, like translatory symmetry, mathematically infinite. (And in this it is therefore all the more unlike mirror symmetry, which does not go on to infinity but is self-contained.) And, at least since Descartes, this idea of a motif or device theoretically going on forever has been essential in mathematics. It is something we should particularly associate with the age of the Baroque. (We noted in chapter 4 that Borromini's plan for Sant'Ivo composes easily into an Archimedean tiling that is infinite.)

In figure 5.9, courtesy of modern graphics software, we have Vaudoyer's drawing redone as a piece of glide symmetry. The palmettes are mirror-reflected across the horizontal axis and, as they're reflected, each palmette glides along one notch—always on that same horizontal axis—and theoretically forever.

Fig. 5.9. Vaudoyer's drawing of a frieze in Fig. 5.8 redone as glide symmetry

WALLPAPER SYMMETRY

Wallpaper symmetry brings us back to cubices rationes and to the square and cube; though, Kepler-fashion, we will now be able to branch out into, or generate, other shapes. And wallpaper symmetry is at the same time a branch of reflection (and of translation). It has mirror axes and identical handed hedrons. In architecture, at least, and apart from its function in decorating rooms, wallpaper symmetry appears chiefly in plans—more specifically, as repeated shapes set into the columns and rows that make up plane lattices.[13]

Most of all, wallpaper symmetry is a variation of tiling. But it is a variation that makes use of what is called the Dirichlet domain. The tiles we looked at in earlier discussions about Kepler were all plain shapes. Any patterning was achieved by contrasting the shapes of the tiles with one another. In wallpaper symmetry, however, the "tiles" are internally patterned. And that imposes certain new laws. Dirichlet domains are the name for those laws, or shall I say for the arenas in which those laws prevail. Dirichlet domains may be defined as the exoskeletons of ornamental motifs—motifs that are built around some point, some crossing of coordinates, in a plane lattice. The domains are then repeated, in one or more regular ways, throughout the lattice.

And, not for the first time in this book, we confront the idea of a geometrical elite—an exclusive club. What P. G. L. Dirichlet, a nineteenth-century German mathematician, discovered was that for all the immense variety of wallpaper patterns, their basic layout always obeys one of five different underlying types. These are his five "domains."[14] One can, in other words, fill any domain with an infinity of patterns, and one can alternate different patterns within a single lattice. These rules—five different domains and no more, but an infinity of possibilities within the domains—had been observed, quite untheoretically, by wallpaper designers and block-printers of fabrics ever since these things came into fashion. And this happened, we should note, during the age of the Baroque. So wallpaper symmetry is a bit like the Alhambra's symmetry groups—something known about for centuries before the mathematicians got hold of it and started analyzing it.

Printed papers pasted onto interior walls came in as substitutes for the decorative brocades that had traditionally been used as wall-hangings. Any

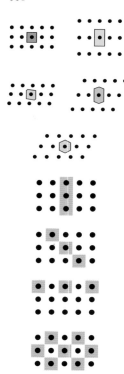

Fig. 5.10. The five types of Dirichlet domain for a planar lattice. From Keith Devlin, *Mathematics: The Science of Patterns* (New York: Scientific American Library, 1994).

Fig. 5.11. Variations on the domain of the violet square. From Devlin, *Mathematics*.

sort of repeat pattern could appear on the brocades. But printing tended to impose limitations. The printing blocks were modeled on those used for pictorial prints. Instead of printing, from the same block, many copies on different sheets to be sold separately, the wallpaper-maker would print his many copies on sheets intended to be displayed together as an overall entity. While there could be overprinting, and while patterns were often hand-colored or printed with different-colored inks, the blocks themselves were generally handled as in tiling—that is, in rectilinear or diagonal arrays. This sharply reduced the possibilities for the varied repeats you could get with hand-painting or embroidering.[15] In a way, the latticed layouts of the printing blocks are the conceptual ancestors of Dirichlet's domains.[16]

The five domains are (1) a square, (2) a rectangle, or (3, 4, 5) some sort of hexagon. The grids within which the domains are distributed can be (1) rectangles, (2) squares, or (3, 4, 5) rhombic parallelograms (see fig. 5.10). Each domain or repeat pattern must tile with its neighbors.

The domains do not have to be tight-packed but can be "cushioned" in a variety of ways (fig. 5.11). They can form vertical or diagonal rows, single or multiple. And, of course, their interior patterns may vary: the violet squares in the diagram in figures 5.10 and 5.11 stand not for infinite extension but for another sort of infinity—that of the possible interior patterns.

In the following discussion, with one exception, I will consider Dirichlet domains of the violet-square type only, though the others can no doubt be found in Baroque architecture and design—in wallpaper, of course, but also in other sorts of overall planar lattice patterns such as floors, gardens, forts, and cities.

So, let's look at the wallpaper symmetry in a Baroque garden. Figure 5.12 illustrates a 1618 engraving of part of the gardens of the Quirinale, Rome. We see a lattice of rectangular flowerbeds that I will call Dirichlet domains (i.e., the areas between the coordinates). The coordinates themselves are the garden paths. Each domain or bed is framed by stone parapets with prominent finials at the corners. These emphasize that the beds are repeats. As in wallpaper with multiple motifs, the differing inner designs are variations on set themes—a centralized pattern and pathways and/or plantings shaped like lozenges or rhombs, circles, chevrons, and the like. Some other beds are solidly filled with trees. As a further variation, each pair of domains flanks, horizontally, a fountain shaped like a conical shell.

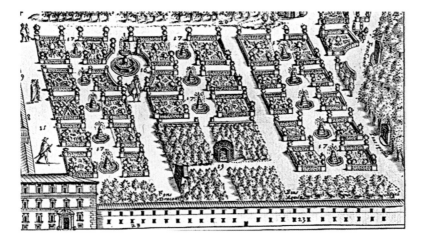

I have noted that the garden matches the rectangular arrangement in the violet-square Dirichlet domain (above, left in fig. 5.10)—that is, as built. However, as we see the garden in the engraver's perspective view in figure 5.12, the lattice is canted so as to resemble (left-handedly rather than right-handedly) two other types of domain—that with the green hexagon and that with the brown in figure 5.10. So, in a way, the Quirinale Gardens represent *two* of the five possibilities for wallpaper symmetry—one as built and one as seen.

Thousands of different architectural schemes could be laid out using the five Dirichlet rules. In other words, we could easily transform the Quirinale into something completely different in function though identical in symmetry. It could be an ideal town. The fountains could be churches, the flowerbeds blocks of houses, and the garden alleys boulevards. Or one column of the lattice could be the layout of a church, with the fountains as domical bays, the beds as chapels, and the pathways as aisles. Or we could put the domains into new arrays that would correspond to one of the other kinds of domain. We could have diapered, or hexagonal, compositions, rather than parterres latticed into rectangles.

If wallpaper was a Baroque invention, or at least specialty, and if wallpaper symmetry lends itself to urban design, let us now note the penchant for overseas settlements during this period. These involved something that practically never happened in Europe: the building of towns from scratch. Since, also, the settlements mostly had to be fortified, their layouts often embodied

Fig. 5.12. Detail of the gardens of the Quirinale (Rome). Engraving by J. Lauro, 1618.

Fig. 5.13. Ideal military camp. From Robert Barret, *Theorike and Practike of Moderne Warres*, 1598. The letters refer to the different subdivisions of the military—cavalry, infantry, and so on. There are also provisions for a market, artificers, and cattle.

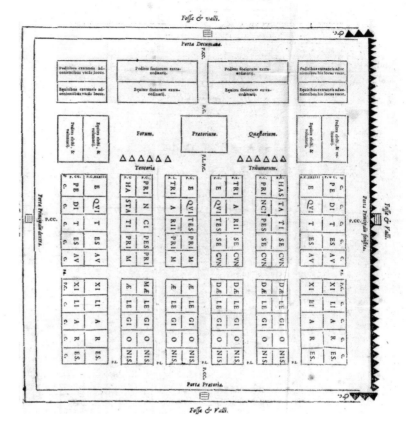

the principles of the science of castrametation—that is, the layout of military camps and outposts. And, at least in its more theoretical forms, castrametation involved wallpaper symmetry.

Renaissance editions of Polybius, Vegetius, and other Roman writers on castrametation, and Renaissance books derived from these classical writers such as Robert Barret's *Theorike and Practike of Moderne Warres*, 1598, show the kind of lattice I mean.[17] Barret's ideal military camp (see fig. 5.13) is basically a square, 750 paces per side, made up of seven vertical columns and eight rows across. Most of the subdivisions are squares, but with some distortions due to the river flowing down the middle, and to the encampments in the second left-hand column, which are sesquitertial rectangles. There is a drill area called the "Place of Armes Generall" and provisions for a market, *G*, and artificers and cattle, *I; E* and *K* are bastioned forts and *A* is the general's tent. As Anthony Garvan points out, the plan is very similar to the city plan used by François I to rebuild the town of Vitry-le-François in the Marne region of northern France.[18]

This camp lattice makes use of an arrangement very similar to those in the wallpaper diagram in figure 5.11, which have their filled domains arranged as a front row and the others, unfilled, arrayed behind in strict columns and rows. Other shapes, many of them utterly irregular, are also found in the settlement colonies erected in the seventeenth and eighteenth centuries. But the regular lattice, and the military camp with its "domains," are equally frequent.[19]

There was another impetus toward wallpaper symmetry in these layouts: the scriptural tradition of Moses' desert camps. Numbers 2:1 tells of the twelve tribes of Israel assembling around their tents in military array. As the Vulgate puts it: "Each [tribe] of the sons of Israel laid out its camp [*castrametabuntur* (2:2)] with its multitudes, trumpets, ensigns, and the houses of its people, around the Ark of the Covenant" (the chest containing the tablets with the Ten Commandments). And later: "the encampments were built [*castrametati sunt*] for the multitudes, their families, and the houses of their fathers" (Numbers 2:34). *Castrametor* is neo-Latin. It adds the verb for "to measure out," *metor*, to "camp," *castra*. So the implication, in the Vulgate text, is that the tribes' settlements were geometrical and indeed were wallpaper lattices like those advised by Vegetius, Polybius, and the other Roman authorities.

As the Hebrew settlements developed from camps to towns, the settings for the Ark and its temple got to be more palatial and less camplike. The earliest description of an architectural setting for the Ark consists of God's directives to Moses on Sinai (Exodus 27:9–19). These describe the Ark's surrounding atrium. It was to be oriented exactly to the main compass points, a double square 50 by 100 cubits and 5 cubits high. On the long sides were to be twenty bronze columns with silver capitals, on the short sides ten such columns. Tapestries or curtains were to be hung on each side of the atrium, and there was to be an elaborate entrance feature at an unspecified place, but almost certainly in the center of one of the exterior walls.

The apogee of ancient Jewish thought about architectural measurement was the palace complex erected in Jerusalem on the Temple Mount.[20] In its heyday, during the age of Solomon (970s B.C.), this complex was a small city housing hundreds, perhaps thousands, of people. Measurements pervading its descriptions always specify round numbers with frequent repetitions, and with everything centered, bilateral, and equal. Unlike similar pagan complexes, Solomon's palace applied principles we would recognize as those of a regular lattice with varied Dirichlet domains—or you could evoke cubices rationes.

And then there are the temple visions of Ezekiel (Ezekiel 40–42) and of the New Jerusalem in Revelation (Revelation 21:9–23.). In Ezekiel's vision the prophet's guide—none other than Jehovah himself—appears with a coil of rope and a measuring staff. As he shows off the temple he measures out its main dimensions (Ezekiel 40:3). The precinct's outer walls are each 100 cubits long, we learn, each facing a cardinal direction. The interior buildings are centered within the square—or at least the text can be interpreted that way. Also square is the city surrounding the temple, 540 cubits—that is, about 810 feet—per side. Both guide and visitor seem as interested in number—dimension, proportion, repetition—as in the actual buildings.

In St. John's vision the Heavenly Jerusalem is again square, with three gates per side—3 × 4 = the twelve tribes of Israel and/or, proleptically, the twelve apostles. The outlandish size of this city has caused comment (12,000 stadia or a bit more than 1,377 miles per side! Well, it's a vision.). Indeed, and even more extraordinarily, the New Jerusalem is actually a cube, for, we learn, its height is again 12,000 stadia. Jerusalem is cubic in other ways. It uses, almost exclusively, a cubic number, twelve (number of sides in a dodecahedron; number of edges in an octahedron; and the first of cubes, eight, plus the number of sides to a square). The three gates in each side, though not specified as being sited at equal intervals, suggest, if streets lead from them into and across town, that the Heavenly Jerusalem was formed of nine squares that themselves made up a square. In any event the city clearly was a grid of some sort—a veritable piece of wallpaper symmetry.

The importance of nine-square grids in Baroque planning stems in large part from Juan Bautista Villalpando, a Jesuit priest and architect. In 1594–1605 he published graphic reconstructions of the Jerusalem Temple and its surrounding palace, mainly as described in Ezekiel (fig. 5.14). These

CASTRA TRIBVVM ISRAEL
CIRCA TABERNACVLVM
FOEDERIS.

OCCIDENS.

Ephraim · Manaſſes · Beniamin · Dan

MERIDIES

Gad · Gerſonitæ · Meraritæ · Aſer

SEPTENTRIO.

Simeon · Caathitæ · Moyſes, et Aaron · Nephthali

Ruben · Zabulon · Iſſachar · Iudas

ORIENS.

were by far the most elaborate of the many such restorations of the temple and its surrounding palace that had appeared up to that time.[21] Villalpando proposes a Bramantesque complex with strong overtones of the Escorial (only recently completed). His engravings are perhaps the greatest example there is of architectural restoration purely as an act of the imagination. Villalpando didn't need or want historical and archaeological evidence. He had something better: the geometries that God dictated to Moses, Solomon, Ezekiel, and St. John the Divine. Indeed, says Villalpando, before one can properly contemplate scriptural descriptions of Moses' camps and Solomon's palace, one must already have in mind the proper numbers and proportions.[22] One proceeds from the numbers to the words, not the other way round.

Fully in line with Scripture, Villalpando's monument is a military camp—a huge square 500 cubits (approximately 750 feet) per side. Or,

Fig. 5.14. Camps of the Israelite kings around the Ark of the Covenant (Juan Bautista Villalpando). From Jerónimo de Prado and Villalpando, *In Ezechielem explanationes et apparatus urbis ac templi hierosolymitami* (Rome: Carolus Vullietus, 1594–1605).

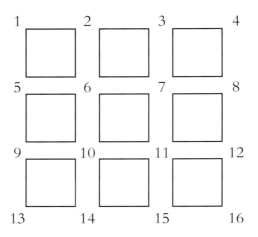

Fig. 5.15. How a 3 × 3 lattice of Dirichlet domains
can develop into a 4 × 4
one

rather, it consists of sixteen square camps (twelve for the twelve tribes of Israel and another four for the kings of the Levites [Numbers 3:14ff.])
grouped into a square. Each camp is exactly one-tenth the size of the whole.
Everything is arrayed around the Ark, which occupies two subsquares in the
great square's center. The streets dividing the camps are two subsquares
wide. For Villalpando, furthermore, this Moses-derived castrametatio with
its Dirichlet lattice is the matrix of the Jerusalem palace.

Do you see not nine but sixteen squares? Look again. Arranged in a 3 ×
3 lattice, nine squares are also sixteen, as the diagram in figure 5.15 makes
clear. In other words, at the corner of each of the nine squares there can be
four subsidiary spaces—street-crossings, *piazze*, towers, whatever. I have used
numbers to show how the lattice of twelve squares turns into one of sixteen.
These sixteen subspaces are essential to the scheme: they are Villalpando's
sixteen tribal tents. And they outline the shapes, as yet invisible, of the 3 × 3
lattice that will generate Villalpando's definitive Jerusalem complex.

Villalpando spells out the order of his castrametatio in tables and astrological charts made of similar lattices. More wallpaper symmetry. And not
just in Villalpando's own book but in later writings by his imitators such as
Bernard Lamy, Nikolaus Goldmann, and Leonhard Christoph Sturm—
thinkers who were as much mathematicians as architects, and who special-
ized in restoring the Jerusalem Temple.[23] The castrametatio exercises
demonstrate the allegorical, astrological, alchemical, musical, and other relationships of the camp/palace and its noble numbers: nine hidden or implied

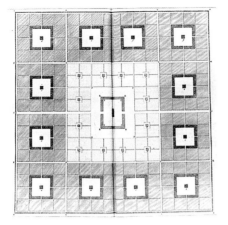

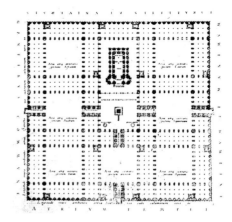

squares, sixteen visible squares, twelve vertices per column of squares, twelve per row of squares, thirty-six in all, and so on. The metaphysical order of Moses' camp and Solomon's palace matches their physical order.

Note, further, that Villalpando's design has crossed central axes both horizontal and vertical, identical flanking axes both horizontal and vertical, and identical left/right and up/down symmetries in both the nine-square complex and its sixteen-square (or sixteen-element) derivative. So the pattern is a much fuller realization of wallpaper symmetry than Polybius's—or, so far as I know, than anything earlier in the history of urban design.[24]

Many later writers and designers pictured the geometrical perfections of Solomon's palace—often with considerable indebtedness to Villalpando, though seldom with this sort of full-court symmetry.[25] However, John Wood the Elder, in *The Origin of Building; or the Plagiarism of the Heathens Detected* (1741), did produce a further exercise in wallpaper symmetry for the temple and surrounding palace, powerfully elaborating Villalpando's 4 × 4 lattice (see figs. 5.16 and 5.17). Solomon's palace is now a veritable symphony of 4 × 4 squares: the great outer square and each of the component domains; then an inner central square composed, in its own way, of sixteen small squares, each of these latter, in turn, being composed of four still smaller squares. Each square in the frame of twelve squares surrounding this inner atrium has within it a central square one-fourth the size of its matrix. Only the central temple itself, which contains the Ark, is a nonsquare: it is a sesquiquartal rectangle.

Fig. 5.16. John Wood the Elder's ground plan of Solomon's temple. From *The Origin of Building; or the Plagiarism of the Heathens Detected,* 1741.

Fig. 5.17. Central part of Solomon's palace with the temple (*upper center*). From Villalpando, *Explanationes.*

FURTHER ADVENTURES OF THE NINE-SQUARE LATTICE

Villalpando's geometric squares, subsquares, and central temple reappeared not only in subsequent restorations of Solomon's complex in Jerusalem (and, as we shall see, as a standard way of articulating Baroque buildings) but in at least one executed New World town.

Since I live in that town I am anxious not to seem guilty of *campanilismo*. So I will immediately point out that the subject was first significantly discussed by André Corboz, a Frenchman. I merely follow along with a few geometrical points. Corboz claims that the first urban realization of Villalpando's Solomonic complex as a modern city is the Rev. John Davenport's nine-square layout of New Haven, Connecticut (fig. 5.18).[26] The original settlement, we are told, derived all its polity directly from Scripture, and Solomon's city figures prominently in the relevant sermonizing.[27] This was in 1639, about thirty-four years after Villalpando's book appeared. So we might think of the name, New Haven, as a trope of New Heaven.

Anyway, Corboz is quite possibly correct; it has been shown that Davenport knew the writings of Valentin Andreae, a Protestant influenced by Villalpando, who wrote a treatise on an ideal missionary city called Christianopolis—though New Haven and Villalpando are closer to each other, formally, than either is to Andreae.[28] We also know that New Haven's original government was based on a legal code written by John Cotton of the Massachusetts Bay Colony, titled "Moses his Judiciaills."[29] So the notion of this New England town as a Mosaic camp was in the air.

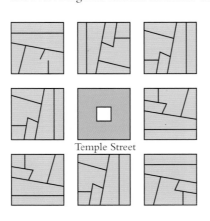

Temple Street

Fig. 5.18. The original nine squares of New Haven, Connecticut, in 1641. After John Brockett. The pattern of lots within each square has been stylized.

Moreover, Davenport's layout and Villalpando's palace complex (fig. 5.17) are strikingly similar in design. They have the same 3 × 3 disposition of Dirichlet domains forming a composite outer square, and the same streets or coordinates whose width is a set fraction of the nine squares. At New Haven, that fraction is smaller, and New Haven's squares are only 175 Biblical cubits

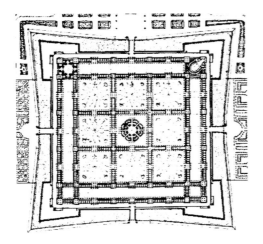

per side (approximately 262 feet) as opposed to Villalpando's 500. But the
New England town does have the same central "atrium" for its temple. Still
today, a thoroughfare called Temple Street runs just in front of the site of that
original meetinghouse (fig. 5.18).[30] As to the irregular patterns of the lots
in the eight surrounding squares, even these can be interpreted as examples
of wallpaper symmetry (though not the Solomonic kind)—independent
inner patterns within identical Dirichlet domains.

    The Rev. Mr. Davenport's ideas for a Solomonic town apparently didn't
take root elsewhere. As far as I know no other New World settlements followed the nine-square principle or anything similar. But, a world or more
away, a play of wallpaper symmetries that is indeed strikingly similar, and in
my view equally derived from Villalpando, did inspire the eighteenth-century Neapolitan architect Mario Gioffredo. In 1750 or 1751 he proposed a
new palace to be erected at Caserta for his monarch, Charles of Bourbon. I
have described Gioffredo's project more fully elsewhere.[31] But here it won't
be out of place to regard it—as I did not do on that earlier occasion—as a
piece of wallpaper symmetry (figs. 5.19 and 5.20).

    Gioffredo's dream was patently Solomonic. It was to build a royal palace
that was a virtual city, housing not just the court and king but all the main
political and cultural elites of the Kingdom of the Two Sicilies—university,
museum, library, cabinet bureaus, military high commands, and so on. More
important, Gioffredo's palace was highly indebted to Villalpando. It is in fact
a 3 × 3 grid of square Dirichlet domains. The centerpiece, in the middle of

Fig. 5.19. Plan for a new
royal palace at Caserta
(Mario Gioffredo, 1750 or
1751). Naples, Biblioteca
Nazionale.

Fig. 5.20. Perspective
view of Gioffredo's
Caserta palace project .
Naples, Biblioteca
Nazionale.

the central square, was a huge octagonal double-helix staircase—just where
Villalpando had located his Altar of the Holocausts. Exactly as in Villalpando's palace, moreover, the coordinates of the lattice are ranges of enclosed space for offices, residences, and the like. It is true that Gioffredo sup-
presses the sixteen ancillary areas Villalpando puts at the corners of his nine
squares, and that he thickens the perimeter of the great square by doubling
the perimeter's width. But otherwise the similarities between the two plans
are overwhelming—in the use and arrangements of shapes as well as in the
distribution of functions. Like Solomon's palace, that of Charles of Bourbon
(undoubtedly Charles was praised by court preachers as the Solomon of the
age) was for the realm's elites.[32]

Gioffredo's conception was indeed as tremendous as Villalpando's—or
more so, since it was actually supposed to be built. It should be better
known. It leads directly on to the megapalaces of French neoclassical theory
(fig. 5.21). Here, as nowhere else, geometry reigns, and architects exploit the
planes and severe surfaces of mathematical models.[33] Villalpando and Gioff-
fredo help us to understand that despite their abstraction, the neoclassical
designs of the French "revolutionary" architects inherited many geometrical beliefs and practices from their Baroque predecessors. One great unify-
ing factor was this love of wallpaper symmetry.

I have claimed that this nine-square construct was significant in the planning and articulation of more ordinary Baroque buildings. And so it was.
Nine-square, square-bordered wallpaper grids are in fact particularly common, almost de rigueur, all throughout Baroque urbanism and architecture.
Figures 5.22 and 5.23, for example, show two versions of Jules Hardouin-
Mansart's notable Paris church of the Invalides. While as it stands the Invalides' nave/chancel complex does not possess more than the most primitive bilateral reflection, the composition is nonetheless formed from a
matrix that very clearly is a 3×3 lattice. That is, by removing the plan's sym-
metry-breaking elements—its main entrance with its steps and columns,

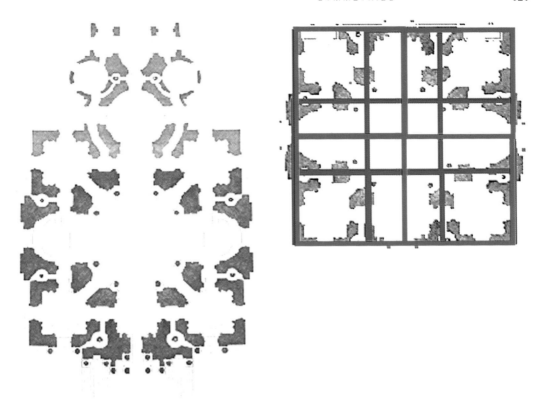

and the chancel extending the church to the east, all of which split the plan into heterodox shapes, the rest of that plan then turns directly into a square building with central rotunda, four flanking domical transepts, four corner chapels, and four entrance massings, all identical in form and placement. And this design is in fact generated by a nine-square grid (in green) superimposed on a four-square one (red). One could make exactly the same analysis of Villalpando's palace and the plan of New Haven, not to mention the example of castrametation we looked at.

To get an idea of how intricately symmetrical was Hardouin-Mansart's use of the system, we have only to look back at Val-de-Grâce (fig. 5.1). In that plan, which by the 1680s was old-fashioned, Mansart had simply erected a large domed cube for his crossing and set it between the two existing transepts, complete with the "défaut de symmétrie" that Bernini complained about. Compared to most of its predecessor churches of the period, Val-de-Grâce's network of real and implied correspondences of wall ele-

Fig. 5.22. Ground-level plan of the church of the Invalides, Paris (Jules Hardouin-Mansart, erected 1679–91). Chancel shown in the original drawing as incomplete. Canadian Centre for Architecture, Montreal.

Fig. 5.23. Church of the Invalides ground-level plan, with main entrance columns, steps, and chancel removed to show the nine-square, four-square matrix (in green and red, respectively)

ments across its interior volumes is a sophisticated new departure. But later Baroque churches, in several countries, took off from these precepts.

SPIRAL SYMMETRIES

Spiral or rotational symmetry is the symmetry not only of spirals and wheels but of circles, globes, and many regular polygons and polyhedrons. Indeed, a considerable number of the shapes we have been talking about have spiral symmetry. Among them are the celestial spheres, Kepler's elliptical planetary orbits, and several of his Platonic and Archimedean solids. Digges's, Newton's, and Galileo's diagrams of planetary motions and forces also have spiral symmetry.[34] And spiral symmetry can be found everywhere in earthly architecture, both in two-dimensional and three-dimensional form—in domes, in staircases, in round and polygonal central-plan buildings, and in every sort of curvilinear ornament—notably two types we will be looking at here, the spiral column-shaft and the Ionic volute.

We can even find it in such things as the nine-square lattice. For if you cross that nine-square setup with central vertical and horizontal axes, the resulting Dirichlet domain in each quarter is a rotation, through 90 degrees, of itself (see fig. 5.24). Therefore the four "different" domains are not really different but are four repetitions of the same domain. Each time, the repetition has been swiveled around on an imaginary pivot located in the corner marked with the green square. The four domains can therefore be labeled as the "identities" C_1, C_2, C_3, and C_4. The concept is really a lot like mirror symmetry with its reflected hedrons, except that with spiral symmetry there are more than two reflected entities, usually, and it is really a question of rotation rather than reflection—swiveling rather than flipping.

And you can reassemble these spiraling motifs in new and different ways. My doctored version of the Invalides plan in figure 5.23, for example, is another C_4 spiral. And not only are all nine-square plans

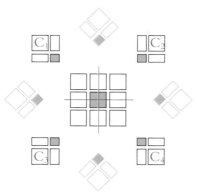

Fig. 5.24. New Haven's nine squares as rotated motifs in a C_4 spiral

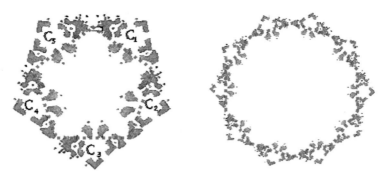

spiral, but so are 2×2, 4×4, or for that matter 121×121 lattices. The only requirement is that in this case the domains must themselves be square and must be arranged in a square.

But the spiralings can go well beyond the confines of the nine-square plan. The lattices can be broken out of their quadrilateral and hexagonal Dirichlet domains and augmented. Our doctored Invalides, for example, can be expanded and rotated into five-way—or for that matter, ten-way—symmetries (fig. 5.25). These experiments show, too, how spiral symmetries can rise up out of the pentagons and the decagons.

One of the most common forms of spiral symmetry in Baroque architecture is found in twisted or Solomonic columns, so called because it was thought that such columns stood in Solomon's temple. The twisted shafts may have been meant to honor the oak tree that was the original Ark of the Covenant (Joshua 24:26:"Joshua wrote all these words in the volume of the Lord's Law, and . . . placed it beneath an oak which was in the sanctuary of the Lord"). This would explain, for example, why Bernini used Solomonic columns in his baldacchino, and why twisted columns so frequently ornament altars.[35]

Anyway, in the seventeenth century, columns generally were held to have special powers. According to an ancient tradition, the supposedly aboriginal Egyptian philosopher Hermes Trismegistus (probably a composite of the Egyptian Thoth and the Greek Hermes) had inscribed his learning on columns or stelae, and, after reading them, Plato, Moses, and Zoroaster (other sages are sometimes mentioned) went forth to found their different philosophies.[36] In the age of the Baroque the contemplation of columns attained the level of what was called *Saülenlehre* and *Saülenphilosophie*, "column

Fig. 5.25. Spiral symmetries of the Invalides: *left,* a C_5 spiral; *right,* a C_{10} spiral

Fig. 5.26. Two of the columns of Bernini's baldacchino in St. Peter's (1624–33). Photograph courtesy of Alinari/Art Resource, New York.

wisdom" and "column philosophy."[37] Columns were thus considered repositories of knowledge. Hence Wren, following Josephus, claimed that Seth's sons "erected Two Columns of Brick and Stone to preserve their Mathematical Science to Posterity."[38]

We don't know that these earliest wisdom-bearing columns were spiral. But spiral shafts did come to be identified, in particular, as sources of religious and scientific insight. Indeed the very fact that they are spirals gives Solomonic shafts a role in philosophy, especially in the sense of Baroque natural philosophy—physics and mathematics.[39] How so? For one thing, Solomonic columns, especially when made, as they frequently are, of bronze, involve fluid dynamics and wave formation. Twisted shafts look like hardened states of originally elastic, even ductile, material. They look as if their bases have remained fixed while the rest of the shaft was gradually twisted—at first a full 360 degrees, and then further, round and round, until the cylinder was whorled like the rubber band in a toy airplane.

Then, as everyone who has played with rubber-band airplanes knows, if the twisting continues a new set of larger, more bulbous whorls begins to appear. I will call these hyperwhorls. You can achieve the same effect not only with a rubber band but (more historistically for our concerns) by twisting a piece of cloth or rope.[40] Architects were very conscious of this physical process of twisting. Note that the two left-hand shafts of Bernini's baldacchino (fig. 5.26) twist to the left, the two right-hand shafts to the right. The plants that garland the upper parts of the shafts twist in the same left- and right-handed fashion. This of course puts the two sides of the baldacchino into bilateral reflection; but it also projects a conscious notional history for the shafts of the twisting process itself, of two oppositely directed flows or waves in an originally ductile substance.[41]

W. Chandler Kirwin's photogrammetry of the baldacchino shows that the hyperwhorls diminish as the shaft rises. Thus if, as suggested, the latter are seen as waves, they are waves with a decreasing amplitude as they move upward from the impetus that created them. This, in turn, suggests further aspects of natural philosophy, borrowed from the world of plant and tree growth. Seen as undulant stems or trunks, gnarled and twisted oaks perhaps, the shafts have concentrated their greatest growth into the lower, "older" parts, with less growth in their "younger" upper regions. This is what botanists call vertical compression.[42] It strengthens the likeness of Solomonic columns to oaks.

Vertical compression also makes twisted shafts slightly conical. And that qualifies them as vortices—the kind of spirals that develop from very narrow cores to widen out like the bells of brass musical horns. Vortices, like other forms of twisting, are once again associated with the fluid dynamics of a bronze column shaft being poured.[43] I will here also mention Descartes's theories about vortices, namely that they filled the heavens and were everywhere on Earth—in the air, invisibly, as well as visibly in water and other fluids. Such thoughts expanded the importance of vortices and spirals in Baroque thought.[44] Yet I've never seen any art-historical comment on these aspects of Solomonic columns. (But then I've never seen any art-historical comment on most of the subjects raised in this book.)

So let's push onward. Figure 5.27 depicts three phases of the Solomonic shaft, now to be regarded as a model of geometrical Saülenphilosophie. The three images are taken from Guarino Guarini's 1686 treatise on civil architecture. On the far left the twisting process has not yet begun. The left-hand shaft is the starting-point, ground zero, with intact vertical flutes. Then comes the first phase of twisting. The vertical flutes are tightly screwed into nested right-hand helices. In phase three the hyperwhorls develop. For the first time we get a true Solomonic column. Finally, just to top up our Baroque Saülenlehre with a bit of the modern kind, I add in figure 5.28 an example of one of twenty-seven symmetry types for twisted columns that are being investigated by Martin Golubitsky and Ian Mel-

Fig. 5.27. *Left to right:*
shaft with straight
flutes; shaft with
twisted flutes; shaft
with twisted flutes and
hyperwhorls. From
Guarini, *Architettura.*

bourne. These take Saülenlehre and translate it into the world of modern
higher mathematics.[45]

Note that Guarini's three shafts are of differing heights. This is because
the architect supplied differing proportional systems for them. But at the
same time if you think about what happens when you twist something—
once again, about the form's notional history—you remember that twisting
something makes it shorter. Indeed if we sense that the shafts are elastic, or
were so once, then they have a powerful upward force-potential. They are
like loaded catapults (or even huge rubber-band motors). This sense is reinforced by Kirwin's thoughts on the shafts on Bernini's baldacchino as cannons—thoughts promoted by the fact that the shafts are hollow and were

made by cannon-founders.[46] To this one might add that the barrels of Renaissance and Baroque cannons were frequently ornamented as if they were
architectural column shafts. In sum, to our metaphors of vortices, waves, and
other column-wisdom, we can add ideas about enormous, barely controlled
potential impetus. Maybe that's the secret of the Solomonic column's suc-
cess.

Another big venue for spiral symmetry in Baroque (and other) architecture—a venue that, statistically, is even more prominent than the twisted
column—is the Ionic volute. There are several ways of generating these.
Some architects seem to have used helical seashells as pantographs.[47] Others generate their spirals geometrically, as in Vincenzo Scamozzi's example
(figs. 5.29 and 5.30). As is normal, Scamozzi uses a module derived from his
column's diameter in order to measure every dimension in the design, right
down to the tiniest. One-tenth of a diameter he calls the *parte*. The diagram
in figure 5.29 shows that the spiral's width diminishes from 4½ parti as it
curves down from under the capital's abacus (to the north), to 4 parti (to the
east), to 3½ (to the south), and to 3 (to the west), and then around again two
more times, shrinking by ½ parte at every quarter-turn. Rationalizing the
fractions, the diminution makes up the arithmetical series 9:8:7:6:5:4:3:2:1.
The result is what mathematicians call an equiangular or logarithmic spiral.

François Blondel had debts to these thoughts of Scamozzi's. He repro-
duces Scamozzi's method of laying out Ionic volutes, although, lower down
in the same plate, he identifies what he calls "a more perfect" method of
doing so. The expansion of the curve in an equiangular spiral is mapped out
with many guidelines in a recursive series of lengths.[48]

Eleven years after Blondel, Guarini was doing the same thing. But he

Fig. 5.28. One of 27
symmetry types for the
twisted-column symme-
tries. Courtesy of Martin
Golubitsky and Ian Mel-
bourne, University of
Houston.

Fig. 5.29 (far left).
Vincenzo Scamozzi's
scheme for drawing the
spiral of an Ionic volute.
From Scamozzi, *Idea
dell'Architettura univer-
sale* (Venice: Expensis
auctoris, 1615).

Fig. 5.30. Ionic volute.
From Scamozzi, *Ar-
chitettura*.

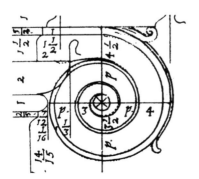

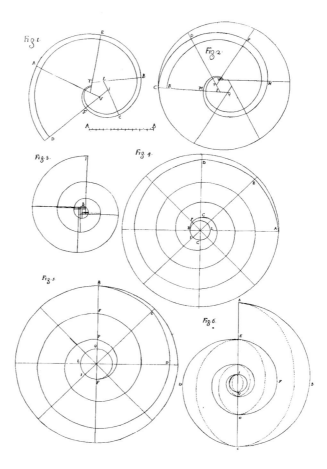

proposed even subtler spirals (fig. 5.31). All of them approach but never
quite achieve continuous curves. The trick with Guarini's spirals is to move
the compass's point every time a new arc is drawn, while at the same time
shrinking the arc's diameter by a set amount. The spiral in Guarini's figure 1
gets its diminutions by measuring from the far side of the central pentagon
as the compass rotates. Figure 2 does the same but with a central hexagon.
In figure 3 Guarini draws a series of tiny squares within the volute's eye and
extends one of each square's sides to form the spiral's continuous angle of
diminution. In figures 4 and 5 he divides the eye's perimeter into equal
parts, numbers them, and sets the compass point successively at each of these
points. The successively smaller arcs will produce the five-whorled spirals

shown. The last figure, 6, shows how to make an oval spiral. After making an ordinary circular spiral (like one of those described), a series of points across this circular spiral's horizontal axis is marked out. These become the places at which to set the compass point for a set of arcs from larger circles that are inscribed inside the arcs of the circular volute. Joining these wider whorls together (and erasing the circular spiral) produces an oval spiral. Blondel included most of these same constructions in his 1675–88 *Cours*, but with uglier drawings.[49]

Mathematicians did not begin to study equiangular spirals until 1638, when Descartes discussed them with Marin Mersenne, the music theorist.[50] It is hard to say whether Guarini and Blondel knew of Descartes's work. Descartes, of course, was interested only in the true equiangular spiral with a continuous curvature, not in aggregations of circular arcs. But since Ionic capitals have always had equiangular volutes, one artisanal solution or another—including the whelk-shell pantograph, which would produce a true continuous curve—must always have been known. Equiangular and other spirals are also found in pinecones and leaf buds.

A third major site for spiral symmetry in Baroque architecture, as suggested earlier, is in the realm of central-plan buildings. Not only are nine-square buildings and their relatives subject to spiral symmetry, but so are buildings (or towns) that are circular, polygonal, or even elliptical; and so too are domes of that description.[51] Some Baroque domes, indeed, are powerful exercises in three-dimensional spiral geometry. I will be content with a single example.

The lantern of Francesco Borromini's Sant'Ivo alla Sapienza in Rome, completed in 1660, is surrounded by a famous comical corkscrew staircase. Many people have written about it, myself included.[52] But that exterior piece of spiral symmetry is only a rather cocky afterthought to that of the church's interior dome. This is symmetry of a kind we haven't looked at yet. The dome juxtaposes two C_3 spirals. In elevation, their arms are parabolic ribs. In plan, each arm or leaf, with its two rotated twins, forms into a triangular shape, one set of these shapes having convex outer rims and the other concave. The two types alternate, becoming, together, a C_6 rotation (fig. 5.32).

It seems to me that the thought behind Borromini's design is botanical. The two juxtaposed rotations seem to mimic the alternating petals and

Fig. 5.32. Interior of the dome of Sant Ivo (Francesco Borromini, Rome, 1642–60). Photograph courtesy of Erich Lessing/Art Resource, New York.

Fig. 5.33. Columbine (*Aquiledia amaliae*). From Hellmut Baumann, *Die griechische Pflantzenwelt in Mythos, Kunst und Literatur* (Munich: Hirmer, 1982).

sepals you find in certain flowers—for example, the columbine pictured in figure 5.33. A similar flower, in which petals and sepals alternate as they spiral, belongs to the strawberry plant. The stamens and pistils in the center of either blossom would be the base of Borromini's lantern with its rays of light and stars. And the alternating, rotating sepals and petals are, in Borromini, his two types of leaves (albeit in Borromini we get a C_3 rather than a C_5 result).

It was commonplace in the age of the Baroque to model the interiors of coffered domes on plant symmetries. The spirals we see in sunflower and chrysanthemum capitula were particularly drawn on.[53] (Perhaps the botanical nature of the idea explains why individual coffers of domes are so often filled with rosettes and other blossoms.) But to me Borromini's petal pattern at Sant'Ivo is a more striking essay in botanical symmetry—not Saülenlehre, you might say, but Kuppellehre.

In their 1992 book *Spiral Symmetry,* István Hargittai and Clifford Pickover include essays on many other kinds of spirals—among them Archimedean, golden section, Pythagorean, dynamic-symmetry, random, and fractal spirals. They also discuss spirals with what is called broken symmetry. One could also mention that there are parabolic, hyperbolic, and cornu spirals. The whole subject stands as a fascinating challenge for architectural writers. And not just in Baroque architecture. Any architect who uses continuous curves—Antonì Gaudí and Frank Gehry are only two of the many who come to mind—can be studied for their use of spiral symmetry.

We have sampled the ways in which the word *symmetry* changed its meaning—or, better, developed and elaborated new meanings—in the Baroque era. As I indicated at the beginning of this chapter, the process led from simpler pre-Baroque concepts of symmetry in terms of style, compositional approach, or commensurability onward to the complexities of reflection, translation, glide symmetry, wallpaper symmetry, and—most complex of all in some ways—spiral symmetry. We have seen how these changes and enrichments played out in architecture. I said at the beginning of this chapter that these new forms of symmetry also involve new ways of working with repetition, inversion, lattices, and rotation. We have seen instances of each. I hope that future architectural writers will begin to step more fully into this fascinating arena.

STRETCHED
CIRCLES
AND
SQUEEZED
SPHERES

F rom the beginning of this book we have been speaking of effable shapes. We looked at their unique regularities, unities, repetitions, and recursions. But Baroque art is full of ineffable, even distorted, shapes as well. Originally effable forms will often end up getting stretched, squeezed, swollen, and pinched. In the same way, we have noted the existence of rectangles that are musically dissonant as well as consonant, and of "irrational" ratios. We saw how column shafts could develop from simple rotational symmetry to a symmetry of double spirals and onward (mathematically) even from that.

THE BEAUTIES OF
DISTORTION

But distortion is partly in the eye of the beholder. After all, ellipses can be seen as distorted circles. We might even see a rectangle as a stretched square. Yet ellipses and rectangles can have their own effable geometry. Anyway, some of the effable objects in nature that served as models for humanmade shapes turned out, on inquiry, not to be so effable—Earth, it seemed, was not Dryden's "goodly Ball"[1] but a slightly squashed one. And even then, as an oblate spheroid, Earth is far from pure, simply as a form. The same goes for the other heavenly bodies, even the Moon's opalescent sphere. As Galileo put it, the Moon "is not perfectly smooth, free from inequalities, and exactly spherical . . . on the contrary, it is full of irregularities, uneven, full of hollows and protuberances."[2] Instead of being filled with perfect geometries of shape and movement, the very heavens—Digges's palaces of God, angels, and planetary intelligences—are all of them somehow distorted.

OVALS, ELLIPSES, PARABOLAS, AND HYPERBOLAS

So let us look with kindly eyes on distortion and its architectural fallout. Nowhere in the world of geometric form does distortion, and especially stretching and squeezing, play a larger role than in the world of curves and curvatures. Ovals, ellipses, parabolas, and hyperbolas, which in the Renaissance are relatively or very rare, are common in the Baroque. Renaissance domes, like those in antiquity, had been hemispheres or other sphere segments. Baroque domes, we have seen, are on the other hand usually paraboloids. And of the three nested domes of St. Paul's, two are even more exotic. Two are cubical catenoids and one is paraboloid.

I will define an oval as any circle stretched symmetrically in a single direction. The other four shapes are matters of more precision, though all of them fit in with the theme of distortion. And this by their very names: parabolas (Greek meaning beyond, outrageous, deceiving, reckless) and hyperbolas (in Greek, "thrown upward"; think also of linguistic hyperbole). "Ellipse" or "ellipsis" means "omission," hence something that is imperfect in another way. But what is "missing" in a geometrical ellipse? Perhaps it tries to be a perfect circle, but "misses."

From figure 6.1 we see that the circle is itself a kind of ellipse, for both are conic sections—ways of slicing cones. When the slicing is done by a perfectly horizontal plane the result is a circle (left). The ellipse (right) is formed when a plane intersects the cone at an angle somewhere between the horizontal and the angle of the cone's own slope. These two conic sections appear all throughout architecture, of course, with great frequency in plans and openings, and they are endemic in all sorts of ornamental work.

The next two forms, the parabola and the hyperbola (fig. 6.2), while they also show up frequently in plans, have, as well, a more specific architectural function. They give shape to different kinds of arches and vaults. They are not closed but open, with a central apse or vertex (the narrow end of each curve) and extending arms. The parabola (left) is formed when the intersecting plane is precisely at the cone's own angle. If the plane is at an angle greater than that of the cone—for example, directly vertical, as on the right in figure 6.2, the result is a hyperbola.

What distinguishes hyperbolas from parabolas? The hyperbola's two arms get straighter and straighter as they move away from the apse or curve at the top. A parabola's arms continue to curve around toward each other. If the arms meet, the parabola becomes an ellipse. The hyperbola's "branches," as they are called, just keep going forever. Hyperbolas look a lot like catenaries. The difference is that catenaries are flat plane figures and hyperbolas are inscribed on conical surfaces.

By the way: why, in defining the hyperbola, show two cones, one upright and the other inverted? This creates the hyperbola's most characteristic form, which is double, consisting of its two disconnected branches.

All these forms, both two-dimensionally (as arches or vaults) and when rotated 360 degrees into solids (domes), have their own proper descriptive and analytical formulas. We have looked at the approximations of continuous curves that can be made with an ordinary pair of bipolar compasses. But, inspired by Descartes and Kepler, by the third quarter of the seventeenth century architects were drawing true continuous curves with newly invented proportional compasses and pantographs.[3] These instruments could be used to draw conic sections, trisect angles, and create all sorts of shapes that, to architects, were fascinatingly new. The first person to draw all the conic sections by such a method was apparently Kepler, who describes it in his *Ad Vitellionem Paralipomena* of 1604.[4] Girard Desargues, discussed in chapter 7, was at the same time inventing more such instruments and elaborating those that existed.[5] As to a heavenly imprimatur for such "new" shapes, while it is true that Kepler first justified ellipses in this sense, Newton found that other conic sections, parabolas and hyperbolas for instance, were also inscribed in the heavens—for example, by comets.[6] Thus shapes that, to the Renaissance, might have seemed distorted and ineffable were, in

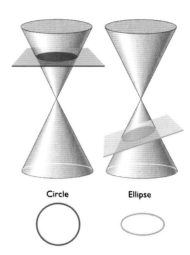

Fig. 6.1. Two cones point to point: *left,* sectioned into a circle; *right,* sectioned into an ellipse. From Devlin, *Mathematics.*

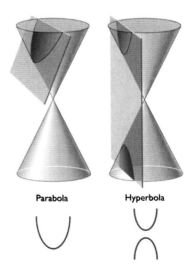

Fig. 6.2. Two cones sectioned into a parabola (*left*); and into a hyperbola with its two branches (*right*). From Devlin, *Mathematics.*

Fig. 6.3. Pseudo-ellipses made with bipolar compasses and (*second from bottom*) a true ellipse. From Valentino Braitenberg, *Vehicles: Experiments in Synthetic Psychology* (Cambridge: MIT Press, 1984).

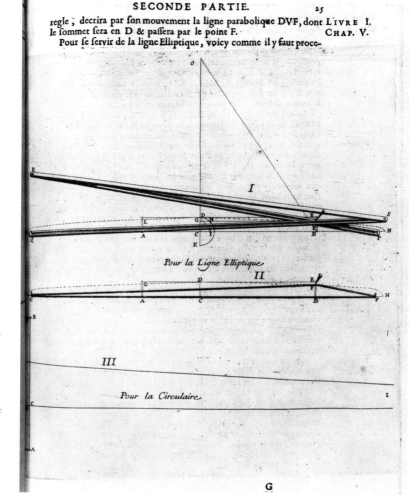

Fig. 6.4. François Blondel. Pantograph or compasses for drawing continuous parabolic, hyperbolic, and elliptical curves. Sliding sleeves change the angle of the compass's "limbs" smoothly as the figure is drawn out. From the *Cours.*

the age of the Baroque, turning out to be quite effable. They were, in fact, heavenly. It was all part of a continuous process—gradually discovering effability in things thought to be ineffable.

In an age of hierarchies, we have to set the ellipse over the Serlian oval. Figure 6.3 is reproduced from Valentino Braitenberg's extraordinary *Vehicles: Experiments in Synthetic Psychology.*[7] This illustrates a number of ovals made of arcs of circles—that is, Serlian ovals—along with a true ellipse. It is easy to tell which is which. I admit that a room, at least a large one, made from a

Serlian oval might be pretty hard to tell from one that made from a perfect ellipse. But the difference would be clear enough in the drawings. The smooth superiority of the ellipse's curve makes all the others look bumpy.

Blondel published designs for pantographs or compasses that would draw these continuous elliptical, hyperbolic, and parabolic curves (fig. 6.4). They consist of gadgets whose multiple arms, by means of sliding sleeve joints, swivels, and the like, create a smooth continuous path for a marker embedded in the pantograph. With the right adjustments (and some skill) one can draw ellipses, hyperbolas, and parabolas as easily as one can make circles with ordinary compasses. Another advantage to Blondel's system is that the curves can be useful for such things as entasis (the gentle outward curve of a column shaft) and the other slight curves that are built into long-lined elements in classical architecture.[8]

The pantograph in Blondel's drawing is anchored by a string tacked to the paper at an upper point. This string is portrayed in two positions, at points D and E. The marker that will draw out the line is located between E and F. The draftsman moves the whole pantograph from point E to point D, and then beyond D to a point symmetrical with the place where he started out. At the same time he gently swivels the arms so that the marker moves gradually along in an upward curve. The dotted line across, contained within the pantograph's arms, is the actual elliptical curve. This will be a true ellipse, its degree of curvature changing constantly with the movement of the arms. Similar arrangements, illustrated by Blondel, produce other continuous curves.[9]

BORROMINI

But let us return for the moment to the old system of constructing ovals, using circle segments. The system itself probably goes back to the remotest antiquity, but as far as I know the earliest writer to illustrate it was Sebastiano Serlio.[10] His systems for doing so—he has several—were employed by many later architects, among them Borromini and Blondel, all throughout the age of the Baroque.

Francesco Borromini, for example—or possibly, in this particular case, his nephew and continuator Bernardo—draws the nave of San Carlino (fig. 6.5) precisely as a Serlian oval (fig. 6.6). To show this, I have concocted my

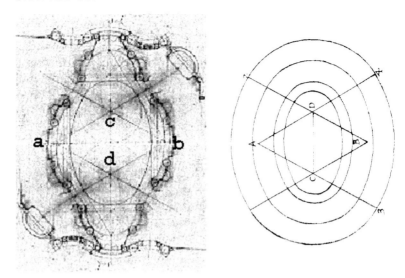

Fig. 6.5. Francesco (or
Bernardo?) Borromini.
Doubled drawing of half
the oval of San Carlino.
Labels added. Vienna,
Albertina.

Fig. 6.6. Serlio's oval.
From Sebastiano Serlio,
*Tutte l'opere di architet-
tura* (Venice: Giacomo
de' Franceschi, 1619).

diagram out of one of the Borromini drawings (the original is the lower half of fig. 6.5 only; thus my diagram, perforce, gives the church two front ends rather than the front and rear it actually has). However, as doctored, the drawing does demonstrate how Borromini constructed his oval. He drew a diamond shape, *abcd*, in the center. The four corners of the diamond then become points from which (common bipolar) compasses swing arcs. The oval's long sides are formed by swiveling the compasses at point *a* (for the side opposite) and then at point *b* (ditto). To create the short sides or apses of the oval, the compasses are swiveled at the crossings of the diamond's diagonals, shown by points *c* and *d*.

So here we have to ask: what are the further differences between an oval and an ellipse? Quite beyond the definitions given so far, the words "oval" and "ellipse" are often used interchangeably.[11] Furthermore, while Borromini clearly used Serlio's system to make his oval, in fact one can use Serlio's system to make ovals that simultaneously come remarkably close to ellipses. One can, with sufficient care, reduce the bumpiness to a near-zero level.

To demonstrate my claim I will use an undoctored Borromini oval (fig. 6.7).[12] This is a typical Serlian oval with inner quadrilateral and paired foci. In fig. 6.8 I show, above, how this form can be laid out under the Serlio system and, below that, how it can be re-created as a true and proper ellipse. In

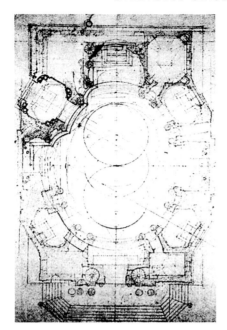

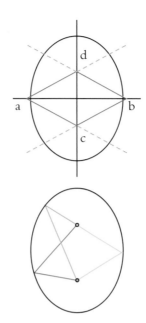

the latter case, since we're making a completed ellipse and not just an elliptical curve, we don't need Blondel's pantograph. Instead, a single loop of
string, its different positions marked in yellow, green, and red, is loosely put
around tacks set at the ellipse's two foci, marked by the two dots. A marker
is then put into the loop and the loop is drawn tight as shown. The furthest
perimeter that the marker can make, moving all the way round with the
string anchored by the foci, will be an ellipse with a continuous degree of
curvature. The red, green, and yellow lines, which all add up to the same
length, show the loop in three different positions. [13]

I admit that scientifically my pseudo-ellipse falls apart into a bumpy Serlian oval if the procedure is redone with thinner, more exact lines. Mathematically, a Serlian oval can never be a true ellipse. Its elliptical nature is really the result of the thick, therefore ambiguous, lines that construct it. But
then, of course, when you're constructing a building, these are just the am-
biguities you face.

Borromini also seems to have used either true ellipses or very good
pseudo-ellipses in creating the type of oval we might call the elongated circle. By this I mean an oval that does not diminish very much toward its ver-

Fig. 6.7. Francesco (or
Bernardo?) Borromini.
Plan for an oval church,
possibly San Carlino (Vi-
enna, Albertina [no.
175]).

Fig. 6.8. The shape
taken from Borromini's
oval church plan as,
above, a Serlian oval
and, *below*, an ellipse.
The two forms are only
roughly identical, how-
ever, and not mathemat-
ically so.

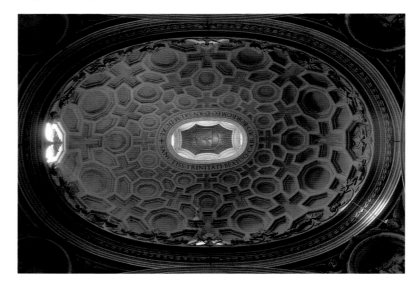

Fig. 6.9. Dome of San Carlo alle Quattro Fontane (Francesco Borromini, 1638ff.). Photograph courtesy of Alinari/Art Resource, New York.

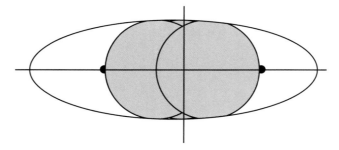

Fig. 6.10. Scheme of stretched circle: the gray area is the perimeter of the dome; the ellipse provides the proper curvature for the bridge between the two circles

tices but stays fairly flat until it begins to curve at each end into something like a semicircle. The dome of San Carlino is an example (fig. 6.9).

As with most geometrical constructions, there are various other ways, besides Serlio's system, to make this shape. These can involve packed circles, overlapped circles, and so on (fig. 6.10). I would suggest that, on the site, a very long ellipse might have been used, however, rather than the huge circular arcs that would have to be drawn with Serlio's scheme. An ellipse, as shown in the lower part of figure 6.8, would be easier than any sufficiently large circle to map out on a building site. For example, to lay out San Carlino's oval, two of the constituent circles would have to have a diameter some four times the length of the church's nave.[14] Later in the seventeenth century full-scale versions of Blondel's and Descartes's instruments would solve some of these problems. One might conclude that while it is easier to use a pair of bipolar compasses to make a *drawing* of an oval, it is easier, on the site, to use the method in figure 6.8, with the bonus being a true rather than a pseudo-ellipse.

Anyway, Borromini's further geometrical thoughts on this famous interior involved complexities and interpenetrations of ovals and/or ellipses well beyond what I have discussed. In figure 6.11 the main oval, in black, is presented as an ellipse. Then, setting the ellipse against the Serlian oval, followed by the upper parts of the nave, and with this followed in turn by the lower parts of that nave, one gets a startling result. That result, in fact, is remarkably like Kepler's diagram of a planet's elliptical orbit—the one already mentioned—shown in figure 6.12 with its real orbit, in black, and the imagined orbit (dotted red) that Kepler used to construct the black ellipse. *F* and *A* are the foci, *PR* its major axis, and *DQ* its minor.[15] Most of these same points, lines, and constructs can be applied to the plan of San Carlino. So I have done this in my diagram—though Borromini, instead of Kepler's invisible circle, has a visible and physical pseudo-ellipse, which is the church's lower nave. Let me hasten at once to add that I doubt very much that San Carlino was intended to proclaim the gospel of elliptical orbits. We are dealing here with the sort of coincidences that arise independently in the course of geometrical play.

Why did Kepler draw out the dotted-red circle and inscribe his ellipse inside it? One notes that the system is like that used by Guarini to make an

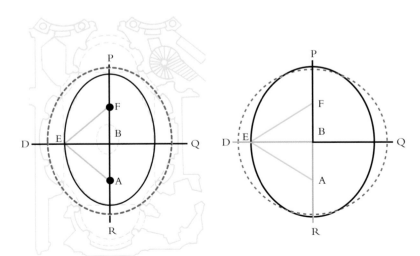

Fig. 6.11. Top view of San Carlino dome and pendentives. Adapted from a photograph courtesy of Alinari/Art Resource, New York.

Fig. 6.12. Kepler's diagram showing how he arrived at an elliptical planetary orbit.

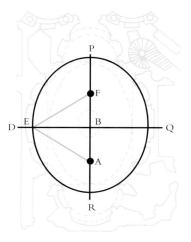

Fig. 6.13. A Keplerian el-
lipse superimposed on
Borromini's plan of San
Carlino

elliptical Ionic volute (fig. 5.31). In Kepler's ellipse, as in all ellipses, the sum of the distances from any point on its perimeter to the two foci, F and A, is always equal to the major axis's total length, PR. From this it follows (and I paraphrase Alexandre Koyré) that the distance from any point located on the ellipse's minor axis to one of the foci, say EF, is equal to the radius of the dotted-red circle, DB. This distance is also one-half the length of the ellipse's major axis, BR or PB. In fact, looking at the diagram, EA (the yellow diagonal) equals DB (the green horizontal radius), or PB (black half of vertical or major axis), or BR (bottom half, in blue, of the vertical or major axis).

Note the ellipse's upper vertex, P, at the top of the circle. When the planet has traversed one-quarter of its orbit, and gotten itself around to point E, its distance from the Sun is exactly equal to the circle's dotted-red radius, DB. Further calculations show that point A must be one of the ellipse's foci. And once you know where one focus is you know where to find the other. There is more to this ingenious and, indeed, epochal proof of Kepler's, involving logarithms and sines. But I think for present purposes I have said enough. Kepler's ellipse is full of simple ratios—effable to a degree.

In figure 6.13 I superimpose a different ellipse, shown in black, on the Borromini plan with its dotted-red ellipse that we just examined. The special qualities in Kepler's ellipse are suggested, but not fully carried out, by the inner oval shown earlier. But when we demarcate the main interior nave wall, as in figure 6.13, we do get a nice Keplerian shape. And, furthermore, transferring Kepler's labels, we find that all the relationships listed above for the planetary orbit in figure 6.12 apply to Borromini's nave wall. In other words, in San Carlino the distances from the foci to the end of the minor axes are the same, and those same distances are also equal to one-half the length of the major axis.[16] So we have yet another way of demonstrating a pseudo-ellipse, and a convincing one, at least at this (architectural) degree of roughness.

ST. PETER'S COLONNADE

A few decades after San Carlino was begun, Borromini's former colleague, Gian Lorenzo Bernini, had a much more monumental, and a much simpler, ellipse in the works. In 1656 Alexander VII decided to redevelop the area in front of St. Peter's as a *theatrum* for pilgrims; Bernini made drawings.[17] A roofed double colonnade surrounding an enormous open piazza was planned. The natural center of such a piazza—the crossing of its major and minor axes—was (or became) the obelisk that Domenico Fontana had set up there in 1585–86. The ellipse's two foci were marked with fountains—one to the left as you face St. Peter's of 1613 by Carlo Maderno and the other, its twin, dating from 1677 (see fig. 6.14).

The final form of the piazza, which was completed in 1667, only emerged gradually out of many a sketch and conference. Bernini's design was the largest construction project of its time in Rome and perhaps the world. There are many early drawings showing oblong circles, ovals, and such. But, in the end, so far as I know Bernini's colonnade became the first truly monumental ellipse of the Baroque era. Which makes it a worthy counterpart to that other monumental Roman ellipse, the Colosseum.[18] The colonnade's use of repeated dimensions is also interesting: the same value, 125 meters, establishes (1) the width of the facade and the upper opening of the trapezoid, (2) the depth of the trapezoid's two arms, (3) the vertical depth of the ellipse at the points of opening, and (4) the distance between the two fountain-foci. So the colonnade has some of the mathematical integrity of Borromini's San Carlino nave—or for that matter of Ezekiel's temple.

In order to frame his ellipse within this colonnade Bernini had to do something completely untoward. He had to take a four-column-deep colonnade and bend it, along every inch of its way, around the ellipse's perimeter: more Baroque distorting, of course, but also an interesting application of the idea of continuous curvature. Single-column colonnades that

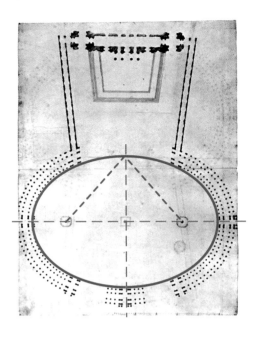

Fig. 6.14. The "Vatican Plan" of Bernini's colonnade (ellipse diagram added). The separated central lower section was never built.

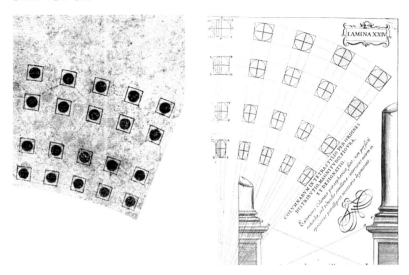

Fig. 6.15. The radiating arrangement of Bernini's columns in the colonnade of St. Peter's. Detail from engraving by G. B. Bonacina in the Vatican Library. Photograph courtesy of Alinari/Art Resource, New York.

Fig. 6.16. Juan Caramuel Lobkowitz, part of a quadruple continuously curved colonnade. From Caramuel Lobkowitz, *Arquitectura civil recta y obliqua* (Vigevano, 1678).

circled and bent were common. But a bent colonnade four columns deep is something else. If the front row curves, the other rows have to fan out accordingly. Similarly, short curved sections have always been common in colonnaded porticoes. But these curves are never anything like Bernini's. In Bernini's plan, the files of columns turn into radiating pencils, as in projective geometry (see chapter 7). And this means that the intercolumniations, which according to Vitruvius and every other architectural writer should be fixed, or should vary only slightly, must instead vary a lot. Indeed, because the curve is continuous these intercolumniations must always be unequal at every point along that curve. And, at each point, if the front row has the proper intercolumniation, the other three rows will all be progressively too far apart. Or else, if the back row is right, the other rows will all be wrong. Note that in Bonacina's plan, figure 6.15, the rear intercolumniations are, on average, approximately two-ninths wider than the front ones.

At this point the fascinating Juan Caramuel Lobkowitz comes into the picture. Caramuel, the polymath bishop of Vigevano in northern Italy, is the author of a 1678 treatise on architecture.[19] His book is divided into two sections: *arquitectura recta*, which deals with Renaissance forms such as circles, squares, and ideal rectangles; and *arquitectura obliqua*. The latter involves everything that is distorted—hyperbolic and parabolic plans, sections, and ornaments; elliptical spiral stairs; and oval chambers, piazzas, and more. In fact there is hardly a right angle or a true circle anywhere in this part of the book. *Arquitectura obliqua* particularly investigates the stretchings and compressions used in forced perspective, as in stage design, where what looks like an expansive hall must be built out of scenery only a few feet deep. Though published after the colonnade of Piazza San Pietro was complete, the "oblique" colonnade that Caramuel publishes proposes a radically different solution to the problem of Bernini's intercolumniations.[20] Note in figure 6.16 that Caramuel's intercolumniations differ among themselves much more than do Bernini's, both along the rows as they follow the curve and within each file of columns running from the center outward. Partly, of course, this is because Caramuel's curve is much tighter than Bernini's.

But this is not the whole reason. Caramuel abandons not only the slightest hint of uniform intercolumniations but uniform columns altogether; and this Bernini did not do. But Caramuel notes: "The exterior columns are paraspheric, not perfectly round but similar to round." "Paraspheric" means "beyond the sphere," so the word has the over-the-top associations of ellipse, parabola, and hyperbola. In fact Caramuel's paraspheric shafts, in plan, are ellipses. The shafts in the back row are just about circular. In the next row forward they become squat ellipses. In the next row after that they are narrowed further, and in the front row the shafts have been squeezed into sausage-like cross-sections. *Arquitectura obliqua* lets us glimpse how a Baroque mind may distort a distortion—further squeezing and stretching Bernini's already squeezed and stretched colonnade.

BLONDEL'S PARABOLIC AND HYPERBOLIC OPENINGS

Unlike Serlio, Blondel was intensely interested in parabolas and ellipses. And he uses them more forthrightly and mathematically than did Borromini. Blondel makes us fully aware that we have reached the 1670s.

Figure 6.17, for example, shows one of his ways of laying out an approximate parabola. The compasses are set at the (unlabeled) branching point of the two symmetrical radii that mark out the polycentric curve *ADB*. This latter is shown as a solid black line. But then, from point *O* down below, "phantom" radii are also drawn, in dotted lines, on the left to point *t* and on the right to point *P*. These cross the line *AB* at (unlabeled)

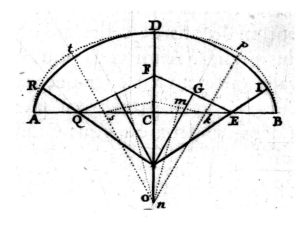

Fig. 6.17. François
Blondel's scheme for
drawing an approximate
parabola. From the
Cours, 1675.

points between *QC* and *CE*. These unlabeled points become the centers for circular arcs drawn out more or less along the
circle *ADB*. But, as shown by the dotted
lines, their curvature puffs out beyond the
smoother, lower curve, *ARtD*. This puffed-
out curve is a straight circular arc. In contrast, the less curvaceous heavy line is
(roughly) a parabola.

Figure 6.18 is another Blondel pseudo-
parabola—or rather my somewhat less
confusing revision of Blondel's confusing
diagram: I substitute color coding for alphabetical labels. Again the result
is a freehand parabola. Two half-circles (gray) are drawn, concentrically,
with the inner circle half the outer circle's diameter. Then a series of horizontals (green) is constructed at regular intervals from the base up to approximately the top of the inner circle. Next, radii (red) are drawn to the
edge of the outer circle, such that each radius hits the inside of that circle
directly above a set of predetermined points on the horizontal lines. The
points are in geometric or some other progression. Then, verticals (also
red) are dropped from the outer ends of the radii to the points on the horizontals determined by the number progression. This happens on both
sides of the figure. Finally, a curve is drawn, freehand, through all points established on the horizontals. This freehand line is shown in black. It is
Blondel's way of making an approximate parabola.

Wren, Guarini, and many another architectural mathematician recom-
mended catenaries, parabolas, and hyperbolas for architecture. Why? For one
thing, unlike semicircles, parabolas are capable of being squeezed and
stretched without losing their geometric integrity. Any symmetrical hyperbola or parabola can be as cleanly and easily analyzed and measured, as easily plotted, as any other. This can't be done with a circle. A semicircle's span
must always be exactly twice its height, no more, no less. Parabolas and hyperbolas can thus span openings in many more ways than can circles. A parabolic or hyperbolic arch can have a span that is just about any fraction, or
multiple, of its height. A vault with a parabolic or hyperbolic profile can
provide a more generous concavity than does a semicircular one, so that if,

Fig. 6.18. Construction of
a second parabola. After
Blondel, *Cours*.

for example, windows are to be set into the soffit they can be taller and admit more light.

In figure 6.19 I have tried to show how wider and narrower parabolic arches can be used to turn the corner of a rectangular bay (that is, a bay with two different spans, one across it and one along its side) while the rigid semicircles (upper left) permit only ugly and impractical results—impractical since the crests of the two vaults with the different spans will have to be at two different heights.

In figure 3.11 I illustrated a true parabola, applied to the dome of St. Peter's. You can build a pantograph for drawing parabolas by making the directrix into a straightedge and moving an adjustable string along the directrix to mark out the curve—the string always being divided into two constantly changing sections, though the two sections will each always have to be equal.

Blondel also has a hyperbola-drawing device that creates some really crazy arches and vaults. These anticipate, or reflect, the radical shapes, the splayed and swollen curves, of Baroque military and civil engineering. In particular they exploit an increasing knowledge of stereotomy (three-dimensional stone-cutting) that was much in the air in the second half of the seventeenth century—that is, when projective geometry was coming into its own.[21]

Indeed, Blondel completely gives up, in these experiments, on what had for centuries been one of the absolute essentials of architecture: vertical imposts and wall ends for arched openings. Blondel's openings are horizontally and vertically canted (fig. 6.20). And even a straight-up-and-down opening can be topped off with a wildly off-center ellipse. So Blondel's illustrations well display the flexibility of these forms. Indeed they revel in them. These parts of the treatise are full of things you wouldn't see in earlier books— wide low spans, canted spans, high narrow spans, rampant spans (one branch longer than the other), spans that do all they can to defy the bilateral mirror symmetry and the sense of predictable solidity and stability that arches and vaults had always enjoyed. Once again: distortion, radical twisting, dismemberment.

Take the five vault profiles illustrated in figure 6.20. The opening on the upper left is a very wide hyperbola generated by a series of maneuvers at least as complicated as one of Kepler's or Newton's mappings of planetary

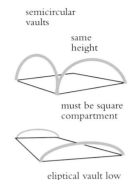

semicircular vaults

same height

must be square compartment

eliptical vault low

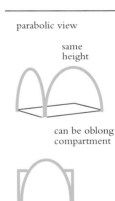

parabolic view

same height

can be oblong compartment

eliptical vault extra height

Fig. 6.19. Semicircular and elliptical arches, with their advantages and disadvantages

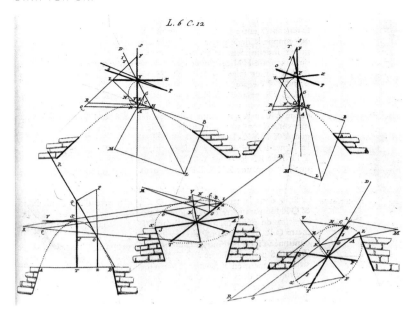

L. 6 C. 12

Fig. 6.20. François
Blondel, canted hyper-
bolic arches. From the
Cours, 1675.

orbits. I will not weary the reader by going through Blondel's "proof," that
is to say the geometrical process he uses to construct his forms. But we
should note, at least, that the line *GM* is extended from the radius of the
small dotted semicircle in the middle. *HL* is another such extended radius,
GH. HB, meanwhile, is the directrix of the hyperbola itself. The other
straight lines are different positionings of the directrix as it moves around to
achieve the curve. In the arch to the right of this one the directrix is shorter,
since the opening itself is narrower and the hyperbola's apse more pointed.
The next opening, on the left in the lower group, is even more sharply com-
pressed.

　　The other two arches in Blondel's illustration (fig. 6.20, lower tier, center
and right) are derived from ellipses that he shows with dotted lines. They are
rakish. They are marked with their major and minor axes, with diagonals and
other lines, all of which establish such things as the height of the wall from
which the arch springs. Thus, for example, the left end of the minor axis in
the far-right arch marks the height of the opening's right wall, and the
right-hand end of the diagonal line, *aZ*, marks the arch's other shoulder.

　　In the middle vault in the lower group, as with the others, the ellipse's
major and minor axes are shown. Blondel has also drawn in the figure's di-

ameter and various other components. Many of these analytical and constructive forms establish elements of the surrounding architecture. Two heavy black straight lines take off, on the left, from *O* to the base or springing point of the arch, and, on the right, from *Z* to the arch's other base.

What were these weird arches and vaults for? Perhaps for sewers or other conduits and tunnels, or perhaps also for military architecture, whose increasingly pronounced stereotomies were leading onward to the slanted, distended forms of projective geometry. Surely Blondel's openings were not being proposed, as, two hundred years later, Gaudí would propose similar shapes for civic and religious buildings. But the conic-section archways in Blondel's *Cours* well accord with everything we've been talking about: distortion, the geometricizing of architecture, even (as we can see in figs. 6.21 and 6.22) influence from cosmography.[22]

SQUEEZED SPHERES

We turn now to the world of three dimensions. Despite their omnipresence in the form of arch and vault profiles, all four of the shapes we've been discussing—circles, ellipses, parabolas, and hyperbolas—can appear three-dimensionally as architectural volumes. Their profiles, rotated through 360 degrees, respectively create the sphere, the ellipsoid, the paraboloid, and the hyperboloid. All these shapes appear in Baroque architecture; and if we can include hemispheres and other sphere quadrants as a subset of spheres, the forms appear exceedingly often. Kircher, we saw, even envisaged machines whose sole purpose was to carve each of these three solids out of wood.[23]

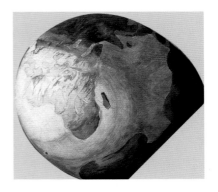

I have noted that the planets, including Earth, were discovered to be squeezed spheres.[24] One key Baroque depiction of Earth, as such, comes in the late 1620s. It is in Andrea Sacchi's fresco of *Divine Wisdom* in the Palazzo Barberini (fig. 6.21). We see the globe, Africa foremost, and Earth itself with exaggeratedly flattened poles—Sacchi has squeezed "Earth's goodly Ball" pretty hard. Moreover, it is way off center in the scene, with the Sun occupying the central place—so it is conceivable that the more revolutionary (in every sense) heliocentric universe, rather than the Earth-centered Ptolemaic one, is being represented.[25]

Fig. 6.21. Detail (rotated 120 degrees) of Andrea Sacchi, *Divine Wisdom* (fresco, 1629–31, Palazzo Barberini, Rome). Photograph courtesy of Art Resource, New York.

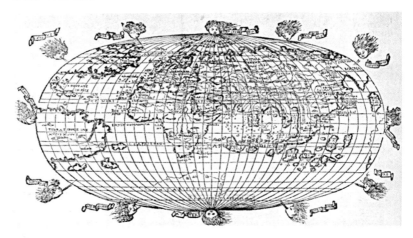

Fig. 6.22. Francesco di Lorenzo Rosselli, World Map, 1508.

One cannot claim, however, that Sacchi was here incorporating Newton's ideas about Earth as an oblate spheroid. That notion still lay the future. Rather, he was probably thinking of contemporaneous traditions for mapping Earth, which, ever since Francesco di Lorenzo Rosselli's map of 1508 (fig. 6.22), proposed a similarly squeezed sphere. But Rosselli, in the spirit of projective geometry, was trying to inscribe the two lateral halves of a sphere, surfaces that were filled up with names and labels that dictated a horizontal format, onto a flat piece of paper. Such projections were much used by cartographers.[26] They stretched the countries, continents, or indeed the globe that they were mapping to accommodate the necessary labels. As we shall see in the next chapter, these instances are all of them examples of isometric projective geometry. That is, the continents, seas, and other physical features have been mapped to present Eurasia and Africa recognizably, in a single view, and with the right number of parallels and meridians. But the body onto which they have been mapped is, as it must be, ellipsoidal or ovoidal.[27]

The older Rossellian tradition blended with the new discoveries that were being made about the planets' actual shapes. What, in exaggerated form, had been convenient fiction turned out, more modestly, to be scientific fact. And if Rosselli's projective tradition made Earth flatter than it really was, some astronomers were saying things that seemed to back up the mapmakers' exaggerations. For example, Galileo went so far as to claim that Saturn was shaped like an olive.[28]

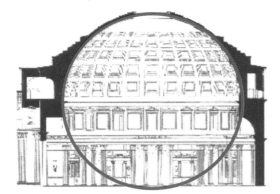 

But how does all this play out in architecture? Once more we go back to St. Peter's. I have already pointed out that in 1564, after Michelangelo's death, Giacomo della Porta converted the perfectly hemispherical profile that Michelangelo had designed for the dome into a paraboloid.[29] And we looked at later paraboloid domes. St. Paul's, we also saw, has a another type of squeezed sphere, cubic catenoids.

As far as I know there was no comparable interest in hyperboloids. But at least one was proposed, and by Blondel. To do it he boldly tampered with a classic. He took from the signature building of ancient Roman architecture, the Pantheon, what many would call its greatest treasure—its dome (fig. 6.23), which, in real life, is a pure hemisphere inside and a spherical quadrant on the exterior. Blondel then proposes a redesign of the building in which both the exterior and the interior profiles are hyperboloids (fig. 6.24). Here, if ever, is a specimen of Baroque distortion—not a squeezed but a stretched spherical segment.

Fig. 6.23. The Pantheon with hemispheric dome (profiles shown in red)

Fig. 6.24. The same, with hyperboloid dome, as suggested by Blondel

PACKED PARABOLOIDS

One of the other things you can do, architecturally, with these three-dimensional constructs on conic sections is called tight packing.[30] This involves stacking identical solids close together into regular lattices. We saw something of this idea when we looked at Matthias Brack's clusters of metal molecules. The result is usually a stable solid such as a pyramid, tetrahedron, cube, or other parallelepiped. In other words, packing allows rounded

Fig. 6.25. A fruit seller's pile of green oranges

Fig. 6.26. The Chigi *monti* on Borromini's tomb of Sergius IV (Rome, S. Giovanni in Laterano, begun 1646). Detail of photograph courtesy of Alinari/Art Resource, New York.

shapes, which might have difficulty standing alone, to do so when they are clustered together. You might call it a three-dimensional form of tiling.

The most familiar application of tight packing occurs at fruit stands (fig. 6.25). The merchants tight-pack oranges and other fruit when they display them in pyramidal piles. The lattices of solids thus created can have either central or longitudinal plans. The piles are not only stable, they are the most compact way there is to cluster spheres and spheroids.

The fruit seller's lattice is of course an architectural as well as a mathematical construct. No doubt these same tight-packed piles existed among the *fruttivendoli* of Bernini's Rome. But, indeed, the tight packing of spheres and other rolling shapes were everywhere in that city, as they are today. For example: the omnipresent Chigi *monti* (fig. 6.26), those six-part pyramidal aggregations of paraboloids. These are tight-packed Baroque domes at miniature scale. Indeed, the monti are often found on or in or around the full-scale domes. Meanwhile the real domes, of Michelangelo and his paraboloid-prone progeny, can themselves be assembled into pyramidal and other geometric groups (fig. 6.27).

Similar things can be said about the plans of these buildings. A horizontal section will reflect the volumes of the domes rising from it. The reflections often involve cylindrical walls, as at Sant'Agnese in Agone (Fig. 6.28). The confrontation of these two different buildings—Michelangelo's elevation for St. Peter's and Sant'Agnese's plan—brings out an important fact about paraboloid domes. We have seen that their elevations and volumes are derived from conic sections. But their plans are circular—or, if you like, their elevations come from slanted conics and their plans from horizontal ones.

Also, these same plans—again as at Sant'Agnese—can often be seen to balance the domes' rotational symmetry with what mathematicians call up-

 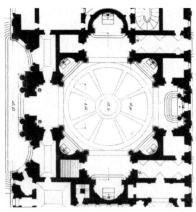

down symmetry, thus complementing the left-right symmetry (also readable as rotational symmetry) that they have already. This happens when the buildings are up-down reflected—for example, in water or wet streets (fig. 6.27). Exactly such occasional, happenstance up-down reflections can be permanently embodied in plans with biaxial symmetry.

And, actually, the packing doesn't have to be all that tight. It only has to be consistently spaced. There is what might be called "cushioned packing"—similar to what I called cushioned tiling—or clustering with regular separations, as for example in the way salt crystals are organized into cubic lattices with atoms of four different types (yellow and blue, large and small, in figure 6.29).

The salt molecule, a paradigm for cushioned packing, can also stand in for the basic lattice of a Baroque (or other) palace. The molecule's lattice is five bays wide and two stories high, the central bay being slightly narrower than those flanking it. We can compare this pattern with the lower part of the street facade of Borromini's Casa dei Filippini, in Rome, of the 1640s, which has exactly this division into bays and stories (fig. 6.30). While here the central bay is wider instead of narrower than the others, the principles of cushioned packing apply throughout. One can even liken the four types of atoms in the salt molecule to the way Borromini has spotted, or cushion-packed, his ornaments (pilaster caps, window headers, panels, and the like) with similar though not identical rhythms and alternations—and this at every visual joint. Note, too, that in both cases the packing lattice gives sta-

Fig. 6.27. G. B. Ricci (?). Detail of a fresco in the Vatican with Michelangelo's and Della Porta's domes (c. 1612). I have treated the domes to up-down reflection across the church's ground-line axis. Adapted from a photograph courtesy of Alinari/Art Resource, New York.

Fig. 6.28. Girolamo and Carlo Rainaldi and Francesco Borromini, plan of Sant'Agnese (Agone, Rome, begun 1652), shown with the main entrance to the left. Courtesy Yale University Art and Architecture Library, Photograph Collection.

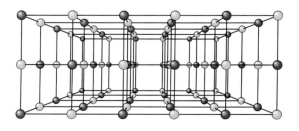

Fig. 6.29. A molecule of table salt. From Devlin, *Mathematics*.

Fig. 6.30. Francesco Borromini. Lower facade of the Casa dei Filippini (Rome, 1640s). Photograph courtesy of Alinari/Art Resource, New York.

bility to elements that, unpacked, would be unstable or unsupported: yellow and blue balls in the molecule and, in the building, similarly repeated, similarly alternated capitals, bases, panels, and hoods.

So. We have looked at some of the ways in which effable Renaissance forms like circles and spheres can be stretched and squeezed. We have come to terms with ovals, ellipses, parabolas, and hyperbolas; and, moving into the world of three dimensions, with spheroids, paraboloids, and hyperboloids. We have seen that these forms appeared in architecture with a certain prominence. My suggestion is that, perhaps, this may have had something to do with Kepler's, Galileo's, and Blondel's newfound techniques for easily drawing out these continuously changing curves.

Borromini's work fascinatingly combines the Renaissance traditions—drafting with straightedge and polar compasses—with a seeming awareness of conic sections. But for now that whole matter remains mysterious. I also showed that Kepler's planetary ellipses were, in new ways, as effable as some of the old Renaissance shapes, or more so. They have their own unities, repetitions, and recursions. It is interesting to see corresponding refinements in Borromini.

Effable "distortions" led to other kinds. Bernini, though often called a traditionalist in architecture, proved to be an estimable innovator with the great ellipse at St. Peter's. He actually bent a four-column deep colonnade, abrogating the whole Vitruvian tradition of regular intercolumniations. And this innovation gave occasion, in turn, to Caramuel Lobkowitz, a wilder spirit, who proposed a colonnade that was much more sharply bent and that would at the same time stretch some column shafts and squeeze others. We looked, too, at the fashion for paraboloid domes in major Baroque buildings. As Earth is a squeezed ball so are these domes (or, anyway, squeezed half-balls). Meanwhile Blondel incorporated all sorts of jaunty hyperbolas and hyperboloids into his system, showing how elliptical and hyperbolic openings are more flexible than their semicircular cousins. He even seems to have thought that the Pantheon would look better with the hyperboloid dome.

But almost always, behind these distortions the invisible, intact presences of the classic forms remain, even as they were being stretched and squeezed. Kepler inscribed his planetary ellipses into circles. Paraboloid, hyperboloid, catenoid, and oblate domes are distorted hemispheres; the distortions generate proper hemispheres in the mind's eye. The fact that hemispherical domes continued right through the Baroque period to be built along with the distorted shapes only continues the contrast.

We have seen, finally, how in architecture these unstable shapes can achieve stability by tight or cushioned packing—a packing that can utilize dihedral reflective symmetry of both the left–right and, at least on rainy days or in canal cities, the up–down sort.

SEVEN

PROJECTION

M ost shapes that we encounter in everyday life, as opposed to geometry, are irregular. Often they are irregular in almost every imaginable way—as to the length of their sides, and as to the sides' angles, direction, and symmetry. Think of the silhouettes of puddles, salads, stains, cities, and mountains. Such shapes can of course have their own demented geometry (e.g., Santin-Aichel's irregular pentagonal and heptagonal piers, discussed in chapter 4). Fractals, not dementedly but magnificently, are a modern insight that helps us think about these things.

We actually began to discuss these highly irregular shapes in chapter 6, when we looked at distortion and at the geometric projections used in map-making. We also saw how packing or tiling—singing in a chorus—can give the shaggiest form a beauty that, as a soloist, it lacks. But now we go further. A new, post-Euclidian geometry full of irregularities and exaggerations, invented by a French architect in the early years of the Baroque, comes into view.

PROJECTIVE GEOMETRY

In 1643 Abraham Bosse printed a book, *La Pratique du trait à preuves* [Practical Proofs in Projection]. Bosse was a disciple of Girard Desargues, the founder of projective geometry. By his title Bosse means that he is discussing the provable geometric analogies among perspective, stereometry, and the art of designing sundials.[1] The common factor in these three disciplines, in short, is that they are "projective." Linear perspective projects three-dimensional scenes onto two-dimensional planes; stereotomy projects two-dimensional templates to create three-dimensional pieces of building-stone—arch voussoirs, quoins, and the like. Sundials project the three-dimensional images or shadows of their gnomons or indicators onto their surrounding clock faces.

Projective geometry is therefore part and parcel of Baroque optics, of the manipulation of light, and of images transmitted by light. For a preliminary definition let us go back to the magic lanterns discussed in chapter 3. These in fact are nothing less than machines for projective geometry. Let us say you have a slide that portrays, perfectly, a square or some more complicated Euclidean construction. Let us say, in other words, that the image is made of right or other simple angles, and of straight lines, circles, and circular arcs. You shine the magic lantern, with this slide in it, aslant onto a wall, or onto a sphere segment, or onto a convex, concave, or bumpy surface. All the straightnesses and curved and angular consistencies of the original slide will go awry. If you are not a projective geometer you say: "Let's get hold of a decent screen and make sure it's directly parallel to the slide."

But if, instead, you say: "Let's study everything that happens to the image on the slide as it travels through the lantern's cone of light and lands on this skewed surface"—if you say that, you are talking projective geometry. In other words you are concerned with the geometry of distortion, of effable shapes that have been squeezed, swollen, stretched, squashed, and otherwise given The Treatment—but optically rather than physically. And this is a geometry that, because it is projected, continues to remember its original condition. Think of the projected shapes as being made of rubber: they can be stretched by skewing the screen, but they can snap back by putting the screen at right angles to the projected pencils.

Figures 7.1 and 7.2 are examples. Guarino Guarini has a plate showing (among other things) how to calculate the area of a circle without using the value of pi (the area of a circle $= \pi r^2$). He does this because pi is an irrational and therefore, if you are a Baroque architect, you avoid it where possible. In Guarini's solution the circle's whole area is filled with as many different-

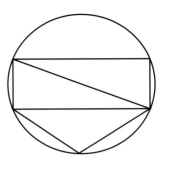 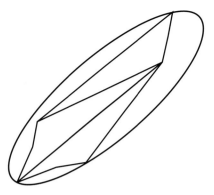

sized triangles as will fit inside it (in his illustration, figure 7.1, he has begun but not completed this process). The areas of these triangles can be calculated by using rational or effable ratios. The total area of all these triangles will roughly equal that of the circle. [2] In mathematics this is called the "method of exhaustion," and it is still used as a way of calculating the area of shapes with problematic perimeters.[3] (On the other hand, most people calculating the area of a circle nowadays are willing to put up with πr^2.)

However, my real interest comes in when we "project" Guarini's effable figure, with its orthodox triangles and perfect circle, onto a slanted screen (fig. 7.2). Let us say that the angle of incidence, in effect, stretches the figure vertically by 40 percent and horizontally by 12 percent. You see the results. The circle turns into an ellipse. The triangles go crazy. You have, that is, a diagram or map of what happens when Guarini's flat diagram is treated as a conic section, bisecting a cone (of light from the magic lantern) by changing both the horizontal and vertical tilt. Projective geometry deals with this distorted diagram. And by this very fact, simply by retracing its steps, it can also reconstruct the diagram. It reverse-engineers it, so to speak, back into its original form.

So far, then, projective geometry, weird as it looks, can discover effability in the seemingly ineffable. But one thing the new science has to do away with, in this process, is the original square-based visual "culture" that we have been discussing throughout most of this book. Projective geometry renders musical ratios, sesquialter proportions, cubices rationes, and the like all useless, or nearly so. In architecture and building these effable shapes and ratios had to be maintained in undistorted forms. In the world of projective

Fig. 7.1. Guarino Guarini's recipe for calculating the area of a circle by using the exhaustion method with polygons. From Guarini, *Architettura Civile.*

Fig. 7.2. The same, stretched vertically by 40 percent and horizontally by 12 percent

geometry we can no longer speak of right-angled parallelepipeds that play tunes. We regretfully say goodbye to sexually active Platonic solids. Alberti *contra*, the cube is not the mother of all number and form—or anyway not of these numbers and forms.

But I'm not going look negatively at such freaks. I'll try to find out their positive qualities. We've already been doing some of this. To a Vitruvius, and even to a Leonardo, Blondel's hyperbolic and parabolic arches (discussed in chapter 6) would simply have looked crazy and ramshackle. It takes someone more advanced in mathematics than they were, someone more at home with conic sections and all their innumerable progeny, to see their effability, not to mention their architectural flexibility, their buildability, and their beauty.

DESCARTES'S LATTICE

René Descartes, so important for us in so many ways, is the ultimate source (but not the founder) of projective geometry. Descartes had a truly revolutionary idea. We go back to our thoughts about close packing (which, I will add here, is a post-Cartesian concept). Descartes's idea was this: think of the physical world as an infinite, three-dimensional lattice filling all of space. Everything physical, everything seen, is packed, in tight or cushioned form, into this lattice.[4] It's a simple enough notion but it has had terrific fallout in many fields. Crystallographers, I have noted, use Cartesian lattices to map the shapes of crystals. We might consider the salt crystal in figure 6.29 a Cartesian lattice, and the Borromini palace facade in figure 6.30 the piece of visual reality that is hung on it. Three-dimensional graphs—more Cartesian lattices—are used in any number of sciences. Architecture, urbanism, and gardening all use lattices—witness wallpaper symmetry. The most recent form of the Cartesian lattice is the global brain network of neuro-computing.[5]

Descartes's lattice was simpler than a neuro-network. But like most lattices it could be looked at either two-dimensionally or three-dimensionally. And it could locate any point in the observed world in terms of some location along its coordinates, formed by horizontal x and vertical y axes (fig. 7.3). Descartes may well have been influenced, here, by Mercator's 1568 three-dimensional lattice projection of Earth (that is, the world projected onto, or into, a three-dimensional lattice). We noticed that, in order to work, Francesco di Lorenzo Rosselli's projection had squashed the planet into a pronounced ellipsoid. Later, in 1568, Gerardus Mercator's projection avoided this, though in compensation the upper and lower regions of the globe are enormously enlarged. But the real point is that Mercator's projection locates continents and cities, oceans and mountains, in accordance with the coordinates dictated by *x* and *y* axes: coordinates that have been wrapped around a spheroid that is, in fact, shaped a lot like Galileo's planetary olive. We know this proleptic version of the Cartesian lattice as the lines of latitude and longitude. And such a lattice, by being regular, brings rational analysis to the otherwise seemingly random zigzagging shapes of islands, continents, and oceans. You can make a visual mess comprehensible, maybe even beautiful, by projecting a lattice onto it—or vice versa.

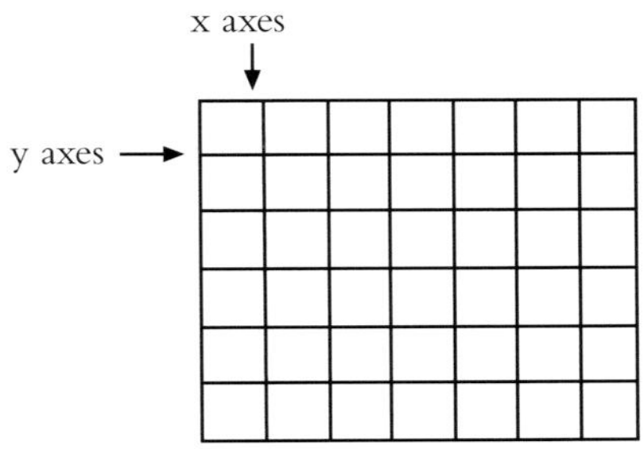

Fig. 7.3. A diagram of the Cartesian lattice

The computer monitor, which expresses everything that appears on its screen as dots and clusters of dots, and does it within just such a Cartesian lattice, is only one of the many recent applications of Descartes's idea. The *Mona Lisa* can be seen as a set of Cartesian coordinates, generated by lines, filled with color and shading, each moment of which—each dot comprising that color or shading—being also a lattice coordinate. The *Mona Lisa*, or Chartres Cathedral. Or, closer to home, the strange angles and distortions of our lantern-slide projector with its squashed and stretched Euclidean diagram sprawled on a slanted screen. All these things can be translated into points on a Cartesian lattice.

THE *COSTRUZIONE LEGITTIMA*

Thus projective geometry is not limited to lattices that are strictly horizontal, vertical, and formed of right angles. Nor are the projective lattices necessarily made up of equal squares—look at longitude and latitude, as projected, either onto a sphere or onto flat paper. The horizontal coordinates are straight when seen dead on but in depth they curve all the way around the globe; and the vertical coordinates curve when seen dead on, also going round the globe. Meanwhile the spaces between the coordinates all differ

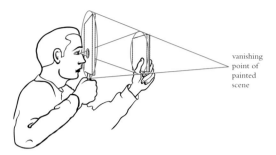

vanishing
point of
painted
scene

Fig. 7.4. An adaptation of
Philippe Comar's recon-
struction of
Brunelleschi's experi-
ment.

from one another. They are all spherical rectangles, but individually they vary from squat
to tall, and most of them slant either to the
right or the left.

Indeed one might say, historically, that the
skewed lattices preceded the straight-up-
and-down ones. One great pre-Cartesian
source for skewed lattices was, in fact, Re-
naissance perspective. This had been a powerful tradition in drawing, painting, and architecture, and it flourished all the more in the age of the
Baroque. Many if not most of the Baroque mathematicians who wrote
about projective geometry also wrote about perspective. For that matter,
most of the architects and architectural writers discussed here also had chapters on perspective.

Oceans of scholarly ink have washed over this subject. But its essence (as
opposed to its controversial outer perimeters) is simple. Perspective of some
sort had always existed. There had always been ways of suggesting, on a flat
painted surface, the recessions of three-dimensional space. But for us the
main events cluster in the wake of Filippo Brunelleschi's circa 1425 attempt
to create a painted optical projection of the Florence Baptistry and the Piazza San Giovanni in which it stood. [6]

Brunelleschi's actual experiment is hard to reconstruct exactly (the attempt has been made countless times); but we do know that it made use of
a panel on which the image of the Baptistry was painted. The upper part of
this panel was mirrored, so as to top off the painted architecture with a reflected real-life sky with moving clouds. In the center of the panel was a
peephole. This peephole was located at the point on the Baptistry just opposite to the eye of Brunelleschi as he stood just inside the central portal of
the Duomo, painting the scene before him. Then, holding the finished
painting in one hand, the viewer looked through the peephole from the
back of the panel. He saw the painting on the panel's front as it was reflected
in a mirror held in his other hand (fig. 7.4). The distance between the
painted image and the mirror was the same, in *piccole braccia*, as the distance,
in full braccia, between the painted panel and the Baptistry itself when
Brunelleschi was painting it. [7]

The whole of Brunelleschi's experiment—that is, the painted image plus

Fig. 7.5. Architectural scene in one-point linear perspective (unknown artist, c. 1470). Lines added. Formerly Staatliche Museen, Berlin.

its reflection in the mirror—was being projected, first from the panel onto the mirror (larger cone in figure 7.4) and then reprojected back from the mirror through the peephole and on into the observer's eye (smaller cone). (The larger cone, meanwhile, passes through the painted scene to end in that scene's central vanishing point.)

We'll get back to cones and vanishing points in a moment. But just now the tiled ground of the Piazza San Giovanni is of greater interest. Undoubtedly Brunelleschi's painting showed a grid of tiles receding into the distance in one-point linear perspective. Though the paving of the piazza has since been renewed many times, the scene today provides much the same sight. It is a receding chessboard or lattice akin to what we see in any number of Renaissance perspective paintings—themselves probably influenced by Brunelleschi's experiment—of streets and squares (see, for example, fig. 7.5).

In sum, looking at this receding grid from what we might call our proto-Cartesian viewpoint, a Renaissance perspective projection is this: you make a lattice of equal squares and then tilt that lattice down by 90 degrees away from your eye.[8] There are several ways to capture on paper what you then see. The most famous of these methods is called the *costruzione legittima*, a construction (of space and of the objects filling it) that is legitimate in the sense that it obeys laws—*leges*. Figure 7.6 presents three views of what happens in the costruzione legittima.

If we could hover over this platform and look directly down on it, we would see a set of tiled squares, each the same size and shape (top left). But we don't actually enter into perspective pictures (though they're intended to

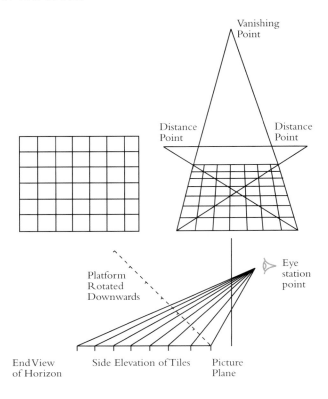

Fig. 7.6. A *costruzione legittima* or perspective platform: *left, above,* as it would exist in real space, in plan, looking straight down on it; *right, above,* as seen in perspective through a picture plane; *below,* seen in side elevation, looking at the picture plane and the tiled platform on edge

give us the illusion that we could). Instead, having tilted the platform away from us, we look down at it from one side (top right). In other words the tiled floor becomes a piece of anamorphosis (Greek for "forming anew")—the cone itself being the pencils of light transporting the image, a cone passing from the platform into our eye. Meanwhile the plane of the drawing or painting that shows all this—for example, the panel on which Brunelleschi inscribed his Baptistry—remains upright. This latter is called the picture plane.

Now we return to a point mentioned earlier. The costruzione legittima is predicated on the idea of a specific observer located at a specific spot in front of the picture plane. That spot has to be located at a distance outward from the picture plane that equals the horizontal distance from the central vanishing point to either of the two distance points (fig. 7.6, bottom). Which, of course, makes the observer a sort of offstage part of the picture.

And all this, in turn, is what makes Renaissance perspective (which, I will maintain, is really Renaissance projective geometry) different from other mechanisms for creating fictive space in art. The observer has to be exactly in the middle of the panel; and he or she has to be a specified distance away from it. And this latter distance, of course, is real rather than fictive. But it will have been dictated by the fictive distance—that between the picture plane and the rear of the perspective scene. This prescribed position for the viewer is known as the station point (fig. 7.6, bottom right).

So much is common coin in discussions of perspective, though it is usu-ally presented with infinitely more ramifications and terminologies, what with Brunelleschi, Paolo Uccello, Piero della Francesca, Leonardo, and many another, each with his own system, coming into the picture (and from which these people do not vanish at any point). Not to mention such mod-ern learned elucidators as John White, Alessandro Parronchi, and Samuel Y. Edgerton.[9]

But here is something that I think has not been brought up: the precise amount of deformity in the tiles on our platform. That deformity is deter-mined by the diagonals slanting across the tilted grid from corner to corner. Each square, now that it has been shrunk and squeezed, turns into an irreg-ular quadrilateral—either a symmetrical trapezoid (for the central tiles only) or, in all other cases, a quadrilateral without bilateral symmetry. One can read and calculate the actual degrees of tilt and squeezing for each and every tile. One can also reverse-engineer their original size and shape. It is through such insights that Renaissance perspective becomes effable.

The age of the Baroque achieved prodigies with the costruzione legit-tima and its brethren. One thinks of the immense perspective ceilings of Fra Andrea Pozzo in churches like Sant'Ignazio, Rome, where temples and skies hurtle upward into the heavens, all as seen from far below. There, the van-ishing point is no dot, but a huge burst of golden light silhouetting God Almighty. (Figure 2.3, the Giaquinto dome filled with angels, is an exam-ple.) Better still, for our purposes, are the theatrical scenes of the Bibiena family, who employed not just the one-point perspective I have described, but elaborations of it with two, three, and more vanishing points, and hence with multiple distance and station points as well.[10]

In the stage design in figure 7.7, for instance, we are looking at a corner of a palace courtyard. The structure is presented in three different views. The lower part of the plate (which by the engraver's mistake is reversed left to

Fig. 7.7. Ferdinando Galli da Bibiena, two-point perspective scene. From Bibiena, *Architettura Civile* (1711; reprint, New York: Benjamin Blom, 1971).

right) comprises the plan of what we seem to see in the perspective version of the courtyard at the top, with the arched loggia on the left, paired columns on pedestals, steps, and so on.

The middle zone of the plate appears to show that same plan in perspective, viewed from a flat angle. But that is not what we are actually looking at. What we really see is a flat, top-view plan—the plan that the set-builders would actually construct, complete with all those acute angles, and the whole thing squashed into a much shallower space than the "virtual" plan below. The architect puts it thus: "The real plan [is] reduced into perspective according to the common rule . . ."[11] Bibiena, in short, is giving us an example of a well-known theatrical device: forced perspective. The resulting scenery (at the top of the plate) would look as if it receded according to the plan at the bottom of the plate. But it would be built in accordance with the middle layout. Forced perspective is a partial three-dimensional construct of a completely two-dimensional construct—you might call it the *costruzione illegittima*—which in turn represents a completely three-dimensional construct! Forced perspective is the reprojection of a projection.

Forced perspective has all the qualities of ordinary perspective—the kind that is painted on a flat surface. The specimen before us has two vanishing points, left and right, each located just inside the edge of the picture plane. In the upright view of the palace the vanishing points of the forced-perspective plan do something else as well. They become—turn into—the station points of the upright view. And the latter, of course, is what the audience would see. In normal practice a principal station point for the whole scene (there are in fact several) would coincide with the eye of the ruler in his center seat at the back of the auditorium.

Finally, the large block with the Palladian archway and inner door, on the left of the perspective view, is not shown in either plan. And, furthermore, this block has vanishing points that are very far outside the edge of the picture plane. So that, in sum, Bibiena's palace consists of two different

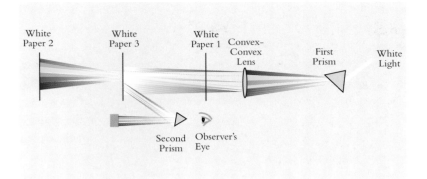

Fig. 7.8. Isaac Newton's
diagram of the division
of sunlight into its com-
ponent colors and its re-
constitution as white
light. Redrawn from
Newton, *Opticks*.

costruzioni legittime, superimposed—or perhaps I should say interlocked and mutually reinforcing. If you consider all the points Bibiena has included—the several vanishing, station, and/or distance points—as the sources of projective cones, there are twelve in all. So unlike a single magic lantern shining its single image, Bibiena's scene is instead like a dozen such magic lanterns, with each cone of images representing only a part of the total scene but at the same time with each projection perfectly interacting with, and supplementing, the others. Projective geometry, in its perspectival aspect, reaches some sort of apogee with the Bibiena family.

Baroque perspective permeated other worlds than those of art and architecture. Newton frequently made use of these same ideas in his cosmic diagrams. Often he would literally draw an observer's eye and then make the diagram a sliced side elevation of what the eye was looking at, much as I did in fig. 7.6. Like a perspective artist, Newton was trying to show that the motions and forces he was diagramming were all being seen from a certain point in space—a cosmic station point no less. One might even think of the other points in Newton's constructions as coordinates on a perspective (or Cartesian) lattice.

Newton was interested in earthly perspectives as well. In the diagram in figure 7.8 we have in a sense two eyes at either end of a perspective sequence, similar to the vanishing point and the station point. In this case one eye is the Sun's white light (on the right) and the other is the observer's (lower center). A ray of white sunlight "looks" through the first prism and separates into a ladder of component colors, running from purple on top down through the other hues of the spectrum to red at the bottom. The resulting colored stripes are put through a lens, which projects them onto white paper 1. But if the white paper is moved to position 2, far left, the colors reverse themselves top to bottom. Finally, says Newton, if the paper is put in between, at position 3, the original white light is restored. The second eye, meanwhile (Newton's), looks through a second prism at white paper 3. This transforms the white light projected from the paper back into its constituent colors, still reversed, with red on top and purple on the bottom. (The experiment also involves a diaphragm and a reflector, which I am omitting for simplicity's sake.)

But note that one sees all this only when the human eye is at its station point; and note that the experiment involves the projecting and reprojecting, the broadening and narrowing of the pencils, via prisms and a lens. In other words: perspective, no? An elaboration of the costruzione legittima, of Brunelleschi's projections and reprojections. (But also, still, behind everything, there is the theory of the magic lantern, and here I should note that this, as a practical projector of painted slides, seems to have come into existence in the 1670s, thirty-odd years before the appearance of Newton's book.[12])

GIRARD DESARGUES'S PERSPECTIVE

Girard Desargues is one of the greatest figures in the history of mathematics.[13] Significantly for us, he is also a bridge between geometry and architecture. Though he built much less than Guarini, Wren, and the others, he was deeply involved in the formal revolutions that took place in mid-seventeenth-century architectural theory. He had a direct impact on Abraham Bosse, for instance, one of the leading figures in Parisian architecture and a great innovator in architectural draftsmanship.[14] Desargues's booklet on perspective dates from 1636,[15] three years before the author's epochal pamphlet on conic sections. The perspective pamphlet is also short, with only one substantive illustration (fig. 7.9), but that is oh, so prescient![16] The essay's major significance lies in Desargues's insistence that his perspective renderings can be understood, mapped, calculated, and "seen" not only as they are projected onto the picture plane but also on all their other sides, even those not visible in the projection. For here we have to note that one can untilt a receding tiled plane and look down on it, and on whatever is inscribed or built up on it, as one looks down on a top view or plan. Yet, earlier, most perspective artists had not bothered to check out their drawings that way. One remains in the dark as to many if not most of the real dimensions of the objects depicted. Desargues solves that problem.

Desargues saw that perspective views didn't have to be a matter of guesswork. His projections give us as much information about the exterior of a design as do a full set of architectural drawings—plans, exterior elevations, and even some sections. The scale may change as the object recedes into space; it may appear on the picture plane with all the requisite diminutions, shrinkings, and convergences. But—and this is the novelty—the precise differences in scale as the recession occurs are, for Desargues, knowable and measurable, which means that the real physical dimensions of the object as it theoretically exists, rather than simply as it appears, are also knowable. His projective geometry is what makes this possible.

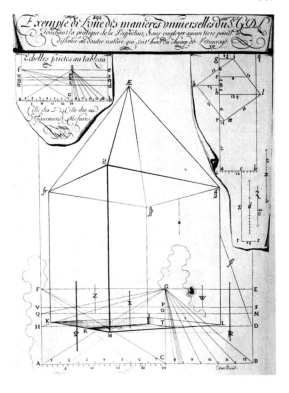

Fig. 7.9. Girard Desargues, perspective view of a pavilion. From Desargues, *Exemple de l'une des manieres universelles du S. G. D. L. touchant la practique de la perspective sans employer aucun tiers point* (Paris: P. Des-Hayes, 1636).

In other words, Desargues's perspective proposes a concept that should by now be familiar to readers of this book—that of the progressively shrinking (or expanding) self-similar series. Only in this case we do not have a series of discrete objects at different scales—no separate, individual shrinking or enlarging series of Russian dolls or Chinese boxes. What we have instead is a series of discrete scales applied to a single object. Not one scale and many objects but one object and many scales.

In the view of a garden pavilion that Desargues prints in order to explain his theory (fig. 7.9), we can calculate the correct measurements of any part of the structure by using the scales on two labels in the upper corners of his plate. The left-hand label demonstrates the exact amount of recession that is mapped by the receding coordinates. Hence it constitutes a constant factor of diminution that we can build into our calculations about the size of any element that is located some distance behind the picture plane. For example, take the inmost, farthest corner of the pavilion. This lies at a point between the horizontals marked *QN* and *HD*. Looking at the label, we learn that at that point the width represented by the picture's bottom edge as twelve *toises* has been reduced, by perspective recession, to three toises. Hence that point is located at $3 \times 4 = 12$ toises in from the picture plane. (A toise is a fathom—i.e., a tall man's height, 1.949 meters or 6'2½".)

In short, we can map an actual pavilion, as it would be built, in terms of this virtual pavilion. Or let us say that we can map it onto an untilted, undistorted Cartesian lattice. Or (each alternative way of thinking about these things is instructive) we could say that Desargues's perspective *is* a Cartesian lattice, but one that has been forced to obey the laws of the *costruzione legittima*.

Since we now know the quantities of Desargues's little house—all its measurements in toises—we could take a pencil, ruler, dividers, and paper, and construct exactly congruent views both of the pavilion's receding and of its invisible sides. We could make a plan, several elevations, and even a bird's-eye view, a worm's-eye view—any view at all—things we would not at all have been able to do with Brunelleschi's projection of the Piazza San Giovanni. Finally, different draftsmen could independently make their own versions of these same drawings, fully confident that each draftsman's work would look like the others'. There again, that would not necessarily occur with Brunelleschi's projection.

All these things lead us to understand Desargues's rather strange description of his drawing:

> a cage simply built up of lines, square in plan and of even width up to a certain level, after which it terminates in a solid point, in the manner of a construction in the form of a roofed pavilion, put down in level country, with all its sides rising vertically from the ground up to the roof level, set into the earth on a level lower than the surrounding terrain, with the measures of several vertical and sloping lines at various places outside and inside the cage, in the earth, on the earth, and suspended over the earth, each line parallel to the picture [plane], which hangs vertically.[17]

This description begins with a station point, yes, but then it circulates that station point, that eye, all around and through the scene. It is almost as if Desargues were describing a mobile airborne and subterranean camera.

But the main point is that his technique reveals the effable, measurable values of his projected image. The seeming distortions of perspective (vis-à-vis plans and elevations) are rationalized. Note, too, that everything Desargues says here about his piece of one-point perspective could equally apply to the multiple-point perspectives of the Bibienas.

DESARGUES'S GEOMETRY

As one might expect, Desargues also investigated the world of conic sections. His most famous work, the *Rough Draft of an Essay on the Results of Taking Plane Sections of a Cone* (1639), was written three years after the essay on perspective.[18] We should pay particular attention to Desargues's theorem. It is basic to all subsequent projective geometry. It derives directly from what we have been saying about magic lanterns, perspective, and the new ways of seeing and looking that go with these things. The color-coded diagram of the theorem in figure 7.10 demonstrates that the whole thing is, in fact, a perspective exercise. The theorem assumes that the observer's eye is at point *O*, looking at the pink triangle *ABC*. Lines or pencils (Desargues still subscribes, at least for didactic purposes, to the notion of visual rays projected outward from the eye) radiate from *O*. These lines, exactly like rays from a magic lantern, strike the corners of the pink triangle *ABC*, then project beyond those corners to strike an imaginary surface or "screen" on which the olive-green triangle *A'B'C'* forms. This latter is of course a projection of *ABC*: a triangle still, but with a new size and shape—with a complete new look, and with different angles.

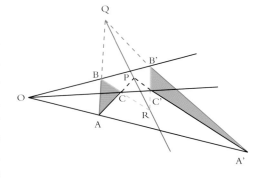

Fig. 7.10. Desargues's theorem

Desargues proved with his theorem that if you extend lines *AC* and *A'C'*, shown in black, to meet at point *P*; and sides *AB* and *A'B'*(shown in blue), to meet at point *Q*; and lines *BC* and *B'C'* (shown in yellow), to meet at point *R*; then *Q*, *P*, and *R* will be points along a straight line (shown in red). And this will happen however much you change the triangles involved, whatever the angle of the projecting rays, wide or narrow, and also whatever the angle of the "screen" on which *A'B'C'* is thrown.[19] So here, as the foundation theorem of projective geometry, and despite the powerful distortions that it sets up between the "slide" and the "screen image," we have a way of seeing certain unexpected internal coherencies in the process of slanted projection. Once again, that which might seem to be ineffable turns out to be effable. Seeming distortions are reconcilable to rational theories about conic sections.

Desargues's disciples continued with his ideas. And they found more new rationalities in the phenomenon of projection. In his *Sectiones conicae* of 1685, Philippe de La Hire, brother of the painter Laurent, proved that squares, circles, and the other components of orthodox Euclideanism distort under projection—yes; but he shows that harmonic ratios do not.[20] No matter how the "screen" is slanted, in other words, and no matter how the specific values change, harmonic those ratios remain. Just as with the projected triangle of Desargues's theorem, the actual shape is changed, but not certain other things between and within the "slide" and its projection.

Even Newton contributed to the establishment of Desargues's ideas. After all, as we have seen, Newton was studying the greatest magic lantern of them all—the cosmos, two of whose point sources, the Sun and Moon, project light down onto Earth. But Newton was interested in projection of the purely earthly type as well:

> If onto an infinite plane lit by a point source of light there should be projected the shadows of figures, the shadows of conic [sections] will always be conics.[21]

Newton continues that the geometric status of many other forms besides conic sections remains constant under even the most vigorous slantings.

SHADOW PROJECTION

Let's return for the moment to the illustration of Guarini's method for calculating the area of a circle (fig. 7.1). But we'll forget about doing it without pi. Let's think, instead, about the complexities of projected light when it hits something. Figure 7.11 depicts the various triangles we have superimposed on the circle as relief elements, with the upper triangle that Guarini has drawn part of the continuous plane of the basic circle. The triangle underneath is recessed onto an inner plane that is parallel to the first plane. This latter triangle's lower edge is a lip or molding sticking out beyond both these

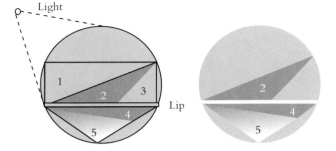

Fig. 7.11. Guarini's exhaustion method transformed into relief elements lit by a 45-degree point source, *left,* with the original edges; *right,* with the shadow pattern only

planes. The lower triangle is cocked at an angle to these planes, projecting diagonally in section so that its point, at the bottom of the circle, comes well forward of everything else. Under a 45-degree point source light from the side, the shadows of these relief features will be projected onto one another, as shown: the upper triangle will project a shadow onto the triangle just underneath it, and then the lip will project its own shadow onto the bottom triangle, and the angled triangle will have a graded shadow leading downward, from its darkest part to a highlight at the bottom of the circle. One could get even more complicated, what with bounced reflections and other graded shadows, penumbras, and the like. But what we should note is that the result is a pattern of cast and graded shadows entirely different from the pattern formed by the triangles' edges.

In figure 7.11, right, I illustrate the cast shadows only. This second diagram is clearly derived from the original. But in appearance it has become very different. Once again, the transformation has been done with projected light and shadow. But now, instead of the straight "slide" and slanted "screen," we have a slanted angle of light meeting the differing angles of the triangles. That angled light projects these angles into shadows of different shapes. All of which could be said to illustrate Desargues's theorem.

Bosse, by the way, distinguishes between *ombre,* which is shadow projected by the object onto something else, and *ombrage,* which is local shadow that is confined to the surface of the object.[22] In this diagram the two cast shadows on the two lower triangles would be ombres, and the graded shadow on the bottom triangle would be ombrage.

One of the main subsets of perspective studies, and of projective geometry generally, is just this sort of shadow play. Projected shadows normally occur at a slanted or distorting angle. Whole books have been written on the subject.[23] Nor is it all post-Desargues. In antiquity the idea was known as sciagraphy (from *skia*, shadow). Sciagraphy is the art of depicting objects whose cast shadows give those objects an added realism (Plato *Republic* 523b). The very invention of painting was attributed to shadow-projection: the daughter of Butades of Sicyon traced the shadow cast by her lover's profile when he went away (Pliny *Historia naturalis* 35.12 [43]). This, we are told, was the first picture ever painted. (In another version Butades's father made a bas relief from the traced shadow; so it was also the invention of sculpture; let us note that the cast shadow was a projection.) And one of the most prominent classical moldings, the scotia, was named after the Greek goddess of shadows.[24] It was a device for casting shadows, in other words. All sorts of associations have gathered around these ideas—above all, the paradox that such frail things as shadows give greater solidity to a depiction. We still sense these associations, perhaps, in our concept of umbrage—suspicion, resentment. Shadows were thought by the ancients to be caused, physically, not so much because of the absence of light as because these areas of darkness are dense with the tiny, motelike souls of the dead.[25] Shadows in life portend death, the ultimate shadow. The Underworld is the land of shadows.

For all the literature on sciagraphy in earlier times, shadow-play first comes to visual importance in the age of the Baroque. Think of the new importance of shadow—of cast shadow, reflected shadow, local shadow, ombres and ombrages—in Caravaggism. Georges de la Tour: where would he be without cast shadows? He is a painter of projections. For centuries, going back to Vitruvius, architectural renderings seem to have done without cast shadows, and even local shadows (making a sphere look round by building up graded shadow and highlight areas but not letting the shadow project onto anything else) were done with the simplest conventions. But, concomitant with the development of projection machines, whether or not they had lenses—and their images, after all, are projected shadows—in line with all this, overlays of projected dark against projected light more and more appeared in representations of buildings.[26]

A good example is the rendering in figure 7.12 by Le Camus de Mezières in the mid–eighteenth century. These magnificent stairs are two helices of stone steps, one twisting right and the other twisting left, nested together. (The sigmoid curve of the steps' ramp was probably supported by iron.)

Like most architectural renderers, Mezières has selected the angle of 45 degrees for the incident light. But here the light is far more than a way of illuminating the stairs. It is a principal actor on stage. We see three great upper windows above the stairs casting three large rhombs of white against the upper hall's shadowy interior. We see more of the light's slanting pencils in the ground-level archway on the left. Like those of spotlights, the exterior rays, penetrating through strategically placed and shaped openings, throw distinct, sharp-edged masses of shadow—well-defined images—over the steps themselves and over the walls of their enclosing cylinder. While the plain neoclassical arch and its support on the left are

Fig. 7.12. Nicolas Le Camus de Mezières, staircase in the Halle au Blé (Paris, 1762–66; demolished). From Robin Evans, *The Projective Cast: Architecture and Its Three Geometries* (Cambridge: MIT Press, 1995).

picked out with delicate linear shadows under and behind their moldings, the arch partially seen on the right, though the same in design, is plunged into near-blackness by the shadow-projections. So the stairway itself, which winds so theatrically in and out of darkness and light, is framed by a shadow-arch and a light-arch. Note that Mezières has incorporated both graded shadows with reflections and re-reflections, and cast shadows, ombrages, and ombres into his drawing. Such projections of shadow-images obey all the laws of the costruzione legittima and of Brunelleschi's experiment, but now put the latter's reflections and re-reflections to new use, incorporating angled and oblique axes.

PROJECTION IN MILITARY ARCHITECTURE

One place where projective geometry quickly became important was in military architecture, indeed in military science generally. As to the latter, it had been known since Galileo that projectiles travel in low, flat parabolas, parabolas that often flatten, at either end of the trajectory, so that the end result is a hyperbola.[27] This meant that soldiers needed to know formulas for conic sections in order to predict the results of their own and their enemies' gunnery. Here, by the way, the main figure is once again Descartes,

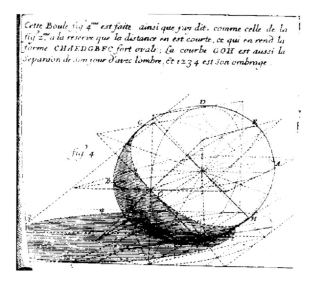

Cette Boule fig 4.me est faite ainsi que j'ay dit. comme celle de la
fig 2.me à la réserve que la distance en est courte, ce qui en rend la
forme CHAEDGBFC fort ovale; la courbe GOH est aussi la
separation de son jour d'avec l'ombre, et 1234 est son ombrage.

Fig. 7.13. Abraham
Bosse, stretched per-
spective sphere and
planes projected by rays
from central points or
"eyes." From Bosse, *La
Pratique du Trait à
preuves de M. Desar-
gues, Lyonnois, pour la
coupe des pierres en
l'architecture* (Paris,
Pierre Des-Hayes, 1643).

who in 1629 worked out foolproof methods for drawing hyperbolas with instruments that some mathematicians, for example Galileo, called "military compasses."
Another fairly mobile name for such
gadgets, or for similar gadgets, was "proportional compasses"; indeed, in a Desar-
guesian mode, these instruments could
also be used to make automatically correct
perspective drawings.[28]

Seventeenth- and eighteenth-century
fortifications were fabricated out of softish
stone bedded on deep masses of earth.[29]
The idea was that enemy cannonballs
would land relatively harmlessly on these
cushioned targets.[30] Meanwhile gun emplacements within the forts—
vaulted chambers offering an approach to 360-degree protection to the gun
crews—replaced the old open-air battlements of the Middle Ages and early
Renaissance. The Baroque fortress is a geometrical labyrinth of tunnels, covered staircases, and vaulted gun chambers. The dominant outer shape, in
plan, was governed by the enormous irregular projecting quadrilaterals of
the bastions. And in perspective those same forms with their acute prowlike
corners and sheer sloping walls once again dominated. Baroque military
building was, indeed, very much in the manner of Blondel's hyperbolic and
parabolic vaults and arches, and of some of the Baroque church designs
we've looked at. Walls are no longer thin flat planes but are solid trunklike
masses shaped into squeezed and stretched polygons blended together. The
technique was stereometric—that is, the forms were full of canted angles,
interrupted arcs, semiparabolas, and planes that sloped, curved, and broke in
three dimensions. It all came out of projective geometry.[31]

To look at it another way we might add to our picture of the magic
lantern projecting its pencils of light, and bearing along its anamorphic
image, another picture: that of a cannon. We would see the cannon hyper-
bolically projecting a projectile onto a "screen" consisting of a densely articulated, many-faceted fortress designed to absorb that projectile—to reflect
it, as it were, or deflect it, almost is if the ball were a projected image to be

bounced off the fort's angled surfaces, or else embedded—captured—on its soft, irregular "screen." But of
course the trajectory of the cannonball is not based
on a cone, as in a magic lantern; instead the multiple
straight-line rays or pencils form a single parabola.

Projective geometry can also be seen in the Platonic and Archimedean solids, and in composites of
these solids, especially as found in military architecture. One simply places the origin of the projection
at the center of the solid. From this center or eye (as
Desargues might call it), "rays" radiate in all directions, generating the stretched sphere. This latter may
have either a smooth or an Archimedean surface.
Abraham Bosse used this model of the radiant sphere
with a central inner eye when he wrote about projecting perspectives onto irregular surfaces; in fact he
introduces his whole enterprise with these spheres
(fig. 7.13). Note, also, its local and cast shadows—ombres and ombrages.[32]

The great figure in Baroque military architecture was Sebastien le Prestre
de Vauban.[33] It was he who mainly erected Louis XIV's massive string of de-
fensive forts around the perimeter of France, thus defining what they called
"le hexagone" (that's how France's shape was seen—a topic written about
up through Le Corbusier).[34]

If we look at the plan of a typical Baroque fortress as sketched by Vauban
(fig. 7.14) we see it, first perhaps, as a flat ring (or part of one), regular or irregular, composed of zigzags. Within the outer zigzags are other repeated
triangles and other shapes—gun chambers, firing platforms, magazines, and
the like. Vauban's plan also includes temporary breastworks for the besiegers. Their field cannons are drawn up at set angles, symmetrical on each
side, to rake the forward bastions with their fire. Vauban has drawn out the
axis of the trajectory of each individual cannon. He was of course well
aware of the ball's parabolic curve. In a word, the besiegers' guns are focused, like magic lanterns, on a zigzagged screen—"*des surfaces irrégulières,*"
as Bosse said in the subtitle of one of his books about the projection of light
and perspective images.

For at least two generations before Vauban, such zigzagging circular

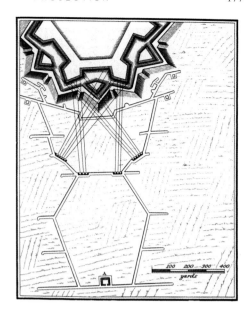

Fig. 7.14. Sébastien
Vauban, plan for attack-
ing a fortress. From
Vauban, *Manière de for-
tifier selon la méthode
de Monsieur de Vauban,*
etc., 1691.

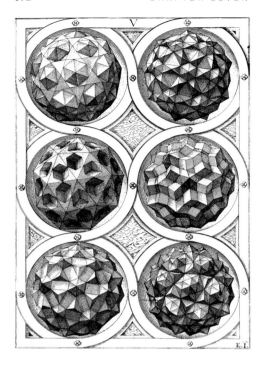

Fig. 7.15. Complex poly-
hedrons. From Wenzel
Jamnitzer, *Perspectiva
Corporum Regularum*
(1568; reprint, Frankfurt:
Biermann, 1972).

forms had been illustrated by geometers, and with ever-increasing complexities. Figure 7.15 illustrates a plate from Wenzel Jamnitzer's *Perspectiva corporum regularum* of 1568.[35] The idea was to interpenetrate one sort of Platonic or Archimedean solid with another so that the corners or apices of the one projected through the faces of the other. One might also, playing this game, convert flat faces into pyramids, or orthodox polygons into stellate forms. In any event a cube, say, will be "engorged," to use Jamnitzer's word, by a regular or a rhombic octahedon. The resulting compound solids would be called, respectively, a cuboctohedron and a rhombocuboctahedron.[36]

What seems clear to me is that Vauban's plans, and those of many other Baroque military architects, are comparable to the horizontal sections of these solids. Why so? It was claimed (correctly) that any material, when formed into such highly plastic shapes, has a rigidity that simpler forms made of that material cannot achieve. (Think of a cardboard egg carton.) In masonry building, corners usually equal reinforcement, the more the better. The same is true for "spheres" or sphere sections made of rhombocuboctahedral components. Thus the Vauban-type plan for a fort, with its "engorged" pyramid sections and stellate polyhedra, can be linked to the same projective geometry that was used to calculate the trajectories of missiles.

In Napoleonic times—that is, beyond the general chronological boundaries of this book—Vauban's great successor was Gaspard Monge (d. 1818). He continued projective geometry into what we now call descriptive geometry—once again, basically in terms of fortification theory. Or you might say that the whole business grew out of castrametation.[37]

PROJECTION AND SPIRAL STAIRS

Baroque spiral staircases could take fantastic forms. We have already admired Le Camus de Mezières' double helix (though that too actually belongs to neoclassicism). From time immemorial the standard type of spiral stair had consisted of a helical run of steps—whorls—usually inside a cylinder but sometimes partly freestanding. We have already looked at such stairs as exercises in rotational symmetry. But they can also be seen as pieces of projective geometry. Look at the plan, the top view, of such a staircase designed by Guarini (fig. 7.16). The steps radiate from a point source, much like the rays of a magic lantern's cone. Think of looking directly into that cone as it shines onto your face. If you subdivide the pencils of light into equal sectors of the circle, you have, in each sector, one of the staircase's treads.

The age also produced variations on the type of projection that I will call sigmoid. Here, instead of being straight, the rays each repeat some curve, jog, or other movement. A good example: the so-called dancing steps at the Kilianskirche, Heilbronn on the Neckar, dating from 1513–29 (fig. 7.17). Here the rays radiate from the projection's point source or central pillar, first in short curves, and then shooting off obliquely, but in straight lines, until they meet the inside wall of their enclosure.

These staircases are projective in the sense that their plans involve radiating pencils that behave like the bent or straight beams in a magic lantern. Or like the light beams, or projection beams, that determine the perimeter of a Baroque fortress built into a shape that resembles a horizontal section through a compound Platonic or Archimedean solid.

In the seventeenth and eighteenth centuries the Neapolitan architect

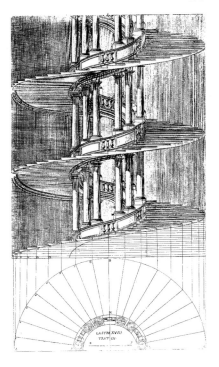

Fig. 7.16. Guarino Guarini, elevation and plan of a spiral stair. From Guarini, *Architettura civile*.

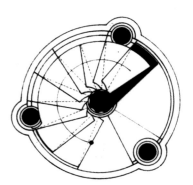

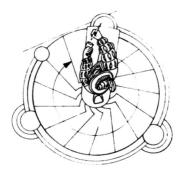

Fig. 7.17. The dancing steps at the Kilianskirche (Heilbronn on the Neckar, 1513–29). From John Templer, *The Staircase: History and Theories* (Cambridge: MIT Press, 1992).

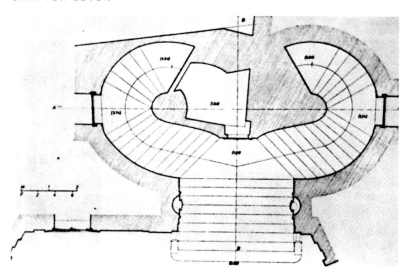

Ferdinando Sanfelice built "projective" stairs that were even more advanced than these.[38] Often they were based on arcs or fragments of spirals—spirals that combine curved and straight courses, derived from squashed as well as true circles, sigmoid curves, and various broken symmetries (see chapter 8). Meanwhile the angling of the treads mimics the squeezed and stretched pencils that produce projection—to use Bosse's term, *sur les surfaces irrégulières.* Some Sanfelice stairs are even epicycloid—that is, they have built-in wobbles or librations like those that Ptolemaic astronomers drew for planets. (Epicyclic architecture is also discussed in the next chapter.) With their arched and vaulted housings Sanfelice's staircases could occupy the whole wall of a courtyard, their tall open-air arches being arrayed in mirrored multistory V's.[39]

Note, in figure 7.18, that Sanfelice's treads can vary from full-radius to partial-radius circle-sectors, and from wide to narrow. Some are simple rectangles. The landings can be trapezoids or flattened spherical triangles. The path of each whorl, as it wanders along its course, may swell or shrink as it goes. Sanfelice's staircases develop out beyond the Baroque proper, moving into the Rococo with its sensibility for broken curves (Sanfelice did not die until 1748). And even beyond that, Sanfelice's stairs make us think of Möbius strips.

Projective geometry is tied up with the optical instruments we looked at earlier, and with what happens to light, to shadow, and to the images that light and shadow bear along with them when the images go through lenses, bounce off reflectors, and expand along conical pathways. Projection is therefore a part of the science of conic sections—as well as of radial symmetry. And it grew out of Renaissance perspective, in which vanishing points, station points, and distance points were the equivalents of the point sources used in projection.

In military science, in fortress-building, projective geometry had another sort of usefulness. Here, architectural effects were achieved that look like sections through compound geometric solids. Many of these ideas flowered in the work of Girard Desargues, founder of projective geometry, and especially in his work on perspective—which sought, successfully, to supplant Renaissance guesswork with the measurable physical realities of what was being looked at.

Another key element in all this is the study of projected shadows— Baroque sciagraphy. From this we learn that pencils of shadow are as important, precise, and dramatic as are rays of light; that most projected images are in fact shadows—transparent colored shadows. Compared to earlier theories of vision, projective geometry introduces radically new concepts both of seeing and of reality itself—new concepts about the optical process; about what is being seen; and about how to capture it, how to present it, and how to understand it. These worlds of broken, bent, and chopped projections find curious resonances in various kinds of spiral staircases such as those of Ferdinando Sanfelice in Naples and the Kilianskirche at Heilbronn.

EIGHT

EPICYCLES

W e have already investigated, slightly, two aspects of Baroque architectural geometry that in this chapter will concern us more fully. After the discoveries of seventeenth-century astronomy, we have seen, epicycles fell out of favor as models for planetary orbits. Yet people interested in mechanics, whether or not they were concerned with that discipline's celestial branch, had for centuries been fascinated with the idea of an object or shape that could rotate or revolve on its own axis at the same time that it also rotated or revolved in a larger orbit. Here on Earth, indeed, this is the basic principle of rotary gears, recognized at least since Archimedes. This same principle, which throughout this chapter I will call the epicyclic principle, had a considerable architectural fallout.

Another aspect of the Baroque was its penchant for what is nowadays called broken symmetry. In the present pages, we formed an impression about broken symmetry from looking at the contiguous arcs with varied radii that, from at least the Renaissance onward, were joined together into ovals. These, since they are formed out of the arcs of circles, are not truly smooth and not truly continuous. And here I will note that while the results may be mere approximations (and not very convincing ones) to today's geometers, these forms were achieved via the mastery of the polar compasses. This was something essential for anyone who would be an architect or geometer. It was a way of drawing ovals and the like, as it happens, that was being advocated in architectural treatises even until the time of Ferdinando Bibiena (1711).[1]

In fact, the whole of this chapter will deal with the fruits of virtuoso compass-twirling. These exploits will include many of the bendings, bouncings, and conical scale-ladders that we observed earlier being done with straight lines in projective geometry. Only now it all happens with arcs, circles, and ellipses. Just such curves—knotted, interwoven, interrupted, overlapped, rescaled—are found, again, in Baroque diagrams of astronomical epicycles. We will look at architectural design that was carried out along these lines.

EPICYCLES (AND EPICYCLOIDS)

In Greek, *epi* means on top of, in addition to, besides, about. Cycle is derived from *kyklos*, wheel. "Epicycle" thus means a wheel on another wheel, a gear on another gear, or, as in astronomy, an orbit on another orbit.

Perhaps the whole idea goes back to Ezekiel's "wheel inside a wheel." It reached from Earth to Heaven (Ezekiel 1:15–21), so it was clearly cosmic. The phrase in the Authorized Version is "when they [the wheels] went, they went upon their four parts; and they did not revolve when they moved."[2] To me these mysterious words, and the rest of the passage, seem to describe orbits as opposed to revolutions. Not objects revolving on their own axes, that is, but "wheels" that didn't move because they were circular tracks in space; it would be a planet, along the track, that did the moving. And when the prophet adds that the "wheels went upon their four parts," to me that means that the planets, moving in those stationary orbits, went all the way round, 360 degrees. The four parts would be north, east, south, and west.

I take this imagery to be epicyclic. I show my suggested explanation in figure 8.1, with the larger wheel or orbit in blue, and the inner "wheels"—revolutions or even micro-orbits—in white. These latter consist of a single small movement that itself circles around the larger orbit, acting as Ezekiel's smaller "wheel" inside the larger one.[3] To suit the prophet's claim that the small wheels didn't turn as they moved, we could imagine the white circles in the diagram as the successive positions of one or more nonturning wheels, or cycles as they move around the greater blue orbit.

The epicycloid, as opposed to the epicycle, got its name from a certain

Ole Römer, who in 1674 discussed the fact that cogwheels with epicycloid teeth—that is, teeth that roll as they mesh with the teeth of another cogwheel—suffer less friction than do normal cogwheels with fixed teeth. But this advantage had been pointed out by earlier experimenters: Desargues, Huygens, Philippe de la Hire, Newton, and others.[4] Anyway, Römer wanted to differentiate the useful cogwheels from the now-discredited planetary motions—epicycles—and he did so by calling the cogwheels epicycloids. For us, however, the difference between the two words is going to be negligible. Indeed my intention is just the opposite of Römer's: I want to reunite the two concepts, earthly-mechanical and celestial-mechanical, and even impart a heavenly nature to earthly epicycles—at least when the latter take architectural form.

The basic idea of epicycles is shown in figures 8.2 and 8.3. In the diagrams an object that is embedded in the system (shown in its successive positions by the red dots, *A*), orbits around a set of smaller orbits, *B*, while simultaneously, in and of themselves, those smaller orbits travel around the larger circle, *C*. Obviously, as it does so, the epicycling object, the red dot, will seem to wander. It was this that explained the wobbles or librations that Ptolemaic astronomers observed in the planets' movements. (The word "planet" means "wanderer.") The red dot rambles, but not too wildly. You could, if you made your observations at the right times, even plot the planet moving effectively in an oval or ellipse, *D*, shown in blue. (This might be what at first suggested elliptical circuits to Kepler.)

The epicycling object might be a wheel or a ball as well as a planet. Or it could be a draftsman's pen. And under certain circumstances the object might only travel through part of its small orbit, say a semicircle, before momentarily joining itself onto the greater orbit. At that point the red dot would click onto another smaller orbit, or rather onto that same smaller orbit when it had gotten to a second position next to its first position. Such continuous hopping from half-orbit to half-orbit, from arc to arc, would produce the scalloped shape we see in figure 8.3. The active parts of these epi-orbits are shown as a ring of red semicircles. The procedure is the same, graphically, as making a Serlian oval.

To this I will add that in all such procedures, the epicycling object is actually following a corkscrew course. So, whether in Heaven or on Earth, epicyclic movements are so many more examples of spiral symmetry.

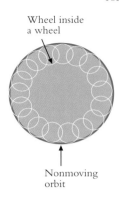

Wheel inside a wheel

Nonmoving orbit

Fig. 8.1. Ezekiel's wheels

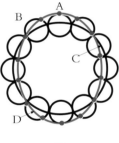

Fig. 8.2. A set of epicycles (metacycles) in full circles

Fig. 8.3. The same, with the metacycles in broken orbits

EPICYCLIC ARCHITECTURE

I would finally point out that such two-dimensional diagrams on paper are, and have to be, completely static. Any actual "movements" are imagined. And throughout our period the main imageries of epicycles, those in the astronomy books, were always drawings of stationary overlapped arcs and circles—just like the ones illustrated here. The interest in the diagrams, simply as diagrams, seems to have been as great as the interest in what the diagrams portrayed. Kepler reveled in them. But, since they are static, the diagrams could almost have been intended to show foundation walls or a horizontal section of a domed building. This is what brings us to architecture.[5]

At this point, indeed, an architectural historian will say that the scalloped pattern of a large circle framed by a ring of smaller circles or epicycles has a strong resemblance to an age-old shape. This is the plan of a martyrium or tomb, round or polygonal, with equal apses surrounding the inner cylinder of the tomb's main walls. The apses, or apsidioles as they can be called, are (usually) some rational fraction of the main cylinder, say a half or a quarter of the latter's diameter and height. In a way not too different from the action of epicycles, the apsidioles buttress and frame the larger cylinder in its "orbit." The plans of these buildings almost exactly reproduce diagrams of Ptolemaic epicycles.

Could there be any historical, as opposed to a purely formal and visual, connection between astronomical epicycles and this architecture? Let us recall that, up through the birth of modern astronomy, epicycles not only explained the movements of the planets, they also constituted the wheels and gears of immense astrological machines that guided our human destinies. It is perhaps in this sense that large and small wheels pervaded Ezekiel's vision; after all he had sojourned in Babylonia, supposedly the original land of astrologers and astronomers.[6] Such shapes and movements would also have been very much in the minds of the builders (and future occupants) of such tombs or martyriums. After all, the rotundas were the earthly houses for the free-flying souls destined for the heavens. Why shouldn't they have a heavenly shape? (Martyrs and heroes—for example, Hercules, Cassiopeia, and Andromeda—often joined the stars.) Heavenly

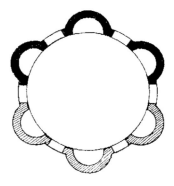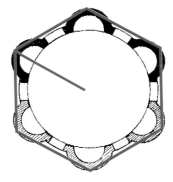

scenes, moreover, with skies, stars, and celestial beings, frequently decorated the interiors of these rotundas.[7]

Furthermore, while such small central-plan structures are usually houses for the dead, they could also be nymphaeums—garden houses with interior pools or fountains, the haunts of water nymphs (figs. 8.4 and 8.5). And nymphaeums had their own heavenly associations. Not only because nymphs were divinities but because their shrines were used to celebrate marriages, marriages "made in Heaven," "under a favoring star"—that is, marriages with cosmic and astrological attributes. In Greek, *nymphasmata* are brides' ornaments, *nympheuma* is marriage itself, the *nympheutes* is the groom, and so on.

Moreover, with their characteristically (though not uniformly) epicycloid forms, nymphaeums survived into Christian times. Their connection with divinity, water, and purification caused the early Christians to use this name, and the architectural shape that went with it, for their baptistries, whether freestanding or built into churches.[8] Often such a baptistry, rather than being centered on a font, would have a full-fledged baptismal pool as the main feature—a particularly clear recalling of the tradition of the pagan nymphaeum. When in the Renaissance Leonardo imitated the nymphaeum or martyrium shape in designing central-plan churches, he was only following precedents he would have known from Florence and Milan. Indeed whole churches had already often been built in the shape of martyriums: in Florence, Brunelleschi's Santa Maria degli Angeli; also, in a squared-off version, the transepts and choir of the Duomo; and, in Milan, San Satiro.

Ancient or modern, these rotundas were usually geometrically effable.

Fig. 8.4. Nymphaeum on the Via Appia, Rome (restored plan). From Louis Hautecoeur, *Mystique et architecture: Symbolisme du cercle et de la coupole* (Paris: Picard, 1954).

Fig. 8.5. The nymphaeum of Fig. 8.4, inscribed in a hexagon and showing the hexagon's long radius

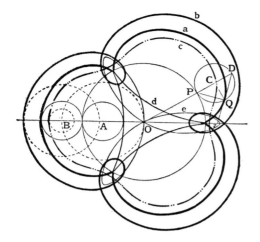

In figure 8.4, the epicycles of an ancient nymphaeum on the Via Appia are separated from one another by short, uniform expanses of the building's central cylindrical wall.[9] Because the central cylinder has six apsidioles, one directly opposite another, the whole plan can be inscribed in a hexagon. The radius of each apsidiole interior is equal to six (the "hexagonal" number) times the diameter of the main cylinder, so that in this sense the number of apsidioles is the same as the value of their radii compared to the radius of the cylinder. One might say that the building is not only hexagonic but hexametric; and that this same radius

Fig. 8.6. Epicycloids. From the *Encyclopedia Britannica*, 11th ed. (1910–11).

also accounts for the width of the wall openings between each apsidiole. No fractions of the module appear, at least along the more normative dimensions, but only its whole value, either by itself or else multiplied by whole numbers. Up to a point, of course, this only means that the building was designed with a module equal to the radius of the apsidiole. Such effability, such easy calculability, is another way in which these buildings are "planetary." They partake of what was supposed to be the heavens' rational simplicity. Indeed, in antiquity there were legends to the effect that some of these buildings actually *could* revolve like the heavens. They were architectural orreries. [10]

In the age of the Baroque such buildings continued to be built, and frequently so. And they could also considerably elaborate the notion of epicycles; so now we can look at epicycles in their more complex forms. The diagram in figure 8.6, for example, shows several types of epicycles superimposed. We need not study all their intricacies except to note that the three lobes are irregular ellipse-like shapes—stretched circles. Their long diameters are greater than the diameter of the basic cycle itself. From this we learn that an epicycle needn't be circular, needn't be regular, and needn't be smaller than its cycle.

Nor need the epicycles revolve and orbit directly on the cycle's perimeter. If they orbit inside it (like Ezekiel's little wheel) they are called hypocycles (*hypo* = under). "Epicycle" and "hypocycle" are in the dictionaries. But here I want to invent new terms to go with these, designating epicycle as the generic name for the whole phenomenon. When the outer orbit rolls entirely outside the central cycle, I will call it a hypercycle (*hyper* = over, beyond). And when it forms apsidioles as in fig. 8.4, I will call it a metacycle (*meta* = half; as in half in, half out). I will further stipulate that these epicycles need not roll just inside, just outside, or centered on the cycle's perimeter. They can revolve well inside it or well outside it (fig. 8.6). One might think of a juggler's balls spinning in the air. They are often separated from his hands, though it is his hands that, like an epicycle's cycle, spin the balls.

In the late 1670s, when he made his plan for the sanctuary at Oropa in Piedmont, it is clear that Guarino Guarini was thinking along similar lines. This project for Emmanuele Filiberto di Carignano of Savoy, destined for a mountain-rimmed shrine, was not built, but it was published in Guarini's book.[11]

The plan (fig. 8.7) is for an epicyclic octagon, the eight lobes consisting of narrow ellipses set lengthwise to form a ring, not unlike the orbiting moons around Jupiter and Saturn. In plan the main choir is an interrupted circle, however, joined to the ellipse at the upper part of the ring, which thereby becomes an entrance into the choir. The latter would have contained the most sacred part of the church, namely the original cubicle erected at the site by St. Eusebius.

Guarini's scheme is as effable as any earlier specimen of epicyclic design. The key to the whole, its number generator so to speak, is the set of three concentric octagons in the interior. As shown by Guarini, these elements—which in plan are plane octagons—form, in elevation, a series of telescoped octagonal cupolas (fig. 8.8). The width of the outermost octagon equals the radius of the circular nave. The smaller octagons, within this outer one, were generated by successively drawing the largest square that would fit into that outer octagon, and then uniformly truncating the square's sides to form the next smaller octagon. This process established the size and shape of all the cupolas.[12] The different widths of the three octagons, by the way, work out to the harmonic sequence 4:7:13.[13] The distances between the foci of the ellipses in the ring of chapels and the sides of the innermost octagon are the same.

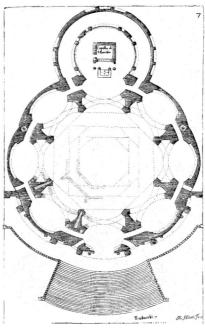

Fig. 8.7. Guarino Guarini, plan of projected sanctuary at Oropa (1678–80). From Guarini, *Architettura Civile*.

Fig. 8.8. Facade and interior section of Guarini's projected sanctuary at Oropa (1678–80). From Guarini, *Architettura Civile.*

Indeed, on looking at Guarini's drawing of the facade and interior vertical section of the proposed church (fig. 8.8), we quickly see that the whole structure is a set of telescoped cupolas. This goes together with the enormous cardioid-shaped openings, which, like the mirrors of a Newtonian telescope, would have transmitted light into the interior successively from each of the four "faces" of the compass wheel or orbit. All of which means that Oropa fits in well with the "optical" architecture we looked at earlier. We can conveniently recall here that, mathematically, cardioids are special kinds of epicycles. And Guarini's project also accords with my interpretation of Ezekiel's wheel, which itself did not revolve but covered all four compass-points. Guarini, in short, carries on the epicyclic possibilities of Baroque architecture in a thoroughly effable manner and makes use of new ways for these possibilities to be realized.

ECCENTRIC EPICYCLES

We have noted that epicycles don't need to be smaller than their cycles and don't need to revolve on the latter's perimeter. Nor must they be concentric and always produce the scalloped, cookie-cutter patterns we've been examining. So let's look at eccentric epicycles. Perhaps the oldest, most familiar example is found in the cogwheels of Baroque clockwork. The train of circular gears in a clock's inner works control the speed and regularity of its hands as they click around in their revolutions. If we want to think astronomically, we might even consider the hands as the radii of objects (the pointers at the ends of the hands) moving at different speeds in concentric circles. The concept of a clock, indeed, is not too far from that of an orrery, or for that matter from the movements of an idealized Ptolemaic planet.

But, beginning with seventeenth-century clocks, this regularity and symmetry on the clock face is achieved via hidden clockwork with radically eccentric gears and toothed drive-shafts. These gears and shafts, to use my terminology, consist of hypocycles, hypercycles, and metacycles, all of different sizes, and often not located on their neighbor's perimeter. And some of the gears drive not one but several other gears, so the epicycles in clockwork may be multicentric as well as eccentric. The epicycles can have epicycles of their own.

One of the earliest pieces of eccentric epicyclic mechanics, if not the very earliest, was invented by Galileo in 1582–83, when he was about eighteen. He called it the *pulsilogium*. At first the gadget was a practical application of his theories about pendulums. It involved matching the rhythm of a pendulum against that of a human pulse to determine the latter's degree of regularity (Galileo had started out as a medical student). Out of this grew the notion of making the pendulum's movements even more regular, and continuing those movements for longer times. For this Galileo used additional gears. His eccentric-geared machine worked well—better than earlier mechanical clocks, apparently. In 1639 Vincenzo Viviani illustrated a full-fledged clockwork, with escapement (to chop up the energy driving the wheels into equal pulses). This clockwork had been developed out of the pulsilogium, and Viviani attributed it to Galileo (fig. 8.9).[14]

It is more than appropriate that Galileo, the future astronomer, should

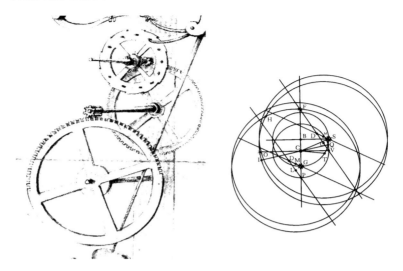

Fig. 8.9. The gears, pendulum, and escapement of Galileo's clockwork.

Fig. 8.10. One of Kepler's diagrams of eccentric epicycles. From Johannes Kepler, *Astronomia nova aetiologica* (1609).

have conceived of his machine as an exercise in eccentric epicycles. Earthly clocks, after all, were checked against the regularity of that ultimate, most reliable of clocks, the heavens. And in these years, of course, the heavens were still thought by most to be epicyclic—though by now the epicycles had gotten very complex, what with hypocycles, hypercycles, metacycles, and the like. And epicyclic Galileo's clock surely is as well. We can call the largest gear, at the bottom, the basic cycle. On it rolls a small epicycle attached to a rod that also turns a slightly smaller metacycle; then, more or less, the same thing happens with the upper metacycle, revolving on the middle wheel.[15]

Kepler is thought of as the overthrower of epicycles, and so he was. But he overthrew them in a strangely reluctant way. It must be the longest goodbye in science. Galileo's experiments with eccentric epicycles in clockwork, in fact, matched Kepler's diagrams of planetary motions (fig. 8.10). Indeed in the *Astronomia aetiologica nova* (1609), the very book in which Kepler first broached (and proved) that the planets moved elliptically, he nonetheless spends many pages giving the details of his fruitless attempts to prove the existence of epicycles. He anatomizes his failures with something close to relish. All this in order to prove not only that ellipses were right but, as a more or less separate enterprise, that epicycles were wrong. (And, in contradistinction to today's scientists, to prove what a lot of work his ultimate achievement was.)

Like Galileo's clockwork, Kepler's epicycles in the *Astronomia nova* are eccentric. They are also of various sizes and are set up along tilted axes. There are hypocycles that roll well inside their cycles. There are also overlapped doublings of all orbits, which you don't find in the clockwork. We should keep in mind, too, that both these epicyclic exercises, with all their added complications, came about in order to establish the utmost possible precision for the ticking off of intervals of time and motion. The "irregularities" of the clockwork's train of gears—by which I mean the eccentric mounting of the wheels—made the rotations of Galileo's clock-hands, and Kepler's planet, more predictable, more regular, than such things had been before.

A further point about Kepler. Using these epicycles, a given planet will orbit only on arcs, on fragments, of the complex of cycles and epicycles that he has drawn, switching back and forth from one arc to another. It was this sense of multiple broken circles that drove Kepler toward the simpler, more rational realm of ellipses. He fully saw all the messiness of the epicyclic system—even though, trying to clean it up, he only made it messier. Kepler indeed frequently comments on his difficulties. In the *Astronomia nova* he often bewails the trouble and confusion that spill onto his page when, as he picturesquely puts it, he seeks to "harness the planetary driving forces to the mouths of the orbits."[16]

Kepler, then, gave up on epicycles, but only after exploring them and illustrating them in their every possible permutation and combination. In architecture, such fragments and interrupted orbits, these epicyclic overlappings, doublings and the like, such hypo-, hyper- and metacyclings, continued to be gladly employed.

So in this spirit let's return to Borromini and San Carlo. Earlier we looked at a composite plan, doctored by me, which illustrated methods for drawing out ovals and ellipses using just these fragmentary or overlapped orbits (fig. 6.5). But that doctored plan had a lot more bilateral mirror symmetry than did the plan of the church as built (fig. 8.11). If we plot out all the circles establishing the built plan's main features, completing, as epicyclic orbits, all its rich arrays (shown in blue), we see it in fact as nothing less than

Fig. 8.11. Francesco (or
Bernardo?) Borromini,
plan of San Carlino as
built (circles added).

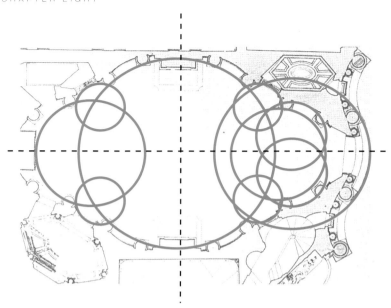

a cluster of eccentric epicycles. Though it does have up-down symmetry,
otherwise it is a fit companion piece to Galileo's clockwork and Kepler's *Astronomia nova* diagram.

ELLIPTICAL EPICYCLES

Many Baroque designers seem to have made their ovals in the Serlian manner. But we also saw the true and proper ellipse coming more and more
onto the scene. After Kepler, the main stage manager of this event was the
Italo-French astronomer Giovanni Domenico [Jean-Dominique] Cassini,
Louis XIV's Astronomer Royal. It was for him that Claude Perrault built the
original building for the Observatoire in Paris.[17] Cassini himself worked
brilliantly away on the geometrical problems we've spoken about. He studied spherical geometry and topology, inscribed ellipses and hyperbolas on
bent or dished planes, and investigated ellipsoids and paraboloids.[18] It was
Cassini, in fact, who discovered the formula for the area of an ellipse, πab
(fig. 8.12).[19] Obviously this gave a considerable boost to the usefulness of
ellipses and ellipsoids in architecture and design.

Ellipses also play their role in the world of epicycles. Quite apart from
what we have just seen in Borromini, many Baroque and especially Rococo

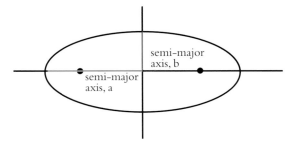

architectural forms are created from eccentric, intersecting ellipses—that is, from elliptical hypercycles, metacycles, and hypocycles. (Indeed, given seventeenth-century standards of precision in architectural drawing, I could have plotted the plan of San Carlo in figure 8.11 in ellipses rather than in circles, or in a combination of the two.)

Fig. 8.12. Diagram of Cassini's formula for the area of an ellipse (πab), with *a* as the (blue) semimajor axis and *b* as the (red) semiminor. The dots are the two foci.

Today, most notably, it is the violin family of musical instruments that preserves this tradition of elliptical epicycles. In fact, the three greatest violin makers ever, Niccolò Amati, Antonio Stradivarius, and Giuseppe Guarnieri del Gesù, were Cassini's contemporaries.[20] The perimeter of a violin, viola, violoncello, or double bass (see fig. 8.13) is nothing more nor less than a play of interrupted, intersecting elliptical epicycles similar to the epicycle fragments that Kepler drew (fig. 8.10), though Kepler's were always circular. In the violin family, each ellipse gets its own name—"top bout," "C bout," "lower bout," and so on. The segments are not always regular. And in some of the showier instruments they will be garnished with moldings that swell and recede in the form of Rococo arabesques, terminating with spiral scrolls or vegetal shoots.

What have violins to do with architecture? Rococo design is based, like the shape of the violin, on the principle of eccentric elliptical or oval epicycles. One might call the work of a typically Rococo architect like Domenico Antonio Vaccaro, of Naples, a violin-derived style. His plans, his frames for openings, his panels, and his cartouches are all assemblages of elliptical arcs. Everything in his buildings swerves, swells, and sweeps around just like the perimeter of a fiddle.

Figure 8.14, for example, shows a window of a monastic building by Vaccaro, the Palazzo Abbaziale di Loreto, in Avellino (1734–49). In and of itself that window frame is practically a contrabass. Note its upper central semicircular metacycle, its jogged shoulders, its long S-curved sides, and its

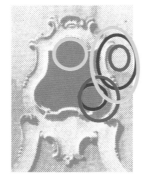

Fig. 8.13. The Vieux-
temps Guarnieri violin.
From *The Cambridge
Companion to the Violin*
(Cambridge: Cambridge
University Press, 1992).

Fig. 8.14. Domenico An-
tonio Vaccaro, Palazzo
Abbaziale di Loreto
(Avellino, 1734–49). De-
tail of ground-floor win-
dow.

Fig. 8.15. The elliptical
epicycles that create the
perimeters of the violin
(*left*) and the window (*right*)
in figs. 8.13 and 8.14

zigzagging Rococo bottom—though it is decked out with more moldings, scrolls, shells, and blossoms than a stringed instrument would have.

Let us draw out most of the elliptical epicycles that create the profiles of the violin and the window frame depicted in figures 8.13 and 8.14. (It is true that some of the "orbits," both of the violin and of the window, are circular, or close to it. But recall that, mathematically, a circle is really an ellipse with coincident foci.)

Note, by the way, also, that both designs have left-right but not up-down symmetry, so we are not talking about the kind of biaxial, indeed multiaxial, tilted eccentricity we see in clockworks, gear chains, and Keplerian epicycles. Otherwise, however, once the ellipse had achieved its new role in cosmology, and its newfound calculability, the sort of design illustrated in figure 8.15 seems almost inevitable.

Even Vaccaro's plan of the Avellino monastery in figure 8.16 seems violin-derived. It is reminiscent of his window frames, so that it is formed of similar clustered curvatures easily seen as further examples of elliptical or circular epicycles. Once again, too, as in stringed instruments, we have left–right symmetry but not up-down. Indeed the facade of the building is structured like one of these windows, with the central opening in this case being the courtyard, and with the rows of cells and other rooms, the corridors, the closets, and so on around that courtyard replacing the arabesques, scrolls, shells, and blossoms of the window surround.

Note, finally, the effect on the facade, simply as a facade, of Vaccaro's fiddle formula (fig. 8.17): the orders have been banished. No pilasters or columns, no entablature, no pedestals, no dado. The six openings in the il-

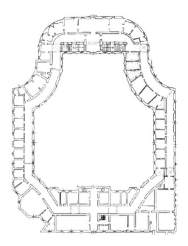

lustrated facade confront the viewer like a string orchestra consisting of two violins (the lower pair) and two cellos (the pair of upper windows). Then, in the center, one on top of the other, are two contrabasses. These are the central doorway and the upper window of appearances. They anchor the architectural music with their deeper sonorities. Note also that the outer margins of the facade—even here there is no traditional columnar lattice—consists simply of more Stradivarian arabesques.

Fig. 8.16. Vaccaro's plan of Palazzo Abbaziale di Loreto (Vaccaro, Avellino, 1734–49).

Fig. 8.17. Detail of facade in Vaccaro's plan of Palazzo Abbaziale di Loreto.

Vaccaro designed many other buildings in this mode, though the fiddle-like openings tend to predominate over facade compositions such as the one at Avellino. Just in Naples alone, these include the church of the Immacolatella near the Bacino Angioino; the high altar of the Chiesa di Rosario di Palazzo near Santa Brigida; the portal of the church of the Concezione a Montecalvario (1718–24); and, in Piazza Dante, the church of San Michele Arcangelo al Mercatello (1730).[21]

BROKEN SYMMETRY

In epicyclic design, the intercutting, interpenetrating, and interlocking of different orbits, one with another, breaks open the circles and ellipses of which the cycles and epicycles are composed. We see interruption, sudden shifts, and abandoned courses. And that, in turn, brings us face-to-face with the phenomenon, mentioned a few pages back, of broken symmetry.[22]

First of all, what is it? Or at least what can we understand it to be? We have broken symmetry when a symmetry system is established and then somehow abandoned, undermined, smashed, inflated, or squeezed. As its ultimate outcome, broken symmetry can produce chaos. But always, for broken symmetry to exist, the original symmetrical intention must remain recognizable. To the mathematician, broken symmetry can bring a feeling of inconsistency, betrayal, or at least of unwonted absence. As Stewart and Golubitsky say, "When symmetry breaks, we're left with the nagging feeling that it must have gone somewhere."[23] Broken symmetry is a sort of mathematical cult of ruins wherein, as in the wake of some catastrophe, an artifact is still readable, still imaginable, even though it is mainly demolished.

And here is a cautionary aside: despite the astronomers' longtime struggle to see perfected—that is, unbroken symmetries—in the universe, paradoxically such breaks and intersections, such bumps and bulges among all the perfect circles, had long been seen and even appreciated. That is, on the one hand you had Copernicus famously claiming that the planets had to be spherical in themselves, and had to be perfectly circular in their orbits.[24] And on the other hand you had Ptolemy himself, and presumably at least some of his Baroque followers, holding that these motions could and should have bumps and breaks—that it was all right for them, in Koyré's words, to wobble, to "bristle with nodes."[25]

Over the centuries, therefore, broken symmetries have held their own in counterpoint to the more perfect and completed kinds. Kepler's fragmentary intersecting epicycles in the *Astronomia nova* are further examples—and, as we shall see, fascinating ones. Indeed, even the simplest, most perfect set of Ptolemaic epicycles could be described in terms of broken symmetry: after all, the circular orbit is "broken" whenever the planet slips off into an epicycle. And it's not just a question of planets in epicycles, or even of the diagrams of epicycles without the planets. Any compound form may seem "broken" when in the middle of being one shape it stops that and starts being another shape. Of course this sort of "breakage" can be repaired if the whole scenario—starting, stopping, and then starting something else—is regularly repeated, as with translatory or rotational symmetry. In such a situation a piece of broken symmetry is mended, or amended, into a larger piece of perfect symmetry.

Something like this has been true of many of the other matters we have looked into. Thinking always about symmetry that is complete, we have often been in the occult presence of broken symmetry. At the very least Serlio's pseudo-continuous curves, all of which are broken, allude to the idea. In Val-de-Grâce, Mansart's nonmatching transepts were a défaut de symmetrie that, simply by being a "default," were already a matter of breakage, of absence (fig. 5.1). They were formal implications about something that had been begun and then was inconsistently realized. And, again to revert to chapter 5, there we saw how, at the Invalides, Hardouin-Mansart "broke" his nine-square lattice to permit the insertion of his entrance and chancel. In the same spirit Bernini broke open his St. Peter's ellipse and gouged out an opening down its minor axis, again to permit entrance and exit (fig. 6.14). The Oropa plan does the same (fig. 8.7). Indeed the idea of broken symmetry—of a geometrical system that is established, then interrupted, then continued—is endemic in Baroque architecture. In a way, I suppose, breaking a symmetry emphasizes, maybe dramatizes, the act of breakage; but it also dramatizes the original symmetry itself—the thing that was broken, the thing that had "gone somewhere."

In nature we see just such forms, first ruptured, then patched together, everywhere. One homely example is the hen's egg. It is found not only in chicken coops and on breakfast tables (fig. 8.18) but in practically every Ionic, Corinthian, and Composite molding complex (fig. 8.19). There must be millions, billions of these ornamental eggs worldwide, most of them arranged in very long rows—that is, with translatory symmetry (see fig. 5.8).

In and of itself, however, each one of these eggs exhibits broken symmetry. The curve of the egg in figure 8.18 is composed of three overlapped ellipses, shown in red. A main ellipse measures the egg's entire height, then an upper, horizontal ellipse accounts for the flattish curve around its top, and finally a small narrow ellipse at the bottom gives the egg its characteristic pointed "chin." The similarity of these ellipse clusters to eccentric elliptical epicycles is obvious.

The broken symmetries of nature's egg are only exaggerated in architectural eggs (fig. 8.19). Compared to the real egg, the top part of the architectural one is wider and flatter, and its chin sharper. The architectural egg, indeed, comes close to being a spherical triangle with rounded points. But to see the broken symmetry we must imagine overlapped ellipses, in this case with the upper ellipse much larger than with the real egg, and with the

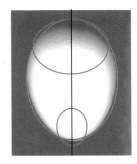

Fig. 8.18. Ellipses overlapped to make a hen's-egg shape or compound oval

Fig. 8.19. An egg and dart molding (detail of Fig. 5.8)

Fig. 8.20. A sphere that has been deformed by a uniform radial compressive force. Computer graphic by R. J. Thompson. From István Hargittai and Clifford A. Pickover, eds., *Spiral Symmetry* (Singapore: World Scientific, 1992).

lower ellipse narrower. So, like the nodes in planetary orbits, hens' eggs and their architectural copies suggest that we can look benignly at broken symmetry.

The mathematical phenomenon of catastrophe theory has fallen out of fashion.[26] But catastrophic acts are endemic in the concept of broken symmetry. Earlier I mentioned smashed symmetries. The application of brute force fascinates mathematicians. As Ian Stewart points out, you can "break" the perfect spiral symmetry of a cylinder, say a Coke can, with a hammer-blow on top. It's fun to do.[27] More soberly, the same thing can happen to other strict solids. The once-perfect sphere that is mapped in figure 8.20 exhibits the broken symmetry that came into it when it was crushed by a uniform pressure. Its circular perimeter stayed put, though the whole thing got smaller. But the surface buckled—much more uniformly than a hammered Coke can would have done—into a set of mounded horizontal ridges or ribs. You can liken this effect to the whorls and then double whorls that appear when you twist a column shaft. If you can imagine the sphere's overall lattice of vertical and horizontal coordinates as having originally been simple continuous arcs without the wiggles they have now, then you see the sphere before it was crushed. The wiggles are precise markers—measurers—of the brokenness of that sphere's symmetry. Note that the force being exerted also opened up a dent or hole in the sphere's top, giving that opening a sort of stand-up collar, or neck, which makes the sphere now resemble an amphora.

Then, if you like, you can think of the crushed sphere as the next, more extreme result of the deformations we witnessed in Guarini's column shafts in figure 5.27. Only, with the column shafts, the deforming force would be inside rather than outside the cylinder and would inflate it into a globe that, in a second stage of symmetry breakage, a second catastrophe, would be squeezed by an outside force.

Or: you can look at the ribbed amphora as a three-dimensional construct of epicycles, with each epi-orbit morphing into a continuous horizontal rib while the main cycle, now spherical rather than plane, stays firm. Of course in this case the orbits would also no longer be planes but would cover a three-dimensional range. The sphere of the orbiting planet would describe not circles, circle-fragments, or ellipses but rather spheres, sphere-fragments, and/or ellipsoids. More Baroque domes, domical vaults, and trompes or wave-form turrets, in short.

Better still, we can repropose the plan of Oropa (fig. 8.7). Turn the squashed sphere back into a plane and think of it as a plan. It becomes, more or less, the perimeter of the plan of Oropa. Or else think of the latter as being revolved 360 degrees into a spheroid. Guarini's plan is a cross-section through the center of that spheroid. Each elliptical chapel is a section of a horizontal mounded rib, exactly as in the crushed sphere. The latter's neck and upper opening, in turn, become Oropa's circular choir area. And the latter's circularity (now, of course, revolved into sphericality) serves to suggest the original sphere that was then crushed into the larger, ribbed shape.

In short, broken symmetry, we have seen, is a constant counterpoint, sometimes obvious and sometimes not, to the symmetries we discussed in chapter 5; to epicycles; and indeed to many other things in this book.

To recap: whatever their heavenly fate here on Earth, epicycles developed, elaborated themselves, and flourished—in gears, in clockworks, and in architecture. There was a lot of fascination in the age of the Baroque with things that rotated or revolved in and of themselves while at the same time they rolled in one or more larger orbits. And, more to the point, there was an equal fascination with diagrams that statically mapped those movements. Indeed the planets or gear-teeth (or architect's pen) could roll in several such orbits. Martyriums, tombs, nymphaeums, and baptistries traditionally model these epicyclic shapes while retaining the epicycles' heavenly significance.

As to broken symmetry in this period, we found that this too was related to epicycles. Both phenomena have to do with clustered arcs, with varied, interrupted forms of circularity. Indeed, much of projective geometry, with its structures of bent, bounced, and up- or downscaled self-similar repetitions, can be restated in these terms. Here again, architecture and architectural ornament come into the picture. The resulting shapes can also be subjected to, or variously structured by, eccentric, elliptical, and eccentric-elliptical epicycles.

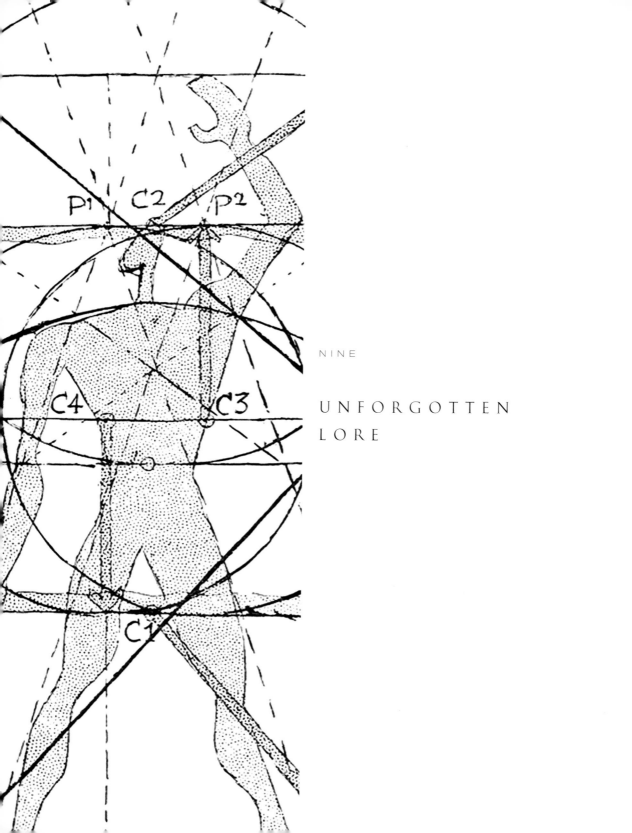

NINE

UNFORGOTTEN
LORE

T oday's architects and the-   GEOMETRY IN
orists are fully conscious   THE TWENTIETH
that they owe a lot to the   CENTURY
lore of the Baroque age.

Baroque drafting instruments, the military compasses, the perspective machines, and elaborations of pantographs stand behind many contemporary
devices. I have even suggested that a computer screen is a Cartesian lattice.
Not to mention that without the likes of Descartes, Newton, and Leibniz,
our architectural engineering would be a lot less further along than it is. Last
but not least, of course, we owe to Baroque architecture some of the defining monuments of our culture.

Nonetheless, most architects nowadays design with no sense of rational
or effable proportions and dimensions; with no idea of how musical ratios
might play into architectural ratios; with no sense of the ways of symmetry,
of geometric attraction and reproduction; with no belief in hierarchies of
shapes, ratios, and dimensions. Nor do conic sections and the intricate obliq-
uities of perspective, projection, and the like seem to play a role—at least not
as these things are worked out scientifically. That is, designers may call for
complex lattices, crazy cones, and squeezed spheres, but they no longer do
it by means of consciously applied geometry. These days, such things are
done freehand and then translated into machine language by CAD (com-

puter-aided design). This effectively lets the machine do the thinking. When an architect wishes to draw out an ellipse, scale it to the finished building, and then have it laid out at the site, she has no need to know Cassini's formula for the ellipse's area, or even how to draw an ellipse mechanically. Instead, the computer does the calculations, draws the shape, and, if desired, neatly prints out quantities and values for scale, area, perimeter, and the like. Nor, I should add, do most of my colleagues in the field of architectural history pay much attention to geometry (though they often brandish the word about). In contrast, during the age of the Baroque, we have seen, architecture and geometry were dominantly present, intensively analyzed, and ardently admired together as a pair. This to me is a crucial contrast between architecture in Wren's period and in ours.

And yet I shouldn't forget that complaints about antigeometrical, or at least ad hoc, ageometrical design appeared even during the height of the Baroque itself. Wren, for example, writes: "It seems very unaccountable, that the Generality of our late Architects dwell so much upon [the] ornamental, and so slightly pass over the geometrical, which is the most essential Part of Architecture."[1] And perhaps it is true that some of Wren's chief rivals—for example, William Talman, who was "late" [young] when Wren wrote these words in the 1670s—did place ornament over geometry, or even thought of ornament as somehow a replacement for it.[2] Maybe, throughout history, geometry in architecture simply revolves in and out like an epicycle, or like population, business, weather, and hemline cycles. If so, Wren clearly lived in one of the geometric periods and, equally clearly, we don't. [3]

And yet some of the geometric principles of the Baroque, and the analytical techniques that reveal those principles, can be observed in two of the greatest early modernists, Frank Lloyd Wright and Le Corbusier, some two centuries after the death of Wren. Geometrical analysis will help us discern kinships between their work and the things we've been studying. We will reveal ties that, most unexpectedly, extend back from these men to the worlds of Descartes and Newton, of Borromini and Guarini. We will be looking, in particular, at twentieth-century recrudescences of Baroque rotational symmetry and at the notion, discussed under the rubric of cubices rationes, that the human body generates ratios.

FRANK LLOYD WRIGHT

In my view Frank Lloyd Wright was one of the most geometric of all architects, ever. [4] But he was no theoretician; instead, he had the graphic equivalent of perfect pitch. I have written a little about his geometry in my recent study, *The Monumental Impulse: Architecture's Biological Roots* (1999). There, however, I limited the discussion to things like honeycomb lattices and plans shaped like molecules or crystals.[5] But, as Lionel March and Philip Steadman bring out in their extraordinary *Geometry of Environment*,[6] there is a lot more than this to Wright's geometry.

As everyone knows, as a child Wright was strongly influenced by a set of architectural toys known as Froebel blocks. About them he famously wrote: "For several years I sat at the little Kindergarten table-top . . . and played . . . with the cube, the sphere, and the triangle—these smooth wooden maple blocks . . . All are in my fingers to this day . . . I soon became susceptible to constructive pattern evolving in everything I saw. I learned to 'see' this way and when I did . . . I wanted to design."[7] Norman Brosterman has recently assembled considerable data concerning Wright's exposure to Froebel blocks and has also published a number of stimulating comparisons of works by Wright with Froebel designs.[8]

Despite all that has been written about Wright and the Froebel blocks, however, the ways in which the blocks tie into traditional Renaissance and Baroque geometry have not been discussed. Perhaps the very idea seems too weird; but I have my evidence. First of all, the blocks themselves are highly Keplerian. They are based on the idea of a standard-sized cube (in America, with one-inch edges), and the ability of that cube to reproduce itself into new forms. Just as in Kepler's *Harmonices Mundi,* the Froebel blocks consist of full cubes, of cubes sliced diagonally along the face, and of parallelepipeds derived from these cubes or from cube-halves. There is also a 4× cube (i.e., with two-inch edges) with a sphere and a cylinder that are exactly inscribable within this 4× cube. [9]

This I illustrate in figure 9.1. The new shapes are all inside the old ones, but, as in biological reproduction, they can emerge with varied new physiques. Froebel, in fact, made much of this highly Keplerian point.[10] The sphere and the cylinder are similarly inside the "womb" of the larger cube. As I have drawn them, each flat rectangle is the face of a different type of

Basic
One-Inch
Cube Face

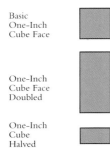

One-Inch
Cube Face
Doubled

One-Inch
Cube
Halved

Basic
One-Inch
Cube Face

One-Inch
Cube Face
Doubled

One-Inch
Cube
Halved

Sphere Inside
Two-Inch Cube

Two-Inch Cylinder
Inside Two-Inch Cube

Basic
One-Inch
Cube Sliced
Diagonally
Into Gables

Fig. 9.1. How Froebel
Blocks fit inside each
other

Froebel block; in other words, you can attach the half of the basic cube's face to the cube face's doubled form, making a parallelepiped; or to the basic cube face, making a much smaller parallelepiped. Thus would Kepler call the Froebel blocks effable.

And the blocks have effabilities of frequency as well as shape. Among the total of 80 blocks, each type is packaged separately into boxes of 6, 8, 12, or some other even integer, the box being called a "gift." As the child plays, he or she progresses from gift to gift, with each step leading onward to new components, new constructions, and larger arrays. The blocks' cubic origins, the ways in which they are split and joined, and even the recursive sequences into which they are grouped—all these things make them excellent neo-Baroque players in the game of cubices rationes.

In figures 9.2 and 9.3 I contrast one of Froebel's diagrams with an example of the cubices rationes approach to roots, squares, and cubes as practiced in the sixteenth century.[11] Note that Froebel's panels of nine cubes, set 3×3, are arranged in squares, that is, as 3^2; and in $3 \times 3 \times 3$ sets, or 3^3. The different arrangements anatomize basic mathematical possibilities for arranging these entities—cubed cubes compacted into a $6\times$ cube, and sets of 3^2 arranged in square panels, vertically and then horizontally, and also in a single line of nine cubes. The right-hand part of Froebel's diagram in figure 9.2 adds in the diagonal blocks to create various rhombic shapes. All of these lessons (or "gifts") are laid out, says Froebel, to teach the principles of addition, subtraction, multiplication, and division, as well as roots and powers.

Froebel makes it clear that while he wants the child to recognize different geometric shapes, this knowledge must clearly encompass, also, the mathematical notions of roots, squares, and cubes as perceived through shape—shape and its cubic components. This is what makes the Froebel system a survival of Renaissance and Baroque practice. For one thing we might note the relationship between Froebel's diagrams and Vincenzo Galilei's plans of organ pipes (fig. 2.1), which involved similar squared ratios and modules, and similar lattices with subsets.

Froebel's illustrations are even more remarkably like those published by Robert Record, the Welsh geometer who wrote about cubices rationes in his treatise *The Whetstone of Witte*, 1557 (fig. 9.3). This book had an aim similar to Froebel's—the education of the young in geometry, or, rather, in geometrized visions of arithmetic. Lionel March adds that from classical

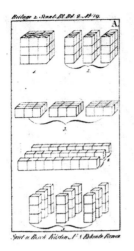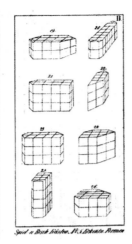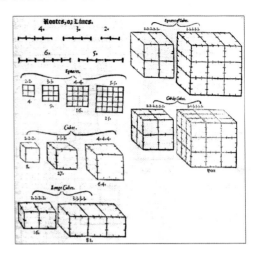

Fig. 9.2. Friedrich
Froebel, the fifth gift,
1838–40. From Froebel,
*Kindergarten Gifts and
Occupational Material*
(New York: E. Steiger,
1876).

Fig. 9.3. Robert Record's
diagram of the powers
of numbers as modules
or building blocks: roots,
squares, cubes, squares
of cubes, and cubes of
cubes. From Robert
Record, *The Whetstone
of Witte* (1557).

times these cube-derived numbers, roots, and powers had been given architectural designations such as bricks and beams.[12] Thus can elementary arithmetic take a strongly architectural form.

The Froebel blocks also teach architecture itself. They can make up all sorts of exercises in rotational symmetry. Other basic architectural lessons are about modularity, lattices, and how to achieve varied or complicated forms with simple standard components. The blocks are much more architectural than most children's blocks; even the fact that they are not brightly colored helps here. It is easy to assemble an approximate Larkin Building or a Unity Temple out of the blocks, and even a competent Coonley House. And it is equally easy to think up complex rotations and lattices in the manner of Guarini or Juvarra, or for that matter of Boullée or Durand.

Brosterman offers a host of comparisons that reveal affinities not only between the Froebel patterns and Wright but between Froebel and Braque, Le Corbusier, Kandinsky, and many others who were the beneficiaries of this kindergarten training. Indeed one might even claim that Froebel and his numerous followers were primary conduits introducing this traditional kind of geometry, at the time long abandoned by secondary schools and professional mathematicians, to the basic training of innumerable five- to nine-year-olds—the future modernists.

In the literature that accompanies the blocks (they are still being manufactured[13]) hexagonal rotations are frequently found. Figure 9.4 illustrates

Fig. 9.4. Three rotational patterns possible with Froebel blocks. From Froebel, *Kindergarten Gifts and Occupational Material* (New York: E. Steiger, 1876).

three such patterns. Each is a C_6 rotation consisting of differently shaped "rotors" (to coin a term). For example on the left, T-shaped rotors comprising a small cube and a small parallelepiped form one rotation; inside it is another, again with six rotors, alternately consisting of a Y-shaped composite of small cubes and larger parallelepipeds. In the center, the tails of these Y's become a C_6 rotation of six more parallelepipeds, with small cubes being joined to each rotor's inner end. The other two patterns vary these ideas.

Such double and triple rotations had long been favorite Baroque devices for dome interiors, for central-plan buildings, and for decorative motifs. Note that Froebel, born in 1782 in Thuringia and later an architectural student in Frankfurt-am-Main, would have absorbed a strong sense of such patterning.

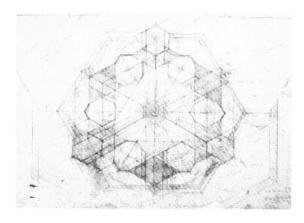

Fig. 9.5. Frank Lloyd Wright, plan of the steel cathedral (New York, 1927, project). Courtesy Frank Lloyd Wright Foundation, Taliesin West.

If Froebel's geometry is thus Baroque, or neo-Baroque, so can Wright's be. Wright's 1927 project for a huge steel cathedral in New York City (fig. 9.5), which was to be higher than the Eiffel Tower, is a monumental version of a Froebel rotation. And by the same token (were it not so huge), it could easily serve as the plan for a South German Rococo pfarrkirche.[14] In the steel cathedral, however, the rotors are, for the first rotation, irregular three-dimensional octagons and, for the

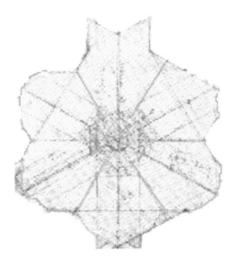

second, three-dimensional rhombs. (Individual Froebel blocks don't have these shapes, but you can easily assemble them. In fact, with two or three sets of Froebel blocks one could map out the approximate plan of the steel cathedral.)

But, even more, Wright's scheme reflects a specific Baroque monument: Borromini's much-studied dome for Sant'Ivo alla Sapienza (fig. 9.6). Borromini's pattern consists of two C_3 rotations of two different rotors alternating to form vectors 45 degrees apart, so as to complete a C_6 hexagonal pattern. Note that Borromini's alternating rotors are strikingly similar to the inner pattern, in gold, set within Wright's outer array of octagons and rhombs in figure 9.7 (in which I have strengthened the radial axes in Wright's drawing, which is too faint in the reproduction).

This may well be the first time that Wright has been likened to Borromini. Note that what they have in common is not style but geometry.

Fig. 9.6. Francesco Borromini, bottom view of dome of Sant'Ivo alla Sapienza (Rome, c. 1648). From Borromini, *Opus architectonicum* (1725).

Fig. 9.7. Inner core of the Wright plan for the steel cathedral (radial axes strengthened)

LE CORBUSIER

As a geometer, and in just about every other way, Le Corbusier was completely different from Wright.[15] Wright's geometry, though present everywhere in his work, never developed into anything resembling a theory of architecture. With Le Corbusier, on the other hand, we have a comprehensive, indeed fantastic geometrical theory. Nowadays we can admire it without necessarily believing in it. But as presented in his book, *Le Modulor* (1950), Le Corbusier's geometry has a lot to do with the things we've studied in these pages. (The word was obviously coined from the French *module* and *moduler*, meaning something that creates modules and also something that modulates—that is, like a model, which "modulates" from small to large scale.)

The modulor is closer to Baroque geometrics, to Fludd, Kircher, and Kepler, than to the more down-to-earth sciences developed by Galileo, Descartes, and Desargues. It also belongs with the proportion theories that run from Vitruvius through Blondel, and further onward into the twentieth century. Nor did Le Corbusier deny this; indeed, in the introduction to the second edition of his book he praises the 1951 Milan Triennale, which featured an exhibition of theorists from Villard de Honnecourt through various Renaissance and Baroque proportioneers, ending with the modulor itself.[16]

On the other hand, Le Corbusier does elsewhere disparage the parts of that tradition that concern us. He complains that his seventeenth-century predecessors advocated what he calls star-shaped geometric plans. Such plans, he says, fail to take into account that a building's viewer or visitor sees only in monodirectional cones directed outward from his or her eyes.[17] (A strange opinion, but never mind.) In other words, Le Corbusier didn't like rotational symmetry. He particularly criticizes stellated polygons. Very well: this sets the scene for his own brand of geometrics, which will be rigorously antisymmetrical and, in distribution, anti-uniform, anti-regular, and anti-repetitive. Notwithstanding all this, however, Baroque geometrics is far from absent in Le Corbusier's work.

How so? For one thing, like his Renaissance and Baroque predecessors, Le Corbusier celebrates the virtues of the musical analogy, of the human body as the generator of ratios, and of noble numbers and shapes arranged in noble series and sequences. As a believer in these things, he pioneered canons of ideal lattices—antisymmetrical lattices, but canons notwithstanding. Often, too, the cells in these lattices were ideal rectangles of the Renaissance and Baroque type. This is not surprising. Le Corbusier's dimensioning and proportioning system was, he says, based on our old friend the Fibonacci sequence.[18]

Also, Le Corbusier derived his modulor from the proportions of the human body. He even erected, in several buildings—for example, the Unité d'habitation at Marseilles (1948)—sculptured reliefs of a number-generating male physique with raised arm—as if with that gesture to indicate that "all this"—the building—was derived from the figure.[19] "A man with an arm upraised," Le Corbusier writes, encapsulating his theory, "provides . . . foot, solar plexus, head, tips of fingers of the upraised arm—three intervals which give rise to a sequence of golden sections called the Fibonacci sequence."[20]

THE MODULOR MAN

On the far left of Le Corbusier's illustration (fig. 9.8), measuring from the man's foot to his umbilicus, we have (in centimeters) 108, then from the umbilicus to the top of his head 66½, and from the top of his head to the end of his upraised hand, 41½.

Recall the Fibonacci sequence from chapter 1: 1, 1, 3, 5, 8, 13, 21, 34, 55, 89, 144, 233, 377 . . . (You could have different numbers in the sequence if you started with 2, or with 3, or with 4, and so on, instead of 1. But the orthodox definition always begins with 1, and the numbers given above are what mathematicians know as the Fibonacci sequence.[21]) Our first point should therefore be that none of Le Corbusier's quantities is in fact a Fibonacci number, nor is his sequence convertible to Fibonacci ratios. Nor do these ratios match those of the golden section, since 66½ ÷ 41½ = 1.602, rather than the proper ratio of 1:1.618 and 108 ÷ 66½ = 1.624.

Le Corbusier's modulor man actually generates five different number sequences. But none of them, despite what he says, is either golden section or Fibonacci. In the center, subdividing the height of the lower half of the body, is a scale that, going up, reads: 2, 7, 9, 16, 25, 41. And then, measuring from the umbilicus to the top of the head, 66 (rounding the 66½ in the diagram that measures that distance). On the right of Le Corbusier's drawing are three more scales. Le Corbusier's fifth scale, on the far right, reads 2, 9, 11, 20, 31, 51, 82.

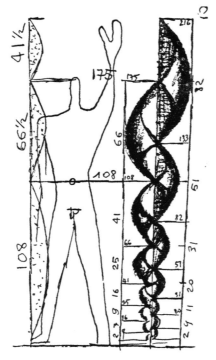
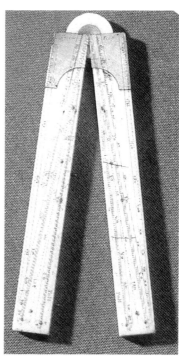

By the way: what do Le Corbusier's differently numbered scales, inscribed along parallel parts of the drawing, bring to mind? That much-used
Baroque calculating instrument, the sector (fig. 9.9).[22] This instrument has
two arms (a bit like the modulor man's legs) that can be set at any angle.
Each arm has different scales that increase from the hinge outward. The
scales are devoted, first, to a line of equal parts, which enable the user to
make proportional calculations (as in sesquiterial, etc.), and then to lines
with successive areas and volumes for set planes and solids. Thus by applying
the sector to a given cube, one can measure its edge and then calculate the
area of its faces and its volume. The scaled markings allow the user to extrapolate for cubes of any size. Sectors can also do arithmetic. They were the
predecessors of the scale ruler, the slide rule, and, we shall see, of the modulor system.

But the modulor man is a somewhat aberrant sector. To repeat: some of
the series and sequences Le Corbusier has marked out are true to Fibonacci
ratios, and some approximate the golden section. But others are way off.

Nor do the numbers correspond to the physical distances up and down the human body that are indicated on the drawing. How could they? The points marked 2, 9, and 11 could never fit the body as drawn; 2, 4, 8 or possibly 2, 4, 9, would be more like it.

But none of this means that Fibonacci values are entirely missing; far from it. On the right in figure 9.8, towering up like a svelte tornado, emphasized by hatching, is a helix of graduated whorls. Though hard to measure exactly, as a set of ratios these whorls could well correspond to the first seven numbers (after the 1's) in the Fibonacci sequence, 3, 5, 8, 13, 21, 34, 55. In other words the top whorl could relate to the lowest as 55:3, the second from the top as 34:3, and so on. And this helix, which really does seem to have Fibonacci values, appears beside the sculptured image of the modulor man in many Le Corbusier buildings.[23]

THE OTHER FATHERS OF THE MODULOR MAN

Behind the modulor man, of course, there lies a considerable patrimony (quite apart from the sector). It is the long story of the ideal human body, usually male, which generates numbers and ratios. The tradition comes out of Vitruvius (*De architectura* 3.1.1) and is embodied most famously in Leonardo's 1485–90 drawing of the naked man inscribed in a square and circle.[24] We discussed Baroque aspects of this tradition in the chapter on cubices rationes.

The age of the Baroque imbued this number-generating body with increased significance. With Fludd, we saw, the whole of the cosmos was shaped to it. And while Le Corbusier is never cosmic, the modulor, like all these earlier bodies, did have a wide social purpose. *Le Modulor*, the book, was a manifesto designed to reconstruct post–World War II European culture via housing, cities, and transport, all of which would be harmoniously standardized. The modulor man was to stand invisibly (and sometimes visibly) within these great projects.

But one must say more. Not only is the modulor man not based on real Fibonacci or golden section ratios but unlike his Renaissance and Baroque predecessors, the man does not himself have "correct" proportions, especially in his extremities (fig. 9.8). It is curious that scholars have remained so

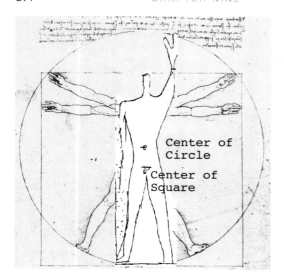

Center of
Circle

Center of
Square

Fig. 9.10. The modulor
man in Leonardo's
square and circle

silent about this matter. And this, even though Le Corbusier himself wrote: "The registered trademark used by us up to the present [1948] may benefit from an improvement of the drawing."[25] Well said.

For it is, of course, perverse that a human figure, proposed as the source of modules for a vast range of designs from tables to cities, should itself be so ill-shaped. I would instance the curious blank stub that is the man's head and face. This has to be seen against Vitruvius's focus on the placement of the features and their exact distribution. Leonardo and his successors also got important sequences and series from the head and its features. And then there is the modulor man's hand. It seems to be wearing one of Mickey Mouse's gloves, and is as grotesquely large as the man's head is grotesquely small. And, once again, compare this to the delicate importance of the hand and its fingers as ratio generators in Vitruvius, Leonardo, and a host of others. I would chalk these oddities up to Purism, the modernist movement Le Corbusier helped found in 1918, and to the distortions, the visual vandalism, that modernism, often with positive results, delighted in.

Nonetheless, the modulor man's vertical measurements do follow Vitruvius, Leonardo & Co. The penis hangs precisely halfway up, measuring from the bottom of the feet to the top of the head. The umbilicus is halfway between the feet and the end of the upraised arm. And, again as in Vitruvius and Leonardo, one could inscribe a circle and a square around this man, the circle's center being at the umbilicus and the square's center at the penis. In this way both the circle and the square sit solidly on the ground with the man's feet. Indeed, one could inscribe Leonardo's entire drawing, without change, around Le Corbusier's modulor man (as I have done in figure 9.10).

By preserving umbilicus and penis in their Vitruvian locations, and by preserving, too, Leonardo's proportions of lower to upper body, of leg length and arm length, Le Corbusier achieves something else essential to this tradition: the man was generated by the circle, for its center is just at his umbilicus. And the man then generates the square: his penis is precisely at the

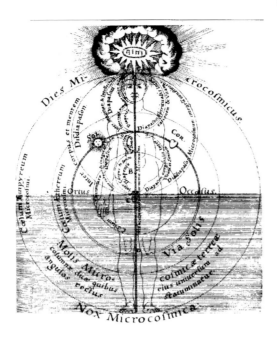

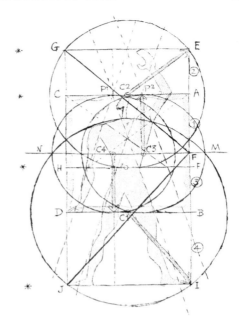

square's center point. Meanwhile the modulor man's upraised arm confirms, in a new way, the body's relationship to the circle. Or we might say that Leonardo's man has swung his right arm up and lowered his left arm—transforming symmetry into asymmetry. We'll be seeing that this is a very Corbusian thing for him to be doing.

But the modulor man has more to do with Robert Fludd than with Leonardo. In chapter 4 we looked at one of Fludd's ratio-generating male bodies embedded in interpenetrating crystal spheres (fig. 4.1). In figure 9.11 I illustrate another of these men, along with a second version of the modulor man.[26] Note, however, in the latter, that Fludd's idea of the generating penis, what he had called the centrum of the whole, is gone. (That the modulor man's penis also occupies the center of Leonardo's square, in my montage, is only a coincidence in the Le Corbusier system.)

In figure 9.12 is the final version of the modulor man in Le Corbusier's book. Le Corbusier tells us that one of his collaborators, Elisa Maillard, like other members of the office in the rue de Sèvres, had been given the job of further working out the modulor's capacity to generate modules and lattices. What Le Corbusier eventually wanted was a lattice of square and rec-

Fig. 9.11. Robert Fludd, "Man the Microcosm." From Fludd, *Utriusque cosmi* (Oppenheim: typis Hieronymi Galleri, 1617).

Fig. 9.12. Le Corbusier and Elisa Maillard, the final modulor man (1948). From Le Corbusier, *The Modulor*. Courtesy Fondation Le Corbusier, Paris.

tangular cells, each one of different proportions and/or dimensions but all based on his versions of what the office conceived to be the Fibonacci sequence and the golden section. A designer could keep this lattice on her drawing board to use whenever she needed a shape.

On December 4, 1948, Maillard brought Le Corbusier her suggestions for deriving lattices from the modulor man. Like the other experimenters, she had begun with a set of three superimposed squares; then, to achieve further modules, she had generated widths or bands onto the squares, which made them into what she called golden section rectangles. The resulting nonuniform lattices could then produce many other canonical ratios. Note how such a system would recapitulate some of the principles of sesquialter rectangles discussed in chapter 1.

But Maillard also turned her concept in a Fludd-like direction. She added various circles, generated by the centers of the squares, to her basic layout (fig. 9.12). These, exactly like the circles in Fludd's image, interpenetrated and were of different sizes. The squares and resultant rectangles within them, and the circles, could also all be considered three-dimensionally. In other words, they could be rotated into cubes, parallelepipeds, and spheres. Then, says Le Corbusier, as the final touch, he himself drew in the gesticulating modulor man. "This sketch," he writes, "closes our investigation of the 'Modulor' by confirming the initial hypothesis. And here the gods play."[27]

I am far from suggesting that Le Corbusier or Maillard were consciously concerned with Robert Fludd. But Fludd's microcosm is nonetheless the modulor man's Baroque ancestor. It is less a question of conscious influence than of geometric genes. Both results were independently generated—and by traditions that were paramount during the age of the Baroque.

MODULOR LATTICES

I have noted that the modulor is not built out of genuine golden section and Fibonacci ratios. Now I must add that, anyway, it is not really Le Corbusier's purpose to import these values and proportions directly into architecture. Nor, for that matter, and despite what he says, does he really want to discern Fibonacci proportions in the human body. If he had, he could easily have altered the tripartite division that is the basis of his system, as demonstrated in table 9.1. (I am counting the Fibonacci numbers 21, 34, 55 as double cen-

TABLE 9.1 *Modulor, Fibonacci, and Golden Section Divisions of the Body*

Distances Measured	Le Corbusier	True Fibonacci	True Golden Section
Head to Hand	41.5 cm	21 (42 cm)	40 cm
Umbilicus to Head	66.5 cm	34 (68 cm)	66 cm
Foot to Umbilicus	108 cm	55 (110 cm)	106 cm

timeters.) Plenty of well-shaped men and women could have been found whose bodies measured out perfectly either in Fibonacci or golden section proportions.

But, as I say, I don't think the great man really cared about these discrepancies. With Elisa Maillard and their other colleagues, Le Corbusier accomplished what he really wanted to do: add rectangles, circles, and solids to a system that, in the drawings of the modulor man himself, is purely linear. Let us return to the original complex of superimposed squares that generates modules. This complex remains the essential mechanism of the "modulor" as a module-maker. My diagram in figure 9.13 is simplified from one that Le Corbusier discusses along with his drawing of the modulor man.[28] In this diagram the distance from feet to umbilicus, 108, is made into the square on the left. This is then doubled to 216—216, Vitruvius's magic cube-number, we recall—to make a double square reaching exactly to the tip of the man's raised hand (shown by the two middle squares). Then, from the middle of one of the sides of the original square, you swing a diagonal to that square's corner (shown in red). That diagonal is then swung, again, up to the point where it meets the opposite side of the upper square. This, keeping to the modulor man's measurements, is 67 centimeters above the base of that square. And, Le Corbusier claims, 175:108 is Φ, 1.618 . . . , the golden section.

So, by adding these squares to the number-generating man, you get a golden section that can be used not just linearly, like his earlier ratios, but to make rectangles. You can form these rectangles by mingling the five scales that bracket the modulor man. Which means that you have a great variety of rectangular shapes, squares and rectangles, shapes that can be very squat or very narrow. But all are generated by this restricted, and restricting, source. And then you can tile the rectangles to make lattices. These in turn can become villa plans, wall panelings, doors, windows, gardens, cities.

The only trouble, once again and now as we might expect, is that Le Corbusier didn't give us true golden sections. The ratio of 175:108 equals 1.6203 . . . , only slightly off, it is true, from 1.618. But the other ratio of 143:83

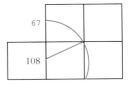

Fig. 9.13. Squares generated by the modulor man. Adapted from Le Corbusier, *The Modulor*. Courtesy Fondation Le Corbusier, Paris.

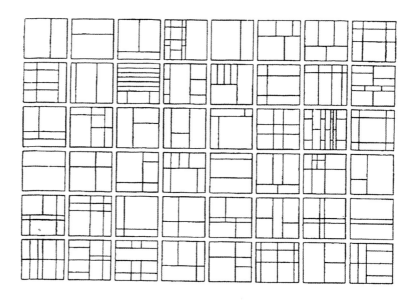

Fig. 9.14. A panel exercise of lattices generated by Le Corbusier's modulor system. From Le Corbusier, *The Modulor*. Courtesy Fondation Le Corbusier, Paris.

equals 1.720—wildly far from Φ. Nonetheless, misnamed as they are, the principles do generate a canon of "noble" lattices. And that was the point.

But Le Corbusier's lattices also had to suit his sense of modernism. That is, they had to be rigorously lacking in every form of symmetry we've discussed. Because of this lack, the modulor's lattices might at first seem to be completely counter to the Baroque tradition. Reader, don't despair. For all his puritanical antisymmetry, Le Corbusier can continue to be hailed as neo-Baroque. Or at least neo-Palladian. Let's look more closely.

Figure 9.14 depicts what Le Corbusier calls a panel exercise. Each lattice is applied to an identical square. But, given the flexibility that the modulor provides with its many different cell-shapes, the results (as to size, shape, and distribution) can be exceedingly varied, as here. Each panel is a square, each panel is subdivided, each panel is different. Most panels avoid center axes. Each avoids, like the plague, any pairing of one of its regions with another.

But here comes the paradox I've been building up to. Looking at Le Corbusier's panel exercises, few students of modern architecture will not immediately think of a similar set of lattices published, for the first time as a book, in 1949—the year before the first edition of *Le Modulor*—by Rudolf Wittkower in his landmark *Architectural Principles in the Age of Hu-*

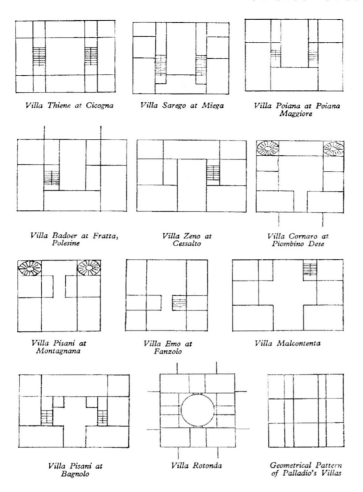

Villa Thiene at Cicogna   Villa Sarego at Miega   Villa Poiana at Poiana Maggiore

Villa Badoer at Fratta, Polesine   Villa Zeno at Cessalto   Villa Cornaro at Piombino Dese

Villa Pisani at Montagnana   Villa Emo at Fanzolo   Villa Malcontenta

Villa Pisani at Bagnolo   Villa Rotonda   Geometrical Pattern of Palladio's Villas

manism. Wittkower's lattices are abstract mappings of some of Palladio's villas (fig. 9.15).

Wittkower's book was seminal in relating Renaissance proportional theory to modernism—an influence chronicled by Wittkower himself in successive prefaces to new editions of the book.[29] And one of the things in the book that is most responsible for this influence was the very page of Palladian lattices shown in figure 9.14. By portraying him through these abstract linear images, Wittkower turned Palladio into a pioneer of the modern movement: Palladio redone by Mondrian. Or else we might call Le Corbusier's "panels" Palladio (or Wittkower) as redone by Le Corbusier.

Fig. 9.15. Rudolf Wittkower, lattices of Palladio villas. From Wittkower, *Architectural Principles in the Age of Humanism* (Cambridge: MIT Press).

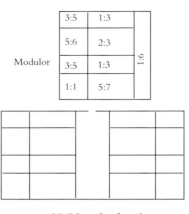

	Modulor		1:6
	3:5	1:3	
	5:6	2:3	
	3:5	1:3	
	1:1	5:7	

Modulor x 2, reflected

Fig. 9.16. A lattice from Le Corbusier's Modulor set (Fig. 9.14) transformed into the plan of a Palladio-type villa

One notices differences, of course. The most important is that Palladio's plans are all mirrored along the vertical center axis. But actually that difference is less of a factor than it might seem. It is a difference, in fact, that has its own symmetry—the symmetry of inversion. By this I mean that the modulor and the Palladian lattices are easily convertible from one to the other (after all, modulor as noted comes from *moduler,* to modulate).

In the top part of figure 9.16 is one of the panel exercises from the Le Corbusier plate just illustrated. All we have to do to repair its antisymmetry is to reflect it (fig. 9.16, below). I have done this in such a way as to turn the long thin vertical strip on the left of the modulor lattice into half of a central corridor. The Corbusian "panel exercise" thus turns neatly into the plan of a Palladian villa.

Indeed an ideal-geometric dividend stems from our little piece of surgery. All the spaces in the resulting villa accord with Palladio's canon of room shapes.[30] I have inscribed their proportions on them in figure 9.16. Not one of Le Corbusier's ideal "panels" falls outside the canon of rectangles in general use throughout the Renaissance, Baroque, and neoclassical periods.

Here's another dividend: the same transformation works equally well in the opposite direction. We reverse-engineer back from Palladian symmetry to Corbusian modulority. For if you cut two different Palladio lattices in half and join them, those two half-lattices become antisymmetrical in a completely satisfactorily Corbusian, Purist fashion. I have done this with the left half of Palladio's 1555ff. villa Poiana at Poiana Maggiore (as published by Wittkower), adding to it the right half of Wittkower's basic scheme for Palladio villas generally (fig. 9.17). Any two other half-plans, in the Palladio, would accomplish the same sort of results. In all these ways the mod-

ulor lattice, like the modulor man, is a
modernist recrudescence of Renaissance and Baroque geometrics.

A final note. I have said that Le Corbusier probably didn't concern himself
much with people like Robert Fludd.
But he may have been interested in
Fludd's counterparts among his contemporaries, such as France's "Section
d'Or" artists of 1912, and in Jacques
Villon,[31] not to mention the highly effable Jay Hambidge. And he certainly
knew about Wittkower.[32] In a way
Wittkower, Wittkower of the Warburg
Institute—as a quondam colleague of
Frances Yates, D. P. Walker, and other
denizens of that revered institution
with its vast Neoplatonic library—can

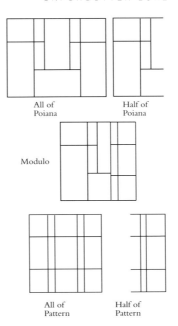

All of Poiana   Half of Poiana

Modulo

All of Pattern   Half of Pattern

be viewed as representing a group of neo-Fluddian geometers. Though of
course the Warburg scholars remained fascinated unbelievers rather than
practitioners. Or so they always claimed.

Fig. 9.17. The left half of
the Palladio Villa Poiana
at Poiana Maggiore
joined to the right half of
Wittkower's basic pat-
tern for Palladio villas,
creating an antisymmet-
rical Modulor lattice

CONCLUSION

We have seen some of the geometric discoveries and techniques embodied by Baroque architecture. It was indeed an age of wonders. Its musical analogies, conic sections, projective distortions, and other optical and acoustical flowers blossomed brilliantly. But I hope I have not implied that all such knowledge first appeared only at this time and in these places. Ellipses, hyperbolas, and parabolas, and their three-dimensional equivalents, appear in many unrelated geographical and historical contexts. There are African indigenous buildings with hyperbolic arches and Roman amphitheaters with elliptical plans. Archimedean and equiangular spirals are everywhere in pre-Baroque and in non-European architecture.[1] But I will also say that it was only in the age of the Baroque that people could accurately plot hyperbolas, compute the areas of ellipses, and understand a spiral as a logarithm.

Beyond that, what I really hope the investigation has established is that the analysis of geometrically constructed plans and elevations can reveal connections between architectures that, from a strictly stylistic viewpoint, seem unrelated. In other words geometry brings together things that up to now have been considered too separately. Geometry—both the traditional kind and its modern extensions—shows affinities between musical chords and architectural moldings, and between the epicycles of the cosmos and those of gears and chapels. It can, as noted, express unsuspected kinships between Borromini and Wright, between Robert Fludd and Le Corbusier.

Furthermore, arching out over everything else, is this: one can look at the whole history of geometry as an ever more inclusive progress leading from simple classic shapes like cubes, pyramids, and spheres to shapes that are ever more complex, turbulent, and chaotic. Gradually, however, unsuspected effabilities were found in these far-out forms. (Of course, the effabilities had always been there. It was only the discovery that took so long.) And, as we saw, these discoveries are embodied in buildings and projects by Bernini, Guarini, Wren, and their gifted peers.

As to the more recent afterlife of Baroque geometry, one of its main underground conduits, from the designs of Wren to those of Wright, is the Froebel approach to kindergarten education. With their ability to see number in concrete form (and vice versa), these geometric toys do much to explain early modernism as a whole. And they are a link between modernism and the Baroque past.

So I hope that this thought will now occur to the reader: perhaps the preeminent role of Wright and Le Corbusier in the history of architecture is linked to their geometrical powers, conscious and unconscious, powers that constitute a fascinating and little-known continuum with the practices of the great masters of the seventeenth and early eighteenth centuries.

CHAPTER 1

1. Guarino Guarini, *Architettura Civile* (1737; reprint, Milan: Polifilo, 1968), 48.

2. An excellent bibliography of period writings on this theme, mainly Italian and French, is given in the annotations by Bianca Tavassi La Greca in Guarini, *Architettura Civile*, passim, and esp. 33ff.

3. See Torgil Magnuson, *Rome in the Age of Bernini* (Stockholm: Almquist and Wicksell, 1986), 2:49; and Paolo Portoghesi, *Borromini nella cultura europea* (Rome: Laterza, 1982), 224ff.

4. Guarini, *Architettura Civile*, 3.

5. M. Stifel, *Arithmetica Integra* (Nuremberg, 1544), fol. 1103r: "irrationalis numerus non est verus numerus."

6. Guarini, *Architettura Civile*, 48, and note by Bianca Tavassi la Greca.

7. Even though the system had been advocated centuries earlier by Leonardo Fibonacci. See his *Liber Abaci*, ed. B. Boncompagni (Rome, 1857), introduction.

8. The best and fullest older discussion of the system, so far as I know, is by Athanasius Kircher, *Musurgia universalis sive ars magna consoni et dissoni* (Rome: F. Corbelletti, 1650), 1:82ff. Kircher even shows you how to add, subtract, multiply, and divide with the system. Guarini also discusses it in *Architettura Civile*, 48ff. For a modern introduction, see Lionel March, *Architectonics of Humanism: Essays on Number in Architecture* (London: Academy Editions, 1998), 58ff.

9. In the seventeenth and eighteenth centuries these ideas blossomed as perhaps never before. Still today, in fact, we are "geometrical" about the first two powers or exponents. In English we don't say "five to the second power" or "six to the third power" but "five squared" and "six cubed." Only when we depart from the three visible dimensions of width, depth, and height, and go into the unvisualizable (or at least undrawable and unbuildable) fourth dimension, do we begin to speak purely numerically and say "three to the fourth power."

10. Approximately. The real formula is $1:(1+\div 5)/2$. And you have to assume a long set of decimal places after the 618.

11. A prominent debunker is George Markowsky, "Misconceptions about the Golden Ratio," *College Mathematics Journal 23* (1992): 2ff. The best treatment for the visual arts is in Linda Dalrymple Henderson, *The Fourth Dimension and Non-Euclidian Geometry in Modern Art* (Princeton: Princeton University Press, 1983). See also Jay Kappraff, *Connections: The Geometric Bridge between Art and Science* (New York: McGraw-Hill, 1990), 75.

12. Ironically, Bernini and others later criticized this facade for being too low. And, of course, a double golden section rectangle, as constituted here, really has the proportion 1:3.236 (1.618 + 1.618), which is roughly the unusual proportion of a supertripartiens quartas. A double 5:9 is only slightly less squat. The combined ratios of the two rectangles are both seriously ineffable and not subject to the reproductive possibilities that, as we're about to see, a single golden section has. For Bernini's criticism of St. Peter's facade, see Magnuson, *Rome in the Age of Bernini,* 1:129; and Howard Hibbard, *Carlo Maderno and Roman Architecture, 1580-1603* (University Park, Pa.: Penn State Press, 1971), 160ff.

13. Michael Frame and Theodore Bick, *The Geometry of Nature: From Compass to Computer,* forthcoming.

14. Guarini, *Architettura Civile,* 54. His demonstration is incorrect. His rectangle is 1:1.73205 rather than 1:1.61803. I thank Michael Frame for working this out.

15. R. V. Jean, *Phyllotaxis: A Systematic Study of Plant Morphogenesis* (Cambridge: Cambridge University Press, 1994), with earlier bibliography.

16. See Fibonacci, *Liber Abaci,* introduction; idem, *The Book of Squares,* trans. and ed. L. E. Sigler (Boston: Academic Press, 1987); and N. N. Vorob'ev, *Fibonacci Numbers* (Oxford: Pergamon Press, 1961).

17. Pico della Mirandola, *Adversus astrologos,* 3.5, in *Opera* (Venice: Bernardus Venetus, 1498).

18. Isaac Newton, *Opticks, or a Treatise of the Reflections, Refractions, Inflections, and Colours of Light* (1730; reprint, New York: Dover, 1952), lxx et seq.

19. Sidney Berkowitz, *Empire of Light: A History of Discovery in Science and Art* (New York: Henry Holt, 1993), 65.

20. Nor has the word quintessence disappeared from astronomy. The "negative energy" or antigravity force just mentioned has been called quintessence. John

Noble Wilford, "Scientists Ponder 'Missing Energy' of the Universe," *New York Times,* May 5, 1998, F5.

21. Alexandre Koyré, *The Astronomical Revolution: Copernicus—Kepler—Borelli* (New York: Dover, 1973), 263.

22. Johannes Kepler, *Harmonices mundi* (Linz: Gottfried Tampach, 1619), book 4, 110ff.

CHAPTER 2

1. Vincenzo Galilei, *Dialogo della musica antica, et della musica moderna* (1581; reprint, Milan: A. Minuziano, 1947), 134.

2. I should explain that baroque musical terminology is a variation on the geometric language discussed in chapter 1. A ratio in which the lower and the higher number differ by only 1, such as 2:3 (a perfect fifth, C–G), is called superparticular: "one above." A ratio in which that difference is more than 1, such as 3:5, is superpartient, "a part or fraction above." Thus the two intervals illustrated, the fourth and the minor third, are both superpartient.

3. 9:16 represents a ratio of areas of the pipe bottom, which corresponds to the ratio of the pipe lengths. If you want to raise a pipe's pitch by a fourth, from C to F, you can either lengthen it from 3' to 4' or increase its area from 9" to 16". The volume will increase as the cubes of the lengths, 27:64.

4. Sirens are normally shaped like women, but they can also have birds' bodies and women's heads. Other shapes are possible. Cf. *Paulys Real-Enzyklopädie der klassischen Altertumswissenschaft* (Neue bearb. herausgegeben von G. Wissowa: Stuttgart, 1894ff.), s.v.

5. But see Walter Burkert, *Lore and Science in Ancient Pythagoreanism* (Cambridge: Harvard University Press, 1972), 350ff., who shows how complicated and ambiguous the tradition is.

6. Nicomachus of Gerasa, in *Antiquae musicae auctores septem,* ed. Marcus Meibonius (Amsterdam: Elzevir, 1652), book 1, ch. 3, and esp. 69ff. Flora R. Levin, *The Harmonics of Nicomachus and the Pythagorean Tradition* (University Park, Pa.: American Philological Association, 1975), 36. See also Bruce Stephenson, *The Music of the Heavens, Kepler's Harmonic Astronomy* (Princeton: Princeton University Press, 1994), 16ff., for a good recapitulation of classical and early modern theories.

7. Nicomachus, *Antiquae musicae auctores,* 1:6.

8. Burkert, *Ancient Pythagoreanism,* 374ff.

9. Pointed out by Joscelyn Godwin, *The Harmony of the Spheres: A Sourcebook of the Pythagorean Tradition in Music* (Rochester, Vt.: Inner Traditions International, 1993), 409, note 7.

10. Marin Mersenne, *Harmonie universelle: Livre septième des instruments de percussion,* Proposition xvii (Paris: Baudry, 1635–36), was apparently the first on record to test, and disprove, Pythagoras's theory. I am grateful to Claude Palisca for this reference.

11. Friedrich von Schelling, *Philosophie der Kunst,* in Schelling, *Werke* (Munich: Beck, 1958), 576, 593. See also Ernst Behler "Schellings Ästhetik in der Überlieferung von Henry Crabb Robinson," *Philosophisches Jahrbuch* 83 (1976): 146.

12. Mentioned as early as Plato in his myth of Er in the tenth book of the *Republic.* See Stephenson, *The Music of the Heavens,* 17.

13. Athanasius Kircher, *Musurgia universalis: sive Ars magna consoni et dissoni in X libros digesta . . .* (Rome: Typographicum haeredum Fratelli Corbinetti, 1650).

14. Ludwig Pastor, *History of the Popes from the Close of the Middle Ages* (1891; reprint, New York: Kraus, 1969), 29:12. Quoted by W. Chandler Kirwin, *Powers Matchless: The Pontificate of Urban VIII, the Baldachin, and Gian Lorenzo Bernini* (New York: Peter Lang, 1997), 42.

15. Alexandre Koyré, *The Astronomical Revolution: Copernicus—Kepler—Borelli,* (1973; reprint, New York: Dover, 1992), 177.

16. Stephenson, *Music of the Heavens,* 238ff.

17. Ibid., 7.

18. Alexandre Koyré, *From the Closed World to the Infinite Universe* (Baltimore: Johns Hopkins University Press, 1957), 35ff.

19. Thomas Digges, *A Perfit Description of the Coelestiall Orbes* [1569], in Leonard Digges, *Prognostication of Right and Good Effect* (Aldburgh, England, 1592).

20. See Wilmer T. Bartholomew, *Acoustics in Music* (Westport, Conn.: Greenwood Press, 1980); and Frederick V. Hunt, *Origins of Acoustics* (New Haven: Yale University Press, 1978). Also see H. F. Cohen, *Quantifying Music: The Science of Music at the First Stage of the Scientific Revolution, 1580–1650* (Dordrecht: D. Riedel, 1984).

21. George C. Izenour, *Roofed Theaters of Classical Antiquity* (New Haven: Yale University Press, 1992).

22. Marin Mersenne, *Harmonicorum libri in quibus agitor de sonorum natura,* etc. (Paris: Baudry, 1635–36), preface.

23. Diodorus Siculus 26.17.18. The best analysis of this legend, which describes it as an actual scientific possibility, is in David Park, *The Fire within the Eye: A Historical Essay on the Nature and Meaning of Light* (Princeton, N.J.: Princeton University Press, 1997), 22ff.

24. Galileo Galilei, *Dialogues Concerning Two New Sciences* [1637], translated by Henry Crew and Alfonso de Salvio [1914] (New York: Dover, 1954), 41 (Day 1, section 87).

25. Kircher, *Musurgia universalis,* 2:231ff.

26. Ibid., 2:231.

27. Ibid., 2:248.

28. Ibid., 2:279.

29. Ibid., 2:266.

30. Mersenne *seems* to assume the existence of fundamentals and harmonics in his *Harmonicorum* of 1636, a book, we have seen, that Kircher knew. On the other

hand, the *Harvard Dictionary of Music*, s.v. Acoustics IV, says harmonics were not known about until they were described by Hermann Helmholtz, *On the Sensation of Tone as a Physiological Basis for the Theory of Music* (1863; reprint, London: Longmans, Green, and Co., 1930), passim.

31. Kircher, *Musurgia,* 2:285ff.

32. Andrew Landale Drummond, *The Church Architecture of Protestantism, an Historical and Constructive Study* (Edinburgh: T & T Clark, 1934), 19ff., gives an interesting account of some of the "Vitruvian" theater-churches, not dissimilar to Kircher's theater of echoes, erected in North Europe in the seventeenth and eighteenth centuries.

33. For measured drawings of Wren's City churches, see J. Clayton, *The Dimensions, Plans, Elevations, and Sections of the Parochial Churches of Sir Christopher Wren* (London, 1848–49); see also Paul Jeffrey, *The City Churches of Sir Christopher Wren* (London: Hambledon Press, 1996), with other bibliography.

34. Quoted by J. A. Bennett, *The Mathematical Science of Christopher Wren* (Cambridge: Cambridge University Press, 1982), 93.

35. Barbara Kienzl, *Die barocken Kanzeln im Kärnten* (Klagenfurt: Verlag des Kärnter Landesarchivs), 1986.

36. Robin Evans, *The Projective Cast: Architecture and Its Three Geometries* (Cambridge: MIT Press, 1995), 195; and Monique Mosser and Daniel Rabreau, *Charles de Wailly, peintre-architecte dans l'Europe des lumières* (Paris: Caisse nationale des monuments historiques et des sites, 1979), cat. nos. 176–84.

37. "Application des Proportions de la Musique à l'Architecture par M. Ouvrard," in François Blondel, *Cours d'architecture enseigné dans l'Académie Royale d'Architecture,* etc. (1675; reprint, Paris: Chez l'Auteur, 1698), book 5, chapter 11, 756ff.

38. René Ouvrard, *Lettres sur l'architecture harmonique, ou l'application de la doctrine des proportions de la musique à l'architecture* (Paris: Roulland, 1679). Reprinted in part in Françoise Fichet, *La Théorie architecturale à l'âge classique* (Brussels: P. Mardaga, 1979), 175ff.

39. Walter Kambartel, *Symmetrie und Schönheit* (Munich: W. Fink, 1972), 81.

40. Helmholtz, *Sensations of Tone*, passim. And, in equal temperament, as employed for instance on modern keyboards, the fifth would be 12:28, the semitone, which is an irrational number.

41. These ratios are in a way idealized, since they work only with strings and with air columns—as in organ pipes and wind instruments—and within a given octave. But this actually accounts for most musical instruments.

42. Daniele Barbaro, *I Dieci libri dell'architettura tradotti e commentati da Daniele Barbaro* (1567; reprint, Milan: Polifilo, 1987), 227ff.

43. For Blondel's influence see Robin Middleton, "Jacques Françoise Blondel and the *Cours de'architecture," Journal of the Society of Architectural Historians* 18 (1959): 141ff.

44. The lower notes of each chord are in dotted lines because they are fundamentals or roots of the chords—heard, says Blondel, even when not sounded.

45. For this question see Kambartel, *Symmetrie und Schönheit,* 82; see also Helmholtz, *Sensations of Tone,* 234ff. Note that in his list of canonical shapes Blondel omits the irrational √2 rectangle, which has no musical equivalent, but which was commonplace in earlier treatises (e.g., those of Francesco di Giorgio, Alberti, Serlio, Palladio, Barbaro, and Scamozzi). He also says nothing about the golden section, which of course is also an irrational. It is interesting that Blondel's pupil Jean-François de Neufforge, in his *Receuil élémentaire d'architecture* (Paris: Chez l'auteur, 1757–68), a multivolume compendium of the author's projects, has an Attic base (vol. 1, pl. 16) of exactly Blondel's components but, reading down from the top, with the sequence 3:7:3:4:3:9:18. No recursion at all, let alone an arithmetic, geometric, or harmonic sequence.

46. Blondel also says that his chords are in plagal church modes, which he identifies respectively as Dorian, Phrygian, and Lydian. Claude Palisca points out that what Blondel has notated are usually known as the first, second, and third plagal modes.

47. The tritone (because it consists of three major seconds) was traditionally to be avoided—the *diabolus in musica*—except in a melodic cadence. For background on all this, see Palisca's classic *Baroque Music,* 3rd ed. (Englewood Cliffs, N.J.: Prentice-Hall, 1991).

48. Kircher, *Musurgia universalis.*

49. Helmholtz, *Sensations of Tone,* 330ff. For Baroque dissonances of this sort, see Christoph Bernhard, *Tractatus compositionis augmentatus* (c. 1660), with an English translation in *Music Forum* 3 (1973): 31–196. I owe the reference to Claude Palisca.

50. See Helmholtz, *Sensations of Tone,* 453ff., for a table of all musical intervals, dissonant and consonant, of less than an octave, including many from non-Western tuning systems.

51. His opinion is corroborated by Helmholtz, *Sensations of Tone,* in his discussion of dissonances, 330ff.

52. Blondel, *Cours,* 756ff.

53. Stephenson, *Music of the Heavens,* 171.

54. Ibid., 184ff.

55. That is, $4/5 \times 3/4 = 3/5$.

56. Sebastiano Serlio, *Tutte l'opere d'architettura et prospettiva,* etc. (Venice: Giacomo de'Franceschi, 1619), bk. 2, fol. 25rff.

57. And, too, a ratio change that substitutes one C for another within a given set of intervals simply emphasizes the fact that the geometric properties involved are strongly related. C–C" is 3:1, C–C' is 2:1—a triple square and a double square, both being direct derivatives of the square.

CHAPTER 3

1. Sidney Perkowitz, *Empire of Light: A History of Discovery in Science and Art* (New York: Henry Holt, 1993), 48.

2. Sir Isaac Newton, *Opticks, or A Treatise of Reflections, Refractions, Inflections, and Colours of Light* (1730; reprint, based on the 4th ed., New York: Dover, 1952), 353ff.

3. Newton, *Opticks*, 126ff. But, as Newton does not note, his is a rather special scale—the descending natural minor. This has a flatted third, sixth, and seventh, as Newton specifies, though in the ascending version only the third is flatted. For Newton's color theory see David Park, *The Fire within the Eye: A Historical Essay on the Nature and Meaning of Light* (Princeton, N.J.: Princeton University Press, 1997), 197ff.

4. See Eileen Reeves, *Painting the Heavens: Art and Science in the Age of Galileo* (Princeton, N.J.: Princeton University Press, 1997).

5. Athanasius Kircher, *Ars magna lucis et umbrae in decem libros digesta* (Rome: Harmann Scheus, 1646), 1:15ff.

6. Cited by Park, *The Fire within the Eye*, 166.

7. Perkowitz, *Empire of Light*, 16ff. See also Lael Wertenbaker, *The Eye: Window to the World* (New York: Torstar, 1984).

8. Patrick Moore, *Eyes on the Sky: The Story of the Telescope* (London: Springer, 1997). Also see Richard Panek, *Seeing and Believing: How the Telescope Opened Our Eyes and Minds to the Heavens* (New York: Viking, 1998).

9. Kircher, without crediting Descartes, borrows much of this discussion, including the diagrams (*Ars magna,* 1:112ff.). But he also carries it much further in applying conic sections to the theater machinery, solar clocks, and the like.

10. See Park, *Fire within the Eye,* 51ff.

11. Perkowitz, *Empire of Light*, 96ff.

12. I'll never know because Diodorus uses the expression *katoptron hetektenen,* translated as "hexagonal mirror." Those who have sought to re-create Archimedes' exploit have used ordinary flat mirrors, which worked. Park, *Fire within the Eye,* 23.

13. It is therefore perhaps relevant that Kircher writes in great detail both about Archimedes' instrument and about magic lanterns. *Ars magna,* 2:880ff.

14. Perkowitz, *Empire of Light*, 129; see also L. Sprague DeCamp, *The Ancient Engineers* (New York: Ballantine, 1974); Eugene Hecht and Alfred Zajac, *Optics* (Reading, Mass.: Addison-Wesley, 1979), 1.

15. Giovanni Battista della Porta, *Magia Naturalis Libri XX* (Frankfurt, 1591). See also G. B. Manzini, *L'Occhiale all'occhio: Dioptrica practica* (Bologna, 1660); and (the most complete treatise of the period) Chérubin d'Orléans, *La Dioptrique oculaire* (1671), which describes the making of telescopes and microscopes as well as lens design. For a modern view, see Marion Fournier, *The Fabric of Life: Microscopy in the Seventeenth Century* (Baltimore, Md.: Johns Hopkins University Press, 1996).

16. See Galileo Galilei, *Discoveries and Opinions of Galileo,* ed. Stillman Drake (New York: Anchor Books, 1957), 29.

17. Perkowitz, *Empire of Light*, 131.

18. Fournier, *The Fabric of Life*, 1. For the architectural importance of the telescope, see M. C. Donnelly, *Astronomical Observatories in the 17th and 18th Centuries,* book 34, fascicule 5, *Mémoires* (Brussels: Académie Royale de Belgique, Classe des Sciences, 1964).

19. See the bibliography in Silvio Bedini, *Science and Optics in Seventeenth-Century Italy* (Aldershot: Variorum, 1994).

20. The first person to put a lens in a camera obscura seems to have been Giambattista della Porta. Park, *Fire within the Eye,* 137.

21. Philippe Comar, *La Perspective en jeu: Les dessous de l'image* (Paris: Gallimard, 1992), 106. I thank Benoit Mandelbrot for introducing me to this amusing and intelligent book.

22. Gian Piero Brunetta, *Il Viaggio dell'icononauta dalla camera oscura di Leonardo alla luce dei Lumière* (Venice: Marsilio, 1997); see also Thomas J. Hankins and Robert J. Silverman, *Instruments and the Imagination* (Princeton, N.J.: Princeton University Press, 1995), 43ff., and bibliography, 241.

23. Kircher, *Ars magna,* 1:177ff. (*"De proiectoionibus scenographicis geometrice expediendis,"* which deals not only with theatrical uses of projected light and images but with the anamorphic and barrel distortions that can be achieved by lens systems).

24. Hankins and Silverman, *Instruments and the Imagination*, 43ff., and bibliography, 241.

25. Lisa Jardine, in *Ingenious Pursuits: Building the Scientific Revolution* (New York: Doubleday, 1999), 76, 80, brings out this parallel.

26. See my *High Renaissance Art in St. Peter's and the Vatican* (Chicago: University of Chicago Press, 1993), 95ff.

27. Quoted by Alberto Pérez-Gómez and Louise Pelletier, *Architectural Representation and the Perspective Hinge* (Cambridge: MIT Press, 1997), 17.

28. For the controversies about Peter's tomb, see Margherita Guarducci, *La Tomba di San Pietro: Una straordinaria vicenda* (Rome: Rusconi, 1989).

29. Pierre Bourget and Georges Cattaui, *Jules Hardouin Mausart* (Paris: Vincent, Freal, 1960); Bertrand Jestaz, *Hardouin Mansart et l'Hôtel et église des Invalides* (Paris: Caisse nationale des monuments historiques et des sites, 1990).

30. John Harris, "Designing St. Paul's," *Country Life* 185 (1991): 80ff.; John Summerson, "J. H. Mansart, Sir Christopher Wren, and the Dome of St. Paul's Cathedral," *Burlington Magazine* 132 (1990): 32ff.; and Kerry Downes, *Sir Christopher Wren and the Designs of St. Paul's Cathedral* [exhibition catalog] (London: Trefoil, 1988). Lisa Jardine, *Ingenious Pursuits,* 72, quotes Robert Hooke, Wren's sometime collaborator and a mathematician-architect, saying that the dome of St. Paul's is "a cubical paraboloid conoid." According to Michael Frame this probably means "a cubical parabo-

loid that has been rotated around its axis 360°. A paraboloid is generated by rotating the parabola $y = x^2$ around the y axis, so wouldn't it make sense to say a cubical paraboloid is generated by rotating a cubical parabola $y = x^3$ around the y axis? A cubical parabola is flatter at its apex than a normal parabola." A conoid, meanwhile, is simply one type of revolved paraboloid.

31. See Galileo Galilei, *Dialogues Concerning Two New Sciences,* trans. Henry Crew and Alfonso de Salvio (1914; reprint, New York: Dover, 1954), 147; and Jardine, *Ingenious Pursuits,* 72, 331ff.

32. Jardine, *Ingenious Pursuits,* 333.

33. J. A. Bennett, *The Mathematical Sciences of Christopher Wren* (Cambridge: Cambridge University Press, 1982); Vaughan Hart, *St. Paul's Cathedral: Sir Christopher Wren* (London: Phaidon, 1995); and Peter Hurman, *St. Paul's Cathedral* (London: Bell and Hyman, 1987).

34. For the dome painting, see Carol Gibson-Wood, "The Political Background of Thornhill's Paintings in St. Paul's Cathedral," *Journal of the Warburg and Courtauld Institutes* 56 (1993): 229ff.

35. Bennett, *The Mathematical Sciences of Sir Christopher Wren,* 53. For drawings of the cathedral, see Arthur F. E. Poley, *St. Paul's Cathedral, London, Measured, Drawn, and Described by Arthur F. E. Poley* (London: the Author, 1927).

36. Adolf Max Vogt, *Boullées Newton-Denkmal: Sakralbau und Kugelidee* (Basel: Birckhäuser, 1969), 157ff.; and Guilhem Scherf, "Pierre Julien et le décor sculpté de l'église Sainte-Généviève à Paris," *Revue du Louvre et des musées de France* 38, no. 2 (1988): 127ff.

37. Elwin C. Robison, "Optics and Mathematics in the Domed Churches of Guarino Guarini," *Journal of the Society of Architectural Historians* 50 (1991): 384ff.

38. See Jean-Marie Pérouse de Montclos, "*De nova stella anni 1784* from Newton," *Revue de l'art* 58–59 (1982–83): 75ff.; Johnnes Longer, "Fels und Sphäre: Bilder der Natur in der Architektur um 1789," *Daidalos* 12 (June 1984): 92ff.; "Sphären der Revolution: Architektur und Weltbild der klassischen Mechanik," *Architecture Plus* 116 (March 1993): 22ff.; and Vogt, *Boullées Newton-Denkmal,* esp. 291ff.

39. "Nature and Nature's laws lay hid in night. / God said, 'Let Newton be!' And all was light." Quoted by Vogt, *Boullées Newton-Denkmal,* 304.

40. Emil Kaufmann, *Von Ledoux bis Le Corbusier: Ursprung und Entwicklung der autonomen Architektur* (Vienna: R. Passer, 1933); idem, "Three Revolutionary Architects—Boullée, Ledoux, and Lequeux," *Transactions of the American Philosophical Society* 42 (1952). For a more recent commentary on the idea, see Anthony Vidler, "Researching Revolutionary Architecture," *Journal of Architectural Education* 44 (1991): 206ff. For Boullée's book on astronomy, see Vogt, *Newton-Denkmal,* 312.

41. Though Vogt explains that Newton also thought that the Earth had been formed as a sphere but had become a spheroid due to the wear and tear of its rotation. Vogt, *Newton-Denkmal,* passim. So the Newton Tomb would perhaps represent

Earth in its pristine form. For the globe in general and its symbolism, see Catherine Hoffmann, Eve Netchine, and Monique Pelletier, *Le Globe et son image* (Paris: Bibliothèque Nationale de France, 1995). See also J. L. Greenberg, *The Problem of the Earth's Shape from Newton to Clairaut: The Rise of Mathematical Science in Eighteenth-Century Paris and the Fall of "Normal" Science* (Cambridge: Cambridge University Press, 1995).

42. See Clara Pinto-Correia, *The Ovary of Eve: Egg and Sperm and Preformation* (Chicago: University of Chicago Press, 1997), 174; also Thomas L. Hankin, "Mathematics and the Exact Sciences" in idem, *Science and the Enlightenment* (Cambridge: Cambridge University Press, 1985).

43. Paul Jeffrey, *The City Churches of Sir Christopher Wren* (London: Hambledon Press, 1996).

44. Quoted by Bennett, *Mathematical Sciences*, 117. For the Basilica of Maxentius, see Udo Kultermann, *Die Maxentius-Basilika: ein Schlüsselwerk spätantiker Architektur* (Weimar: VDG, 1996).

45. Wren might have been attracted to the Temple of Peace, too, because of its Solomonic associations. According to Palladio's text (book 4, chap. 6) this structure was built by Claudius and endowed, by Vespasian, who completed it on his return from Jerusalem, with "vases and valuables" from the sacked Temple of Herod. However, Palladio is mistaken. It was Vespasian alone who built the Temple of Peace, 71–75 A.D. It stood near the Basilica of Maxentius but was an entirely different building. The Maxentius Basilica never seems to have contained any Solomonic or other temple trophies but certainly the Temple of Peace did: Pliny *Historia Naturalis* 36.4.27.

CHAPTER 4

1. George L. Hersey, *Pythagorean Palaces: Magic and Architecture in the Italian Renaissance* (Ithaca, N.Y.: Cornell University Press, 1976), 43ff. See also Lionel March, *Architectonics of Humanism: Essays on Number in Architecture* (London: Academy Editions, 1998), passim.

2. My phrase is a genitive singular followed by a nominative plural, translatable as "the principles [*rationes*] of cubics [*cubices*]." My inspirations are Vitruvius, Kepler, and Robert Record, in *The Whetstone of Witte* (1557). Vitruvius as noted spoke of *cybicae rationes* (*De architectura* 5.pref.3). He traces the term back to the Pythagoreans who, he says, wrote out their treatises *cybicis rationibus*, "according to cubic principles." These he applies to architecture. Record uses the word *cubike*, based on the Greek κυβικός, to mean "cubics"—the science of cubes. Kepler used a cognate Greek-derived form, *harmonice*, to mean "harmonics" in the title of his *Harmonices mundi*.

3. See Frank Zöllner, *Vitruvs Proportionsfigur* (Worms: Wernersche Verlagsgesellschaft, 1987).

4. Robert Fludd, *Utriusque cosmi,* vol. 2, part 1, *Tractatus secundus: De naturae simia,* etc. (Oppenheim: typis Hieronymi Galleri, 1617), 251ff.

5. Fludd, *Utriusque cosmi,* vol. 2, tract. 1, sect. 1, book 12.

6. One is struck with the homunculus's similarity, in concept, to the DNA in the nucleus of each tissue cell, which similarly contains the complete recipe for the mature organism. Nor was all this just a Baroque idea. Seneca had written that "in the seed are enclosed all the parts of the body of the man that shall be formed," including even his beard. Athanasius Kircher, *Musurgia Universalis de natura et productione consoni et dissoni* (Rome: Typographicum haeredum Fratelli Corbinetti, 1650), 2:372. For Fludd on semen (he is copious), see "De spermate et semine," *Utriusque cosmi,* 226ff.

7. Kepler, *Harmonices mundi*, book 2, 48ff. For single-shape tilings, the angle of the shape must evenly divide 360 degrees.

8. Branko Grünbaum and G. C. Shephard, *Tilings and Patterns* (New York: W. H. Freeman, 1986), with full earlier bibliography.

9. In the modern sense "congruent" means figures that can be made to coincide exactly with each other simply by being superimposed.

10. The rule, which I have from Michael Frame, is: to tile the plane with regular *n*-gons (regular polygons of any number of sides), each vertex angle of the *n*-gon must evenly divide into 360 degrees.

11. Kepler, *Harmonices mundi,* 65.

12. Keith Devlin, *Mathematics: The Science of Patterns* (New York: Scientific American Library, 1994), 166.

13. See my *High Renaissance Art in St. Peter's and the Vatican* (Chicago: University of Chicago Press, 1993), 73ff.

14. Grünbaum and Shephard, *Tilings,* 20ff.

15. Martin Raspe, *Das Architektursystem Borrominis* (Munich: Deutscher Kunstverlag, 1994), fig. 51.

16. According to Emil Kaufmann, *Architecture in the Age of Reason: Baroque and Post-Baroque in England, Italy, and France* (Cambridge: Harvard University Press, 1955), 151, Neufforge's penchant for geometry drove him in his later days to design nothing but plans. However there are plenty of (rather old-fashioned) elevations in his *Recueil élémentaire d'architecture,* etc. (Paris: Chez l'auteur), 1757ff.

17. I am using the edition by Sir Thomas L. Heath, *Euclid: The Thirteen Books of the Elements,* 2nd ed. (New York: Dover, 1956).

18. Thus Robert Streitz, in *Palladio: La Rotonde et sa Géometrie* (Lausanne-Paris: Bibliothèque des Arts, 1973), in figs. 6, 7, 8, 15, etc., shows how the plans and sections can all be created with an (adjustable) pair of compasses and a straightedge.

19. One earlier thinker who had dealt with these ideas was Fra Luca Pacioli, au-

thor of a book on the golden section called *De Divina Proportione*. Cf. Alberto Pérez-Gómez, "The Glass Architecture of Fra Luca Pacioli," *Architectura,* forthcoming.

20. The theory was first broached in Kepler's *Prodromus Mysterium cosmographicum* of 1596. For further discussion, see Alexandre Koyré, *The Astronomical Revolution: Copernicus—Kepler—Borelli* (New York: Dover, 1973), 145ff.; and Bruce Stephenson, *The Music of the Heavens: Kepler's Harmonic Astronomy* (Princeton N.J.: Princeton University Press, 1994), 79ff.; also, and especially, J.V. Field, "Kepler's Rejection of Solid Celestial Spheres," *Vistas in Astronomy* 23 (1979): 207ff.

21. Hersey, *Pythagorean Palaces*, 155-60.

22. See ibid., 88ff. Elsewhere in the *Harmonices mundi,* Kepler speaks of the Archimedean solids having intercourse (book 2, 65) and says the same of the "consonances" of circles (book 3, 18). Proclus seems to have inspired him here (Kepler, *Harmonices mundi,* book 4, 115).

23. Kepler, *Harmonices mundi,* book 5, 180ff. The modern mathematical term for Kepler's androgyne is "self-dual." The dual of *any* polyhedron is achieved by interchanging the number of vertices with the number of faces. Thus are the cube and the octahedron duals. The androgynous tetrahedron is termed self-dual.

24. Stephenson, *The Music of the Heavens*, 78ff.

25. Matthias Brack, "Metal Clusters and Magic Numbers," *Scientific American* 277 (December 1997): 53.

26. Ibid.

27. See Paul Jeffrey, *The City Churches of Sir Christopher Wren* (London: Hambledon Press, 1996), 285ff.

28. Kepler, *Harmonices mundi,* 65.

29. Ibid., 61ff.

30. Notably in his book *Euclides adauctus* (Turin, 1671; repr. 1676). See Nino Carboneri, introduction to *Architettura civile,* by Guarino Guarini (1737; reprint, Milan: Polifilo, 1968), xiv. Michael Frame points out to me that Guarini's dome is articulated in a way suggesting Poincaré's non-Euclidean model of a hyperbolic plane covered with lines (called geodesics), which are the arcs of circles that intersect the boundary orthogonally.

CHAPTER 5

1. Hermann Weyl, *Symmetry* (Princeton, N.J.: Princeton University Press, 1952). See also Ian Stewart and Martin Golubitsky: *Fearful Symmetry: Is God a Geometer?* (Oxford: Blackwell, 1992); and Mike Field and Martin Golubitsky, *Symmetry in Chaos: A Search for Pattern in Mathematics, Art, and Nature* (New York: Oxford University Press, 1992), both with full bibliographies. For symmetry in ornament, see Ernst Gombrich, *The Sense of Order: A Study in the Psychology of Decorative Art* (Ithaca: Cornell University Press, 1978), 67ff.

2. Dorothy K. Washburn and Donald W. Crowe, *Symmetries of Culture: Theory and Practice of Plane Pattern Analysis* (Seattle: University of Washington Press, 1988), 5.

3. Edith Müller, "Gruppentheoretische und strukturanalytische Untersuchungen der Maurischen Ornamente aus der Alhambra in Granada" (Ph.D. diss., University of Zürich, Rüschlikon, 1944). See also Aleksei V. Shubnikov and Vladimir A. Koptsik, *Symmetry in Science and Art* (New York: Plenum, 1974); and Branko Grünbaum and G. C. Shephard, *Tilings and Patterns: An Introduction* (New York: W. H. Freeman, 1987).

4. Mitchell Greenberg, *Corneille, Classicism, and the Ruses of Symmetry* (Cambridge: Cambridge University Press, 1986).

5. Michael Layton, *Symmetry, Causality, and Mind* (Cambridge: MIT Press, 1992), passim and esp. 477ff.

6. Washburn and Crowe, *Symmetries of Culture*, 4ff., and with full bibliography of earlier work.

7. The episode is discussed briefly in George Hersey and Richard Freedman, *Possible Palladian Villas (Plus a Few Instructively Impossible Ones)* (Cambridge: MIT Press, 1992), 16ff.; and, in more detail, by Walter Kambartel, *Symmetrie und Schönheit*, 37ff. See also Cecil Gould, *Bernini in France: An Episode in Seventeenth-Century History* (London: Weidenfeld and Nicholson, 1981), 52ff.

8. See Anthony Blunt, ed., *Diary of the Cavaliere Bernini's Visit to France,* by Paul Fréart de Chantelou (Princeton, N.J.: Princeton University Press, 1985), 55 [July 8, 1665]; symmetry is also discussed on pp. 234, 261, and 314. See also Gould, *Bernini in France.*

9. Kambartel, *Symmetrie und Schönheit*, 37ff. Bernini, it must be said, was not speaking French but Italian. His words were translated by his amanuensis, Chantelou.

10. Claude Perrault, *Ordonnance for the Five Kinds of Columns after the Method of the Ancients* (1673; reprint [English edition], The Getty Center for the History of Art and the Humanities, Santa Monica, Calif., 1993), 50, 53. Cf. also idem, *A Treatise of the Five Orders in Architecture,* etc., trans. John James (London: Benjamin Motte, 1707), which probably planted the seed of Perrault's "French" definition of symmetry in England. For Perrault as an engineer, see Antoine Picon, *Claude Perrault, 1613-88, ou, la curiosité d'un classique* (Paris: Picard, 1988): Louvre colonnade, 157ff.

11. Picon, *Perrault,* discusses Perrault's involvements with weighing, measuring, and lifting machines on pp. 95ff.

12. The house was first designed by Matthew Brettingham, c. 1758. The center block was redone in 1761 by James Paine. From 1760 onward Robert Adam began additions to the building, including the magnificent south front. Nikolaus Pevsner, *Derbyshire* (London: Penguin, 1953), 167ff.

13. Though Dirichlet domains, equally limited to five types, do exist in three-dimensional form, set into three-dimensional lattices. See Keith Devlin, *Mathematics: The Science of Patterns* (New York: Scientific American Library, 1994), 163ff.

14. Ibid.

15. Nonetheless, the early patterns on wallpaper were all discontinuous. Jean Papillon the first (c. 1688), apparently, to match up the printed sheets as they were hung on the wall. Thus did he lay the groundwork for the continuous, infinitely repeated patterns we have today. Papillon's innovation brought out the full possibilities of wallpaper symmetry.

16. For wallpaper history: Barty Phillips, *Fabrics and Wallpapers: Sources, Design, and Inspiration* (Boston: Little, Brown, 1991); and Lesley Hoskins, ed., *The Papered Wall: Pattern, Technique* (New York: Abrams, 1994).

17. See also *Flavi Vegeti Renati . . . De re militari libri quatuor,* etc., with chapters from Frontinus, Oleanus, Polybius, and other experts in castrametatio (Lugduni Batavorum: ex officina Plantiniana, apud F. Raphelengium, 1592); and Spiro Kostof, *The City Shaped: Urban Patterns and Meanings through History* (Boston: Little, Brown, 1991).

18. Anthony N. B. Garvan, *Architecture and Town Planning in Colonial Connecticut* (New Haven, 1951), 29ff.

19. Garvin, *Architecture and Town Planning,* 44ff.

20. See Robert Jan van Pelt, "Los Rabinos, Maimónides y el Templo," in *Dios Arquitecto: J. B. Villalpando y el Templo de Salomon,* ed. Juan Antonio Ramírez (Madrid: Ediciones Siruelas, 1991), 82ff. See also Robert Fludd, *Philosophia Moysaica* (London: Moseley, 1659).

21. Helen Rosenau, *Vision of the Temple: The Image of the Temple of Jerusalem in Judaism and Christianity* (London: Oresko, 1979), 91ff. See also Alberto Pérez-Gómez, "Juan Bautista Villalpando's Divine Model in Architectural Theory," *Chora* 3 (1999): 125ff.

22. Villalpando, *Templo de Salomón,* 52.

23. See the articles grouped under the heading "El Rigor de la ciencia: los tratados tradicionales sobre el Templo de Jerusalén," by Juan Antonio Ramírez, Robert Jan van Pelt, Antonio Martínez Ripoll, and René Taylor, in *Villalpando,* ed. Ramírez, 79ff. For Goldmann and Sturm, see idem, *Sciagraphia Templi Hierosolymitani* (Leipzig: Krüger, 1694); idem, *Erste Ausübung der vortrefflichen und vollständigen Anweisung zu der Zivil-Bau-Kunst Nikolai Goldmann* (Leipzig: Richter, 1695); and idem, *Prodromus Architecturae Goldmannianae* (Augsburg: Wolff, 1714). For Lamy, see Bernard Lamy, *De Tabernaculo foederis; de sancta civitate Jersalem et de templo eius,* 1720; and F. Girbal, *Bernard Lamy, 1640-1715* (Paris, 1964).

24. The earliest regular-grid city layout I have been able to trace is that of the Chinese capital of Chang-an as it existed in the seventh and eighth centuries C.E. Its strict lattice was based on cosmology. In its perfected form, the Chang-an was a quadrilateral grid surrounded by walls pierced by twelve gates (corresponding to the twelve months of the year). Nancy Steinhardt, *Chinese Imperial City Planning* (Honolulu: University of Hawaii Press, 1990), 118ff.; Michiele Pirazzoli-T'Serstevens, *Liv-*

ing Architecture: Chinese (New York: Grosset & Dunlap, 1971). I thank Julie Ro for help with this note. Any subsequent investigation of urban design and wallpaper symmetry would start off, I should think, with Chang-an and then move to the great lattice-planned complexes of Hindu Cambodia.

25. We read that René Ouvrard (Blondel's sidekick), for example, had discovered his and Blondel's rules in the proportions in Solomon's temple as described in Scripture. François Blondel, *Cours d'architecture enseignée dans l'Académie Royale d'Architecture,* etc. (Paris: Chez l'Auteur, 1698), 756ff. See also Rosenau, *The Temple,* 133ff.

26. The original shareholders of the settlement came from Yorkshire, Hertfordshire, Kent, and London. Rollin G. Osterweis, *Three Centuries of New Haven, 1638–1938* (New Haven, Conn.: Yale University Press, 1953), 12. As to scriptural sources for the name, see Genesis 49:13 (Authorized), Jacob's testament to his sons: "And Zebulon shall dwell in the haven of the sea; and he shall be for an haven of ships." One other nine-square city is Jaipur, in India, laid out by the Rajah Jai Singh, an astronomer, in 1778. There are probably other such Hindu towns. See Joseph Rykwert, "Letter from Chandigarh," *TLS,* April 23, 1999, 15.

27. Osterweis, *New Haven,* 15.

28. See Katherine A. Lantuch, "The Origin of New Haven's Nine Squares," *Journal of the New Haven Colony Historical Society* 37 (spring 1991): 7ff., with earlier bibliography.

29. Osterweis, *New Haven,* 17. John Cotton, *Discourse about Civil Government* (Cambridge, Mass., 1663).

30. See John Davenport, *Aspects of Puritan Religious Thought* (New York: AMS Press, 1982). Both the Geneva and the Castellion Bibles (1588 and 1551 respectively) contained graphic reconstructions. Cf. also Davenport's *Biblia hebraica cum interlineari interpretationes,* etc. (Leyden: Plantiniana Raphaelengii, 1613).

31. George L. Hersey, *Architecture, Poetry, and Number in the Royal Palace at Caserta* (Cambridge: MIT Press, 1976), 142ff. The present palace of Caserta was built, at smaller scale, by Luigi Vanvitelli (begun in 1751 but never completed).

32. Villalpando, *El Templo de Salomón,* 87ff.

33. Both Gioffredo's and Boullée's projects belong, also, to the building-type I analyze as the Poggioreale Principle. See my *Monumental Impulse: Architecture's Biological Roots* (Cambridge: MIT Press, 1999).

34. See also István Hargittai and Clifford A. Pickover, eds., *Spiral Symmetry* (Singapore: World Scientific, 1992), with many fascinating papers, though none on architecture.

35. J. B. Ward-Perkins, "The Shrine of St. Peter and Its Twelve Spiral Columns," *Journal of Roman Studies* 43 (1952); Juan Antonio Ramírez, "Sinécdoque: Columnas 'Salomonicas,'" in *Villalpando,* 17ff., with bibliography. One is also reminded, looking at spiral columns, of chaos experiments in the field of fluid dynamics. See Ian Stewart, "Broken Symmetry and the Formation of Spiral Patterns in Fluids," in *Spi-*

ral Symmetry, ed. István Hargittai and Clifford A. Pickover (Singapore: World Scientific, 1992), 187ff.

36. See Garth Fowden, *The Egyptian Hermes: A Historical Approach to the Late Pagan Mind* (Cambridge: Cambridge University Press, 1986), 23, 30ff.

37. There is a good bibliography of *Saülenphilosophie* in Joseph Rykwert, *The Dancing Column* (Cambridge: MIT Press, 1996). In a kindred but less exalted spirit, I too have recently discussed Solomonic columns as vessels of information. See my *Monumental Impulse,* chap. 2.

38. Christopher Wren, "Discourse on Architecture," in *Wren Society,* ed. A. T. Bolton and H. D. Hendry (London: 1923–43), 20:140.

39. W. Chandler Kirwin, *Powers Matchless: The Pontificate of Urban VIII, the Baldachin, and Gian Lorenzo Bernini* (New York: Peter Lang, 1997), 67ff., 124ff.

40. Here again I cite Joseph Connors, "Ars tornandi: Baroque Architecture and the Lathe," *Journal of the Warburg and Courtauld Institutes* 53 (1990): 217ff., which shows that in the seventeenth century, producing such whorled and hyperwhorled shapes in wood on a lathe was a gentleman's hobby.

41. Jack Cohen and Ian Stewart, *The Collapse of Chaos: Discovering Simplicity in a Complex World* (New York: Penguin, 1994), 167ff.; and Mario Markus, "Autonomous Organization of a Chaotic Medium into Spirals: Simulations and Experiments," in *Spiral Symmetry,* ed. Hargittai and Pickover, 165ff.

42. Kirwin, *Powers Matchless,* figs. 141 and 142; and Hersey, *Monumental Impulse,* chap. 2.

43. Jay Kappraff, "The Spiral in Nature, Myth, and Mathematics," in *Spiral Symmetry,* ed. Hargittai and Pickover, 15ff. See also, in this same volume, Ian Stewart, "Broken Symmetry and the Formation of Spiral Patterns in Fluids," 187ff., and esp. fig. 2e, which shows how a "Solomonic" spiral can be induced by fluid dynamics.

44. See Stephen Gaukroger, *Descartes: An Intellectual Biography* (Oxford, 1995), 249ff.

45. Martin Golubitsky and Ian Melbourne, "A Symmetry Classification of Columns," in *Bridges: Mathematical Connections in Art, Music, and Science,* ed. Reza Sarhangi, 209–23 (Bridges Conference, April 6, 1998).

46. Kirwin, *Powers Matchless,* 61ff., 124ff.

47. Illustrated in Banister Fletcher, *A History of Architecture on the Comparative Method* [1892], many eds., many publishers (e.g., New York: Scribner's, 1951).

48. François Blondel, *Cours d'architecture enseigné dans l'Académie royale d'architecture,* etc. (Paris: Chez l'Auteur, 1698), pl. xii.

49. Blondel, *Cours,* pl. xii. Blondel does, however, illustrate a right triangle whose hypotenuse is gradually reset at different levels along the altitude, to produce a very gradual diminution on the lengths of the hypotenuses. These hypotenuses can then be transferred to the spiral to create a change of curve that is even subtler than those given.

50. D'Arcy Wentworth Thompson, *On Growth and Form* (1917; complete revised edition, New York: Dover, 1992), 754. See also Descartes, *Oeuvres,* ed. Charles Adam and Paul Tannery (Paris, 1898), 360.

51. See Louis Hautecoeur, *Mystique et architecture: Symbolisme du cercle et de la coupole* (Paris: Picard, 1954).

52. See my *Monumental Impulse,* chap. 3. See also Joseph Connors, "The Spire of Sant'Ivo," *Burlington Magazine* 138 (October 1996): 668ff., for the article itself and for bibliography.

53. See my *Monumental Impulse,* chap. 2. For more on Borromini's dome interiors, see Raspe, *Architektursystem Borrominis,* 85ff.

CHAPTER 6

1. John Dryden, trans., *The Eclogues of Virgil* (London, 1697), vi.52.

2. Galileo Galilei, *Sidereus Nuncius, or the Sidereal Messenger,* edited by Albert van Helden (Chicago: University of Chicago Press, 1989). For Earth's shape, see chapter 3 of this book (on Boullée); for the Moon's, see Isaac Newton, *Principia mathematica,* vol. 2, *The System of the World* [1687], trans. Andrew Motte, revised by Florian Cajori (Berkeley: University of California Press, 1934), 484ff. Newton also proves that the planets are all oblate (ibid., 424ff.).

3. See Stephen Gaukroger, *Descartes: An Intellectual Biography* (Oxford: Oxford University Press, 1995), 89ff. For the drawing instruments, see Maurice Daumas, *Scientific Instruments in the 17th and 18th Centuries and Their Makers* (London: Batsford, 1972).

4. See the commentary by C. Taylor, "The Geometry of Kepler and Newton," *Transactions of the Cambridge Philosophical Society* 18 (1900): 197.

5. J. V. Field and J. J. Gray, *The Geometrical Work of Girard Desargues* (New York: Springer-Verlag, 1987), 153ff.

6. Newton, *Principia mathematica,* 2:498ff.

7. Valentino Braitenberg, *Vehicles: Experiments in Synthetic Psychology* (Cambridge: MIT Press, 1984), 132. The images are originally from G. Scheffers, *Lehrbuch der Mathematik* (Leipzig: Veit & Co., 1911).

8. See Lothar Haselberger, ed., *Appearance and Essence: Refinements of Classical Architecture: Curvature* (Philadelphia: University Museum, University of Pennsylvania, 1999).

9. François Blondel, *Cours d'architecture enseignée dans l'Académie Royale d'Architecture,* etc. (1675; reprint, Paris: Chez l'Auteur, 1698), book 6, chapter 8, passim.

10. Sebastiano Serlio, *Tutte l'opere d'architettura et prospettiva,* etc. (Venice: de'Franceschi, 1619), fol. 13v ff.

11. See, however, the articles on Roman ovals and ellipses by Mark Wilson Jones—for example, "Principles of Design in Roman Architecture: The Setting Out of Centralised Buildings," *Publications of the British School at Rome* 57 (1989): 106ff.

12. See the illustrations in the Italian edition of Hans Sedlmayr, *L'Architettura di*

Borromini: La Figura e l'Opera con un'appendice storico-stilistico, ed. Marco Pogacnik (Milan: Electa, 1996), 182. They are all in the Albertina, Vienna.

13. The earliest person to describe this system for creating ellipses, apparently, was Anthemius of Tralles, one of the architects of Hagia Sophia. See D. C. Heath, *A History of Greek Mathematics,* 2:542.

14. Although the architect and his assistants could have laid out the huge circle in a field and then made a template of the amount of arc they needed.

15. Alexandre Koyré, *The Astronomical Revolution: Copernicus—Kepler—Borelli* (1973; reprint, New York: Dover, 1992), 313.

16. Borromini played other intricate games with his ovals/ellipses. He overlapped them, rotated them on one another, shrank and enlarged them. Some of this has been discussed by Martin Raspe, who also sees, in Borromini's architecture, analogies to musical composition. Martin Raspe, *Das Architektursystem Borrominis* (Munich: Deutscher Kunstverlag, 1994), passim.

17. Roberto Pane, *Bernini architetto* (Venice: N. Pozza, 1953). The documents are gathered by Timothy K. Kitao, *Circle and Oval in the Square of St. Peter's: Bernini's Art of Planning* (New York: New York University Press, 1974). Kitao thinks that the piazza's shape was formed from overlapped circles (Kitao, fig. 5). Franco Borsi, *Bernini Architetto* (New York: Rizzoli, 1984), 64ff., agrees. And the idea is perfectly possible: but how do they know? There is always another way to skin the geometrical cat. For the piazza in general, see T. A. Marder, *Bernini and the Art of Architecture* (New York: Abbeville, 1998), 123ff., with earlier bibliography. For the piazza's geometry, see especially Massimo Birindelli, *Piazza San Pietro* (Bari: Laterza, 1981; originally published as *La Machina heroica: Il disegno di Gianlorenzo Bernini per Piazza San Pietro* [Rome: Università degli Studi, 1980]; and Thomas Thieme, "La Geometria di Piazza San Pietro," *Palladio,* n.s., 23 [1973]: 129ff.).

18. For the Colosseum and its ellipticism, see M. Wilson Jones, "Designing Amphitheatres," *Römische Mitteilungen* 100 (1993): 391ff., with earlier bibliography; note especially J. C. Golvin, *L'Amphithéâtre romain: Essai sur la théorisation de sa forme et de ses fonctions* (Paris: Diffusion de Boccard, 1988). Despite Wilson Jones's valiant efforts, confusion still reigns on the matter of ellipses versus ovals. I hope I haven't increased it.

19. Juan Bautista Caramuel Lobkowitz, *Arquitectura civil, recta y obliqua* (1678; reprint, Madrid: Ediciones Turner, 1984).

20. A. G. Marino, "Il Colonnato di Piazza San Pietro: Dall'architettura obliqua di Caramuel al classicismo berniniano," *Palladio* 23 (1973): 81ff. One can add that the original name for the piazza was "Piazza Obliqua" (Kitao, *Circle and Oval,* passim.)

21. See Alberto Pérez-Gómez and Louise Pelletier, *Architectural Representation and the Perspective Hinge* (Cambridge: MIT Press, 1997), 51ff. and passim; also Robin Evans, *The Projective Cast: Architecture and Its Three Geometries* (Cambridge: MIT Press, 1995), 179ff.

22. For everything discussed above, see François Blondel, *Cours,* 24ff. Blondel also discusses and illustrates column-shaft entasis created with hyperbolic and parabolic curves, using full-scale pantographs at the building site.

23. Athanasius Kircher, *Musurgia universalis: Sive ars magna consoni et dissoni in X libros digesta,* etc. (Rome: Typographicum haeredum Fratelli Corbinetti, 1650), 2:279.

24. See Galileo's *Trattato della Sphaera,* 1586–87.

25. Francesco Barberini, the patron, may have been more given to heliocentrism than other prelates because the Sun was a central emblem of his family. The fresco was painted before Galileo was condemned and while Francesco Barberini was still his supporter. See Torgil Magnuson, *Rome in the Age of Bernini,* 1:342, with bibliography. For Sacchi, see Anne Sutherland Harris, *Andrea Sacchi: Complete Edition of the Paintings with a Critical Catalogue* (Oxford: Oxford University Press, 1977). This account, however, ignores all cosmographical and cartographical questions.

26. Ingrid Preussner, *Ellipsen und Ovale in der Malerei des 15. Und 16. Jahrhunderts* (Speyer: VCH Acta Humaniora, 1987), 51ff.; and L. Bagrow, *Die Geschichte der Kartographie* (Berlin: Safari-Verlag, 1951).

27. Still today world maps are subject to projective geometry. And, in the cause of art rather than technology, the artist Agnes Denes projects world maps onto snail-shaped spirals, dodecahedrons, eggs, and the like, all the while preserving total recognizability. Agnes Denes, "Isometric Systems in Isotropic Space," in *Spiral Symmetry,* ed. Hargittai and Pickover, 389ff.

28. Eileen Reeves, *Painting the Heavens: Galileo and the Lunar Controversy* (Princeton: Princeton University Press, 1997).

29. Magnuson, *Age of Bernini,* 1:37, with bibliography; see also, especially, Rudolf Wittkower, *La Cupola di San Pietro di Michelangelo* (Florence: Nuova Italia, 1964), 77ff.; James Ackerman, *The Architecture of Michelangelo,* 2nd ed., vol. 1 (Chicago: University of Chicago Press, 1986); and Roberto di Stefano, *La Cupola di San Pietro: Storia della costruzione e dei restauri* (Naples: Edizioni scientifiche italiane, 1966). Di Stefano claims that structurally Michelangelo's dome is not a traditional one made of a solid rotated vault but, instead a medieval-type star vault supported on ribs rising from the base of the drum. This shape, Di Stefano implies however, is based on what he calls the "elastic ellipse" (141).

30. A good discussion of tight packing in an architectural setting is Friedrich Christoph Wagner, "Symmetrie-Model-Grundlagen der Gestalten," *Daidalos,* March 15, 1985, 123ff.

CHAPTER 7

1. Girard Desargues, *Brouillon projet d'une exemple d'une maniere universelle du S. G. D. L.* [Sieur Girard Desargues Lyonnais] *touchant la pratique du trait à preuves pour la coupe des pierres en l'architecture,* etc. (Paris: Pierre Des-Hayes, 1643). Stereometry is highly relevant to what I'm writing about; but unlike the rest of what I say, it has

been well covered. For a recent example, see Robin Evans, *The Projective Cast: Architecture and Its Three Geometries* (Cambridge: MIT Press, 1995), 179ff.

2. Guarino Guarini, *Architettura Civile* (Milan: Polifilo, 1968), pl. iii, 6, and p. 57.

3. See Keith Devlin, *Mathematics: The Science of Patterns* (New York: Scientific American Books, 1994), 94ff.

4. Stephen Gaukroger, *Descartes: An Intellectual Biography* (Oxford: Clarendon Press, 1995), 172ff., 224ff., with full bibliography.

5. George B. Dyson, *Darwin among the Machines: The Evolution of Global Intelligence* (Reading, Mass.: Perseus Books, 1997).

6. Antonio di Tuccio Manetti, *The Life of Brunelleschi,* ed. and trans. Howard Saalman (University Park, Pa.: Pennsylvania State University Press, 1970), 42ff.; Giorgio Vasari, *The Lives of the Painters, Sculptors, and Architects* (1550, 1568; reprint, trans. A. B. Hinds, London: Dent), *1,* 272. Samuel Y. Edgerton, *The Renaissance Rediscovery of Linear Perspective* (New York: Basic Books, 1975), is the best of the many modern books. But see also Martin Kemp, *The Science of Art: Optical Themes in Western Art from Brunelleschi to Seurat* (New Haven, Conn.: Yale University Press, 1990), part 1. See also Evans, *Projective Cast,* 107ff.

7. One braccia equals .5836 meters or about 23 inches. See Manetti, *Vita,* 42. I can find no value for *piccole braccia,* but these are obviously a way of scaling down the larger unit for convenience in measuring models and renderings, as when we say a scale is ½ inch = 1 foot. Think of the ½ inch as a "little foot."

8. For a good discussion of this device, which is actually in contrast to distance-point perspective, see Edgerton, "Brunelleschi's First Perspective Picture," *Arte Lombarda* 18 (1973): 187ff. For a mathematician's view, see Morris Kline, *Mathematics in Western Culture* (Oxford: Oxford University Press, 1953), 126ff. (Projective geometry is discussed, as a derivation from Renaissance perspective, on pp. 144ff.) Also see Evans, *Projective Cast,* 107ff.

9. And here I would mention again Philippe Comar, *La Perspective en jeu: Le dessous de l'image* (Paris: Gallimard, 1992), which is probably the most visually alert, and certainly the wittiest, of the many contributions.

10. See Alexandra Glanz, *Alessandro Galli-Bibiena (1686–1748) inventore dalle scene und premier architkteur am kurpälischen Hof in Mannheim,* etc. (Berlin: Gesellschaft für Theatergeschichte, 1991), with earlier bibliography.

11. Ferdinando Galli da Bibiena, *Architettura Civile* (1711; reprint, New York: Benjamin Blom, 1971), 136.

12. Invented by Thomas Walgenstein and first described, as far as I know, in Athanasius Kircher's *Ars magna lucis et umbrae,* edition of 1671. See Gian Piero Brunetta, *Il Viaggio dell'iconauta: Dalla camera oscura di Leonardo alla luce dei Lumière* (Venice: Marsilio, 1997), 183ff.

13. See now J. V. Field and J. J. Gray, *The Geometry of Girard Desargues* (New York:

Springer, 1987); and Marcel Chabaud, *Girard Desargues: Bourgeois de Lyon, mathématicien, architecte* (Lyon: IREM de Lyon, 1996).

14. Bosse was also the author of works on perspective. His approach in all this
work was informed by the spirit and discoveries of Desargues, as his very titles often
make clear. Abraham Bosse, *La Pratique du Trait à preuves de M. Desargues, Lyonnois,
pour la coupe des pierres en l'architecture* (The technique of M. Desargues's geometric
projection for stonecutting for architecture) (Paris, 1643); idem, *La manière universelle
de Mr. Desargues, Lyonnois, pour poser l'essieu & placer les heures et autres choses aux cadrans
au soleil* (On sundials) (Paris, 1643); idem, *Manière universelle de Mr. Desargues, pour pratiquer la perspective par petit-pied comme le geometrale* (Universal Manner of M. Desargues
to create perspective by means of scaling) (Paris, 1648); and idem, *Traité des practiques
géometrales* (Paris, 1665).

15. Girard Desargues, *Exemple de l'une des manieres universelles du S.G.D.L.
touchant la pratique de la perspective sans employer aucun tiers point, de distance ny d'autre
nature, qui soit hors du champ de l'ouvrage* (Paris, 1836): "Example of one of S.G.D.L.'s
general methods concerning drawing in perspective without using any third point,
a distance point, or any other kind, which lies outside the picture field."

16. Field and Gray, *Desargues,* 144.

17. Ibid., 147, slightly edited by me.

18. Girard Desargues, *Brouillon project d'une atteinte aux evenmens des rencontres du
cone avec un plan, 1639* (Paris: Poudra, 1864).

19. Diagram adapted from Kline, *Mathematics in Western Culture*, 148.

20. Field and Gray, *Desargues*, 36ff.

21. Sir Isaac Newton, *The Mathematical Papers of Isaac Newton*, vol. 7, 635. Quoted
by Field and Gray, *Desargues,* 39.

22. Abraham Bosse, *Traité des manières de dessiner les ordres de l'architecture,* etc.
(Paris: P. Aubouin, P. Emery, et C. Clousier, 1688), pl. xliv.

23. Pérez Gómez and Louise Pelletier, *Architectural Representation*, 125ff., with
bibliography. Much more loosely, sciagraphy could also mean just about any kind of
architectural rendering. See, for example, L. C. Sturm, *Sciagraphia templi Hierosolemytani* (Leipzig: Krüger, 1694).

24. George Hersey, *The Lost Meaning of Classical Architecture: Speculations on Ornament from Vitruvius to Venturi* (Cambridge: MIT Press, 1988), 21ff.

25. Richard Broxton Onians, *The Origins of European Thought about the Body, the
Mind, the Soul, the World, Time, and Fate*, etc. (Cambridge: Cambridge University
Press, 1951), 95.

26. See David Murray, ed., *Architecture and Shadow, Via 11* (Philadelphia: Univer-
sity of Pennsylvania Graduate School of Fine Arts, and New York: Rizzoli, 1990).
More definitive, but not limited to architecture, is Thomas Da Costa Kaufmann,
"The Perspective of Shadows: The History of the Theory of Shadow Projection,"
Journal of the Warburg and Courtauld Institutes 38 (1975): 238ff.

27. Galileo Galilei, *Dialogues Concerning Two New Sciences* (1638; reprint, trans. Henry Crew and Alfonso de Salvio, New York: Dover, 1954), 244 [Fourth Day].

28. Galileo Galilei, 1606. Trans. Stillman Drake, as *Operations of the Geometric and Military Compass* (Washington, D.C.: National Museum of Science and Technology, 1978). For Descartes, see Gaukroger, *Descartes*, 299. See also Field and Gray, *Desargues*, figs. 7.3–7.6.

29. Sebastien Le Prestre de Vauban, *Manière de fortifier selon la méthode de M. de Vauban, avec un traité préliminaire des principes de géometrie,* etc. (Paris: Coignard, 1681).

30. Christopher Duffy, *Siege Warfare: The Fortress in the Early Modern World, 1494–1660* (London: Routledge and Kegan Paul, 1979); and idem, *The Fortress in the Age of Vauban and Frederick the Great, 1660–1789* (London: Routledge and Kegan Paul, 1985).

30. Many Baroque treatises on stereometry treat these matters. Compare Desargues's own *Brouillon . . . du trait à preuves*.

31. Abraham Bosse, *Moyen universel de pratiquer la perspective sur les tableaux ou surfaces irregulières,* etc. (Paris: Chez ledit Bosse, 1653).

32. F. J. Hebbert and G. A. Rothrock, *Soldier of France: Sebastien le Prestre de Vauban, 1633–1707* (New York: Peter Lang, 1989), with bibliography.

33. Le Corbusier, "Il faut reconsiderer le hexagone français," in *Architecture et urbanisme* (Paris: Publications Techniques, 1942).

34. Wenzel Jamnitzer, *Perspectiva corporum regularium* (1568; reprint, Frankfurt: Biermann, 1972). The title claims that the Platonic solids are here being presented "in a special new way never made use of or seen before, . . . with which [they] may be endlessly varied and interpenetrated (*gefunden*)."

35. The best short analysis of these forms, so far as I know, is Alan Holden, *Shapes, Space, and Symmetry* (New York: Dover, 1971). He shows the reader how to make these compound solids from wire and cardboard—a necessity, since they are extremely difficult to understand or portray except in three-dimensional models.

36. Unlike the other architecture discussed in this book, Desargues's buildings are little known. In 1646 he was commissioned to design a new town hall for his native city, Lyon (unexecuted). However he did build there the Hôtel de l'Europe, and he added what was apparently a *trompe* or wave-form turret, in the manner of Philibert Delorme, to the facade of a house on the Pont de Pierre. In 1653 he built a staircase or *perron* for the Duc d'Ediguères at the Château de Vizille near Grenoble. Then in Paris came a staircase for the Maison Vedeau de Grammont, another in the Hôtel de Varenne, and a third in the Hôtel de l'Hôpital. In 1660, two years before his death, Desargues designed the grand staircase of the Palais Royale (rebuilt), and also, for a certain Sieur Aubry, a house in the Rue des Bernardines. Much of this work has perished, though some of the vanished buildings have been preserved in prints. The stairs at Vizille remain, and are illustrated in Pérez-Gómez and Pelletier, *Architectural Representation,* fig. 1.44, and by Bosse, *Les Ordres de l'architecture*, part 1, pl. XL.

37. See Christoph Thoenes, "Ein spezifisches Treppenbeusstsein. Neapler Treppenhaüser des 18. Jahrhunderts," *Daidalos* 9 (Sept. 15, 1983): 77ff.; and R. J. Morrice, "Sanfelice and St. Florian: Indigenous Tradition in Staircase Design," *Architectural History* 26 (1983): 82ff.

38. Desargues constructed a hydraulic pump using epicycloid wheels. Christiaan Huygens, *Oeuvres,* vol. 7, 112. See Field and Gray, *Desargues,* 35.

CHAPTER 8

1. Ferdinando Galli da Bibiena, *Architettura Civile* (1711; reprint, New York: Benjamin Blom, 1971).

2. *The Anchor Bible* (Garden City, N.Y.: Doubleday, 1964–93).

3. The prophet also endows his orbits with eyes and fearsome creature-faces, saying that the monsters move simultaneously with the orbits. This makes one think of the Intelligences that Kepler believed moved the heavens. Bruce Stephenson, *The Music of the Heavens, Kepler's Harmonic Astronomy* (Princeton, N.J.: Princeton University Press, 1994), 238ff.

4. Indeed Desargues, we noted, had designed an epicycloid water pump—i.e., one whose wheels and gears performed like Ptolemaic planets, a device that interested Christiaan Huygens. Huygens, *Oeuvres,* 7:112. See J. V. Field and J. J. Gray, *The Geometry of Girard Desargues* (New York: Springer, 1987), 35.

5. For martyriums as a type, see Howard Colvin, *Architecture and the After-Life* (New Haven, Conn.: Yale University Press, 1991), esp. 43ff., the Mausoleum of Augustus, and Santa Tecla, Milan, 107.

6. Ezekiel 20:18–21 in *The Anchor Bible.*

7. Louis Hautecoeur, in *Mystique et architecture: Symbolisme du cercle et de la coupole* (Paris: Picard, 1954), passim and with earlier bibliography. See also Patrick Marchetti, *Le Nymphée de l'agora d'Argos: Fouille, étude architecturale et historique* (Paris: De Boccard, 1995); and Felice Costabile, ed., *I Ninfei di Locri Epizefiri: Architettura, culti erotici, sacralità delle acque* (Catanzaro: Soveria Manelli, 1991).

8. Hautecoeur, *Mystique et architecture,* 19ff.

9. Hautecoeur, in *Mystique,* 97ff., discusses these and many other ancient and medieval "epicyclic" plans.

10. H. P. L'Orange, *Studies in the Iconography of Cosmic Kingship in the Ancient World* (Cambridge: Harvard University Press, 1953), 316.

11. Presumably intended to replace the present building, which is by Marcantonio Toscanella, 1600–1606. I should point out that as an astronomer himself, Guarini does not seem to have embraced Kepler's ideas about elliptical planetary orbits (cf. his *Coelestis mathematicae pars prima et secunda,* 1683), though ellipses are often found in his architecture.

12. And here again I recommend Elwin C. Robison's "Optics and Mathematics

in the Domed Churches of Guarino Guarini," *Journal of the Society of Architectural Historians* 50 (1991): 384ff.

13. That is, a sequence whose reciprocals would be .7:.14:.25.

14. Vincenzo Viviani, in a report of 21 August 1659 to Prince Leopoldo de' Medici, gives a history of the earliest clockwork and includes the illustration above. Cf. Silvio Bedini, *Science and Instruments in Seventeenth-Century Italy* (Aldershot UK: Variorum, 1994), 257ff.

15. Christiaan Huygens received the first patent for a pendulum-regulated clock with clockwork gears in 1657. Bedini, *Science and Instruments*, 35.

16. Alexandre Koyré, *The Astronomical Revolution: Copernicus—Kepler—Borelli* (New York: Dover, 1973, 225ff.

17. Antoine Picon, *Claude Perrault, 1613–88, ou, la curiosité d'un classique* (Paris: Picard, 1988), 95ff.

18. Giovanni Domenico Cassini, *Abrégé des observations . . . la comète de 1680* (Paris: E. Michallet, 1681); idem, *La meridiana del tempio di San Petronio tirata, e preparata . . .* (Bologna: V. Benacci, 1695); idem, *Nuovo atlante geografico universale delineato sulle ultime osservazioni* (Rome: Calcografia Camerale, 1792–1801); Lloyd Arnold Brown, *Jean-Dominique Cassini and His World Map of 1696* (Ann Arbor: University of Michigan Press, 1941); and J.L. Heilbron, *The Sun in the Church: Cathedrals as Solar Observatories* (Cambridge: Harvard University Press, 1999), 82ff.

19. And he could have instructed Bernini in ellipse-drafting, since Bernini was in Paris, talking to Perrault, in these same years (circa 1665). Paul Fréart de Chantelou, *Diary of the Cavaliere Bernini's Visit to France*, ed. A. Blunt (Princeton: Princeton University Press, 1985).

20. For the physics of the violin family of instruments, see C. Taylor, "The New Violin Family and Its Scientific Background," *Soundings* 7 (1978): 101ff.; C. M. Hutchins, "The Acoustics of Violin Plates," *Scientific American* 245 (1981): 170ff.

21. I hesitate to recommend Anthony Blunt's book, but there's not much else in English so here it is: Anthony Blunt, *Neapolitan Baroque and Rococo Architecture* (London: Zwemmer, 1975), 110ff. (with a good earlier bibliography).

22. For broken symmetry, see Ian Stewart, "Broken Symmetry and the Formation of Spiral Patterns in Fluids," in *Spiral Symmetry,* ed. István Hargittai and Clifford A. Pickover (Singapore: World Scientific, 1992), 187ff.; and Ian Stewart and Martin Golubitsky, *Fearful Symmetry: Is God a Geometer?* (London: Penguin, 1993), 53ff.

23. Stewart and Golubitsky, *Fearful Symmetry,* 54.

24. Koyré, *Astronomical Revolution,* 58.

25. Ibid., 51.

26. It referred to sudden violent shifts in systems that ordinarily change slowly—for example, New England weather, the stock market, airline prices. See E. C. Zeeman, *Catastrophe Theory: Selected Papers, 1972–77* (Reading, Mass.: Addison-Wesley, 1977).

27. Stewart, "Broken Symmetry," 187ff. See also R. J. Thompson, *Instabilities and Catastrophes in Science and Engineering* (Chichester: Wiley, 1982).

CHAPTER 9

1. Sir Christopher Wren, *Tract II on Architecture* (mid-1670s; reprinted in Lydia M. Soo, ed., *Wren's "Tracts" on Architecture and Other Writings* [Cambridge: Cambridge University Press, 1998], 159).

2. See John Harris, *William Talman, Maverick Architect* (London: George Allen and Unwin, 1982); and John Summerson, *Architecture in Britain, 1530–1833,* 6th ed. (London: Penguin, 1977), 260ff. But it would be hard to call Talman ungeometrical. And then later, in the eighteenth century, there were strongly geometric architects like James Gibbs, Robert Morris, and William Halfpenny.

3. There have been post-Baroque episodes of architectural geometry—neoclassicism was patently one such, and then there was the less known *architecture chiffrée* espoused at the Paris École des Beaux-Arts in the mid–nineteenth century. It is described in Julien Guadet, *Eléments et théorie de l'architecture* (Paris: Librairie de la construction moderne, 1905).

4. Wright and his colleagues in the Prairie School were particularly geometrical. And yet, for all the torrents of scholarship on them, there has been little or no geometrical analysis. I can cite only a few items—on this American work or even on late Victorian geometric design generally. There are two good articles by Lionel March: "'Proportion Is an Alive and Expressive Tool,'" in *R. M. Schindler: Composition and Construction,* ed. L. March and J. Sheine (London: Academy Editions, 1994), 88ff., which deals with Wright's one-time collaborator; and also "Sources of Characteristic Spatial Relations in Frank Lloyd Wright's Decorative Designs," in *Frank Lloyd Wright: The Phoenix Papers,* vol. 2, *The Natural Pattern of Structure*, ed. L. Nelson (Tucson: University of Arizona Press, 1995), 12ff. Another promising geometric analysis on the period is Christina K. Hough, "The Pattern Designs of William Morris: Nature Conventionalized According to Geometric Principles," *Architectura,* 1992.

5. George Hersey, *The Monumental Impulse: Architecture's Biological Roots* (Cambridge: MIT Press, 1999), 5ff., 67ff.

6. March and Steadman, *The Geometry of Environment: An Introduction to Spatial Organization in Design* (Cambridge: MIT Press, 1974).

7. Frank Lloyd Wright, *A Testament* (New York: Horizon, 1957), 21. Aside from the bibliography given in Norman Brosterman, *Inventing Kindergarten* (New York: Abrams, 1997), 156 n, see (and above all) Lionel March, "Sources of Characteristic Spatial Relations in Frank Lloyd Wright's Decorative Designs," in Jeffrey M. Chasid, ed., *Frank Lloyd Wright: The Phoenix Papers,* vol. 2, *The Natural Pattern of Structure* (Tempe: Arizona State University, The Herberger Center for Design Excellence, 1996), 12ff.

8. Brosterman, *Inventing Kindergarten,* 138ff.

9. For Froebel's system, see Alexander Bruno Hanschmann, *The Kindergarten System: Its Origin and Development as Seen in the Life of Friedrich Froebel* (London: Schwann Sonnenschein, 1897); and Brosterman, *Inventing Kindergarten,* 14ff.

10. Brosterman, *Inventing Kindergarten,* 46.

11. The Froebel diagram was originally published in *Ein Sonntagsblatt . . . von Friedrich Froebel,* vol. 2, no. 19 (1838–40). For the ways in which the blocks teach elementary mathematics, see Brosterman, *Inventing Kindergarten,* 38. For Robert Record, see Lionel March, *Architectonics of Humanism: Essays on Number in Architecture* (London: Academy Editions, 1998), 22ff.

12. March, *Architectonics,* 22. See also my own *Pythagorean Palaces: Magic and Architecture in the Italian Renaissance* (Ithaca, N.Y.: Cornell University Press, 1976), 43ff., on what I call the "sectioned cube" and its more direct applications in architecture in Cesare Cesariano's edition of Vitruvius (Como, 1521).

13. By Uncle Goose Toys, Grand Rapids, Michigan 49504. For the rest of this literature, see Friedrich Froebel, *The Education of Man* (1826; reprint, 1887); idem, *Education and Development,* 1899; *Pedagogics of the Kindergarten* (New York: D. Appleton, 1895); *Kindergarten Gifts and Occupation Material* (New York: E. Steiger, 1876); also Scott Bultman, *Froebel Gifts 2000* (Grand Rapids, Mich.: American Traditional Toys, Inc., 1997).

14. Robert L. Sweeney, *Frank Lloyd Wright: An Annotated Bibliography* (New York, Duell, Sloan, and Pearce, 1978).

15. Curiously enough there are two books on just this subject: Thomas Doremus, *Frank Lloyd Wright and Le Corbusier: The Great Dialogue* (New York: Van Nostrand Reinhold, 1985); and Richard R. Etlin, *Frank Lloyd Wright and Le Corbusier: The Romantic Legacy* (Manchester: Manchester University Press, 1993). Neither is concerned with what I discuss here. Le Corbusier did have one essential thing in common with Wright: he too had been a Froebel pupil, and for several years. Brosterman, *Inventing Kindergarten,* 150ff.

16. Le Corbusier, *The Modulor: A Harmonious Measure to the Human Scale Universally Applicable to Architecture and Mechanics* (Cambridge: Harvard University Press, 1954), 5; idem, *Le Modulor and Other Buildings and Projects, 1944–45* (New York: Garland, 1983); and idem, *Le Modulor 2, 1955 (Let the User Speak Next)* (Cambridge: MIT Press, 1958), which puts together much of the written reaction to the first book and is full of ingenious ways of correcting the vaguenesses of the original system.

17. Le Corbusier, *Modulor,* 72.

18. See Rudolf Wittkower, *Four Great Makers of Modern Architecture* (New York: da Capo Press, 1970), 196ff.

19. Le Corbusier, *Modulor.*

20. Quoted by Willi Boesiger, ed., *Le Corbusier* (New York: Praeger, 1972), 84.

21. Glenn James and Robert C. James, eds., *Mathematics Dictionary*, 4th ed. (New York: Van Nostrand Reinhold, 1976), s.v.

22. See Maurice Daumas, *Scientific Instruments of the Seventeenth and Eighteenth Centuries and Their Makers* (London: Batsford, 1972), 22ff.

23. In 1955 Le Corbusier published an *Anhang* to his original modulor book titled (in the slightly later English version) *Modulor 2, 1955 (Let the User Speak Next)*. This contained corrections, most of them sent in by interested readers. See especially pp. 16, 44, 48, 60, 141.

24. Discussed more fully in my *Pythagorean Palaces*, 88ff.; and in Frank Zöllner, *Vitruvs Proportionsfigur* (Worms: Wernersche Verlagsgesellschaft, 1987).

25. Le Corbusier, *Modulor*, 65.

26. Robert Fludd, *Utriusque cosmi*, vol. 2, pt. 1, *Tractatus secundus: De naturae simia*, etc. (Oppenheim: typis Hieronymi Galleri, 1617).

27. Le Corbusier, *Modulor*, 235.

28. Ibid., 50.

29. For example, Rudolf Wittkower, *Architectural Principles in the Age of Humanism*, 3rd ed. (London: Tiranti, 1967), preface.

30. For the do's and don'ts of Palladio's villa planning, see Wittkower, *Architectural Principles*, 57 ff.; and, more particularly, Freedman and Hersey, *Possible Palladian Villas, Plus a Few Instructively Impossible Ones* (Cambridge: MIT Press, 1992).

31. See Linda Dalrymple Henderson, *The Fourth Dimension and Non-Euclidean Geometry in Modern Art* (Princeton: Princeton University Press, 1983), 66, n. 54 with bibliography.

32. At least by 1955. See Le Corbusier, *Modulor 2*, 189, 192ff.

CONCLUSION

1. Though Descartes, in 1638, first recognized the equiangular spiral as a separate mathematical entity and Sir Christopher Wren was the first to define it logarithmically. D'Arcy Wentworth Thompson, *On Growth and Form* (1916; rev. ed., 1942; reprint, New York: Dover, 1992), 754, 785.

BIBLIOGRAPHY

Ackerman, James. *The Architecture of Michelangelo.* 2nd ed. Vol. 1. Chicago: University of Chicago Press, 1986.

Adam, Charles, and Paul Tannery, eds. *Oeuvres,* by René Descartes. Paris: J. Vrin, 1964.

Bagrow, L. *Die Geschichte der Kartographie.* Berlin: Safari-Verlag, 1951.

———. *A History of Cartography.* Cambridge: Harvard University Press, 1964.

Barbaro, Daniele. *I Dieci libri dell'architettura tradotti e commentati da Daniele Barbaro.* 1567. Reprint, Milan: Polifilo, 1987.

Barret, Robert. *Theorike and Practike of Moderne Warres.* 1598.

Bartholomew, Wilmer T. *Acoustics in Music.* Westport, Conn.: Greenwood Press, 1980.

Bedini, Silvio. *Science and Optics in Seventeenth-Century Italy.* Aldershot, England: Variorum, 1994.

Behler, Ernst. "Schellings Ästhetik in der Überlieferung von Henry Crabb Robinson." *Philosophisches Jahrbuch* 83 (1976): 146.

Bennett, J. A. *The Mathematical Science of Christopher Wren.* Cambridge: Cambridge University Press, 1982.

Bernhard, Christoph. *Tractatus compositionis augmentatus.* Circa 1660. English translation in *Music Forum 3* (1973): 31–196.

Bibiena, Ferdinando Galli da. *Architettura Civile.* 1711. Reprint, New York: Benjamin Blom, 1971.

Birindelli, Massimo. *Piazza San Pietro.* Bari: Laterza, 1981. Originally published as *La Machina heroica: Il disegno di Gianlorenzo Bernini per Piazza San Pietro* (Rome: Università degli Studi, 1980).

Blondel, François. *Cours d'architecture enseigné dans l'Académie royale d'architecture,* etc. Paris: Chez l'Auteur, 1698.

Blunt, Anthony. *Neapolitan Baroque and Rococo Architecture.* London: Zwemmer, 1975.

Boesiger, Willi, ed. *Le Corbusier.* New York: Praeger, 1972.

Borsi, Franco. *Bernini Architetto.* New York: Rizzoli, 1984.

Bourget, Pierre, and Georges Cattaui. *Jules Hardouin Mausart.* Paris: Vincent, Freal, 1960.

Bosse, Abraham. *La manière universelle de Mr. Desargues, Lyonnois, pour poser l'essieu & placer les heures et autres choses aux cadrans au soleil.* Paris: Pierre Des-Hayes, 1643.

———. *Moyen universel de pratiquer la perspective sur les tableaux ou surfaces irregulières.* Paris: Chez ledit Bosse, 1653.

———. *La Pratique du Trait à preuves de M. Desargues, Lyonnois, pour la coupe des pierres en l'architecture.* Paris, Pierre Des-Hayes, 1643.

———. *Traité des manières de dessiner les ordres de l'architecture,* etc. Paris: P. Aubouin, P. Emery, et C. Clousier, 1688.

———. *Traité des practiques géometrales.* Paris: Chez l'Auteur, 1665.

Bottineau, Yves. *L'Art Baroque.* Paris: Mazenod, 1986.

Bourget, Pierre, and Georges Cattaui. *Jules Hardouin Mausart.* Paris: Vincent, Fréal, 1960.

Brack, Matthias. "Metal Clusters and Magic Numbers." *Scientific American* 277 (December 1997): 53.

Braitenberg, Valentino. *Vehicles: Experiments in Synthetic Psychology.* Cambridge: MIT Press, 1984.

Brosterman, Norman. *Inventing Kindergarten.* New York: Abrams, 1997.

Brown, Lloyd Arnold. *Jean-Dominique Cassini and His World Map of 1696.* Ann Arbor: University of Michigan Press, 1941.

Brunetta, Gian Piero. *Il Viaggio dell'icononauta: Dalla camera oscura di Leonardo alla luce dei Lumière.* Venice: Marsilio, 1997.

Bultman, Scott. *Froebel Gifts 2000.* Grand Rapids, Mich.: American Traditional Toys, Inc., 1997.

Burkert, Walter. *Lore and Science in Ancient Pythagoreanism.* Cambridge: Harvard University Press, 1972.

Caramuel Lobkowitz, Juan Bautista. *Arquitectura civil, recta y obliqua.* 1678. Reprint, Madrid: Ediciones Turner, 1984.

Carboneri, Nino. Introduction to *Architettura civile,* by Guarino Guarini. 1737. Reprint, Milan: Polifilo, 1968.

Cassini, Giovanni Domenico. *Abrégé des observations . . . la comète de 1680.* Paris: E. Michallet, 1681.

—————. *La meridiana del tempio di San Petronio tirata, e preparata . . .* Bologna: V. Benacci, 1695.

—————. *Nuovo atlante geografico universale delineato sulle ultime osservazioni.* Rome: Calcografia Camerale, 1792–1801.

Chabaud, Marcel. *Girard Desargues: Bourgeois de Lyon, mathématicien, architecte.* Lyon: IREM de Lyon, 1996.

Clayton, John. *The Dimensions, Plans, Elevations, and Sections of the Parochial Churches of Sir Christopher Wren.* London: Longman, Brown, Green & Longman, 1848–49.

Cohen, H. F. *Quantifying Music: The Science of Music at the First Stage of the Scientific Revolution, 1580–1650.* Dordrecht: D. Riedel, 1984.

Cohen, Jack, and Ian Stewart. *The Collapse of Chaos: Discovering Simplicity in a Complex World.* New York: Penguin, 1994.

Comar, Philippe. *La Perspective en jeu: Le dessous de l'image.* Paris: Gallimard, 1992.

Connors, Joseph. "Ars tornandi: Baroque Architecture and the Lathe." *Journal of the Warburg and Courtauld Insitutes* 53 (1990): 217ff.

—————. *Borromini and the Roman Oratory: Style and Society.* Cambridge: MIT Press, 1980.

—————. "The Spire of Sant'Ivo." *Burlington Magazine* 138 (October 1996): 668ff.

Cotton, John. *An Abstract of Laws and Government, Discourse about Civil Government.* London: F. Coule and W. Ley, 1641.

Daumas, Maurice. *Scientific Instruments of the Seventeenth and Eighteenth Centuries and Their Makers.* London: Batsford, 1972.

Davenport, John. *Aspects of Puritan Religious Thought.* New York: AMS Press, 1982.

DeCamp, L. Sprague. *The Ancient Engineers.* New York: Ballantine, 1974.

della Porta, Giovanni Battista. *Magia Naturalis Libri XX.* Frankfurt, 1591.

Del Pesco, Daniela. *L'Architettura del Seiciento.* Turin: UTET, 1998.

Denes, Agnes. "Isometric Systems in Isotropic Space." In *Spiral Symmetry,* edited by Hargittai and Pickover, 389ff. Singapore: World Scientific, 1992.

Desargues, Girard. *Brouillon project d'une atteinte aux evenmens des rencontres du cone avec un plan.* 1639. Reprint, Paris: Poudra, 1864.

—————. *Brouillon projet d'une exemple d'une maniere universelle du S. G. D. L.* [Sieur Girard Desargues Lyonnais] *touchant la pratique du trait a preuves pour la coupe des pierres en l'architecture,* etc. Paris: Pierre Des-Hayes, 1643.

—————. *Exemple de l'une des manieres universelles du S.G.D.L. touchant la pratique de la perspective sans employer aucun tiers point, de distance ny d'autre nature, qui soit hors du champ de l'ouvrage.* Paris: Pierre Des-Hayes, 1636.

—————. *Manière universelle de Mr. Desargues pour pratiquer la perspective par petit-pied,* etc. Paris: Pierre Des-Hayes, 1648.

Descartes, René. *Oeuvres de Descartes.* 2nd ed. Paris: L. Cerf, 1974–86.

Devlin, Keith. *Mathematics: The Science of Patterns.* New York: Scientific American Library, 1994.

Digges, Thomas. *A Perfit Description of the Coelestiall Orbes.* 1569. Reprinted in *Prognostication of Right and Good Effect*, by Leonard Digges. Aldburgh, England, 1592.

Di Stefano, Roberto. *La Cupola di San Pietro: Storia della costruzione e dei restauri.* Naples: Edizioni scientifiche italiane, 1966.

Donnelly, M. C. *Astronomical Observatories in the 17th and 18th Centuries.* Book 34, fascicule 5, *Mémoires.* Brussels: Académie Royale de Belgique, Classe des Sciences, 1964.

Doremus, Thomas. *Frank Lloyd Wright and Le Corbusier: The Great Dialogue.* New York: Van Nostrand Reinhold, 1985.

Downes, Kerry. *Sir Christopher Wren and the Designs of St. Paul's Cathedral.* Exhibition catalog. London: Trefoil, 1988.

Drummond, Andrew Landale. *The Church Architecture of Protestantism, an Historical and Constructive Study.* Edinburgh: T & T Clark, 1934.

Dryden, John, trans. *The Eclogues of Virgil.* 1697. Reprinted in *The Works of John Dryden*, edited by E. N. Hooker and H. T. Swedenberg. Berkeley: University of California Press, 1956.

Duffy, Christopher. *The Fortress in the Age of Vauban and Frederick the Great, 1660–1789.* London: Routledge and Kegan Paul, 1985.

———. *Siege Warfare: The Fortress in the Early Modern World, 1494–1660.* London: Routledge and Kegan Paul, 1979.

Dyson, George B. *Darwin among the Machines: The Evolution of Global Intelligence.* Reading, Mass.: Perseus Books, 1997.

Edgerton, Samuel Y. "Brunelleschi's First Perspective Picture." *Arte Lombarda* 18 (1973): 187ff.

———. *The Renaissance Rediscovery of Linear Perspective.* New York: Basic Books, 1975.

Elmes, James. *Memoirs of the Life and Works of Sir Christopher Wren.* London: Priestley & Weale, 1823.

Etlin, Richard R. *Frank Lloyd Wright and Le Corbusier: The Romantic Legacy.* Manchester, U.K.: Manchester University Press, 1993.

Evans, Robin. *The Projective Cast: Architecture and Its Three Geometries.* Cambridge: MIT Press, 1995.

Fibonacci, Leonardo. *The Book of Squares.* Translated and edited by L. E. Sigler. Boston: Academic Press, 1987.

———. *Liber Abaci.* Edited by B. Boncompagni. Rome, 1857.

Fichet, Françoise. *La Théorie architecturale à l'âge classique.* Brussels: P. Mardaga, 1979.

Field, J. V. "Kepler's Rejection of Solid Celestial Spheres." *Vistas in Astronomy* 23 (1979): 207ff.

Field, J. V., and J. J. Gray. *The Geometrical Work of Girard Desargues.* New York: Springer-Verlag, 1987.

Field, Mike, and Martin Golubitsky. *Symmetry in Chaos: A Search for Pattern in Mathematics, Art, and Nature*. New York: Oxford University Press, 1992.

Fletcher, Banister. *A History of Architecture on the Comparative Method*. 1892. Reprint, New York: Scribner's, 1951.

Fludd, Robert. *Utriusque cosmi maioris scilicet et minoris metaphysica*. Vol. 2, part 1, *Tractatus secundus: De naturae simia,* etc. Oppenheim: typis Hieronymi Galleri, 1617.

Fournier, Marion. *The Fabric of Life: Microscopy in the Seventeenth Century.* Baltimore: Johns Hopkins University Press, 1996.

Fowden, Garth. *The Egyptian Hermes: A Historical Approach to the Late Pagan Mind.* Cambridge: Cambridge University Press, 1986.

Frame, Michael, and Theodore Bick. *The Geometry of Nature: From Compass to Computer.* Forthcoming.

Fréart de Chantelou, Paul. *Diary of the Cavaliere Bernini's Visit to France.* Edited by Anthony Blunt. Princeton, N.J.: Princeton University Press, 1985.

Froebel, Friedrich. *The Education of Man.* 1826. Reprint, New York: Appleton, 1908.

———. *Kindergarten Gifts and Occupation Material.* New York: E. Steiger, 1876.

Galilei, Galileo. *Dialogues Concerning Two New Sciences.* 1637. Translated by Henry Crew and Alfonso de Salvio (1914). Reprint, New York: Dover, 1954.

———. *Discoveries and Opinions of Galileo.* Edited by Stillman Drake. New York: Anchor, 1957.

———. *Operations of the Geometric and Military Compass.* Translated by Stillman Drake. 1606. Reprint, Washington, D.C., Smithsonian Press, 1978.

———. *Sidereus Nuncius, or the Sidereal Messenger.* Edited by Albert van Helden. Chicago: University of Chicago Press, 1989.

———. *Trattato della Sphaera.* 1586–87. In Galilei, *Opere,* ed. Antonio Favaro. Florence: G. Barbéra, 1953.

Galilei, Vincenzo. *Dialogo della musica antica, et della musica moderna.* 1581. Milan: A. Minuziano, 1947.

Garvan, Anthony N. B. *Architecture and Town Planning in Colonial Connecticut.* New Haven: Yale University Press, 1951.

Gaukroger, Stephen. *Descartes: An Intellectual Biography.* Oxford: Oxford University Press, 1995.

Gibson-Wood, Carol. "The Political Background of Thornhill's Paintings in St. Paul's Cathedral." *Journal of the Warburg and Courtauld Institutes* 56 (1993): 229ff.

Girbal, F. *Bernard Lamy, 1640–1715.* Paris: Presses universitaires de France, 1964.

Glanz, Alexandra. *Alessandro Galli-Bibiena (1686–1748) inventore dalle scene und premier architkteur am kurpälischen Hof in Mannheim,* etc. Berlin: Gesellschaft für Theatergeschichte, 1991.

Godwin, Joscelyn. *The Harmony of the Spheres: A Sourcebook of the Pythagorean Tradition in Music.* Rochester, Vt.: Inner Traditions International, 1993.

Goldmann, Nicolaus, and Leonhard Christoph Sturm. *Prodromus Architecturae Goldmannianae*. Augsburg: Wolff, 1714.

―――. *Sciagraphia Templi Hierosolymitani*. Leipzig: Krüger, 1694.

Golubitsky, Martin, and Ian Melbourne. "A Symmetry Classification of Columns." In *Bridges: Mathematical Connections in Art, Music, and Science*, ed. Reza Sarhangi, 209–23. Bridges Conference, April 6, 1998.

Golvin, J. C. *L'Amphitéâtre romain: Essai sur la théorisation de sa forme et de ses fonctions*. Paris: Diffusion de Boccard, 1988.

Gombrich, Ernst. *The Sense of Order: A Study in the Psychology of Decorative Art*. Ithaca, N.Y.: Cornell University Press, 1978.

Goodyear, William H. *Greek Refinements: Studies in Temperamental Architecture*. New Haven: Yale University Press, 1912.

Gould, Cecil. *Bernini in France: An Episode in Seventeenth-Century History*. London: Weidenfeld and Nicholson, 1981.

Greenberg, Mitchell. *Corneille, Classicism, and the Ruses of Symmetry*. Cambridge: Cambridge University Press, 1986.

Grünbaum, Branko, and G. C. Shephard. *Tilings and Patterns*. New York: W. H. Freeman, 1986.

Guadet, Julien. *Eléments et théorie de l'architecture*. Paris: Librairie de la construction moderne, 1905.

Guarducci, Margherita. *La Tomba di San Pietro: Una straordinaria vicenda*. Rome: Rusconi, 1989.

Guarini, Guarino. *Architettura civile*. 1737. Reprint, Milan: Polifilo, 1968.

―――. *Euclides adauctus et methodius*. Turin: B. Zapata, 1671.

Halfpenny, William. *A New and Compleat System of Architecture*. London, 1749.

Hankins, Thomas L. *Science and the Enlightenment*. Cambridge: Cambridge University Press, 1985.

Hankins, Thomas L., and Robert J. Silverman. *Instruments and the Imagination*. Princeton, N.J.: Princeton University Press, 1995.

Hanschmann, Alexander Bruno. *The Kindergarten System: Its Origin and Development as Seen in the Life of Friedrich Froebel*. London: Schwann Sonnenschein, 1897.

Hargittai, István, and Clifford A. Pickover, eds. *Spiral Symmetry*. Singapore: World Scientific, 1992.

Harris, Anne Sutherland. *Andrea Sacchi: Complete Edition of the Paintings with a Critical Catalogue*. Oxford: Oxford University Press, 1977.

Harris, John. "Designing St. Paul's." *Country Life* 185 (1991): 80ff.

―――. *William Talman, Maverick Architect*. London: George Allen and Unwin, 1982.

Haselberger, Lothar, ed. *Appearance and Essence: Refinements of Classical Architecture: Curvature*. Philadelphia: University of Pennsylvania, 1999.

Hautecoeur, Louis. *Mystique et architecture: Symbolisme du cercle et de la coupole*. Paris: Picard, 1954.

Heath, D. C. *A History of Greek Mathematics.* New York: Dover, 1981.

Heath, Sir Thomas L. *Euclid: The Thirteen Books of the Elements.* 2nd ed. New York: Dover, 1956.

Hebbert, F. J., and G. A. Rothrock. *Soldier of France: Sébastien le Prestre de Vauban, 1633–1707.* New York: Peter Lang, 1989.

Hecht, Eugene, and Alfred Zajac. *Optics.* Reading, Mass.: Addison-Wesley, 1979.

Heilbron, J. L. *The Sun in Church: Cathedrals as Solar Observatories.* Cambridge: Harvard University Press, 1999.

Helmholtz, Hermann. *On the Sensation of Tone as a Physiological Basis for the Theory of Music.* 1863. Reprint, London: Longman, Green, and Co., 1930.

Henderson, Linda Dalrymple. *The Fourth Dimension and Non-Euclidean Geometry in Modern Art.* Princeton, N.J.: Princeton University Press, 1983.

Hersey, George L. *Architecture, Poetry, and Number in the Royal Palace at Caserta.* Cambridge: MIT Press, 1976.

———. *High Renaissance Art in St. Peter's and the Vatican.* Chicago: University of Chicago Press, 1993.

———. *The Lost Meaning of Classical Architecture: Speculations on Ornament from Vitruvius to Venturi.* Cambridge: MIT Press, 1988.

———. *The Monumental Impulse: Architecture's Biological Roots.* Cambridge: MIT Press, 1999.

———. *Pythagorean Palaces: Magic and Architecture in the Italian Renaissance.* Ithaca, N.Y.: Cornell University Press, 1976.

Hersey, George, and Richard Freedman. *Possible Palladian Villas (Plus a Few Instructively Impossible Ones).* Cambridge: MIT Press, 1992.

Hibbard, Howard. *Carlo Maderno and Roman Architecture, 1580–1603.* University Park: Pennsylvania State University Press, 1971.

Holden, Alan. *Shapes, Space, and Symmetry.* New York: Dover, 1971.

Hoskins, Lesley, ed. *The Papered Wall: Pattern, Technique.* New York: Abrams, 1994.

Hough, Christina K. "The Pattern Designs of William Morris: Nature Conventionalized According to Geometric Principles." *Architectura* 1 (1992).

Hunt, Frederick V. *Origins of Acoustics.* New Haven: Yale University Press, 1978.

Hutchins, C. M. "The Acoustics of Violin Plates." *Scientific American* 245 (1981): 170ff.

Izenour, George C. *Roofed Theaters of Classical Antiquity.* New Haven: Yale University Press, 1992.

James, Glenn, and Robert C. James, eds. *Mathematics Dictionary.* 4th ed. New York: Van Nostrand Reinhold, 1976.

Jamnitzer, Wenzel. *Perspectiva corporum regularium.* 1568. Reprint, Frankfurt: Biermann, 1972.

Jardine, Lisa. *Ingenious Pursuits: Building the Scientific Revolution.* New York: Doubleday, 1999.

Jean, R. V. *Phyllotaxis: A Systematic Study of Plant Morphogenesis.* Cambridge: Cambridge University Press, 1994.

Jeffrey, Paul. *The City Churches of Sir Christopher Wren.* London: Hambledon Press, 1996.

Kambartel, Walter. *Symmetrie und Schönheit.* Munich: W. Fink, 1972.

Kappraff, Jay. *Connections: The Geometric Bridge between Art and Science.* New York: McGraw-Hill, 1990.

———. "The Spiral in Nature, Myth, and Mathematics." In *Spiral Symmetry,* edited by Hargittai and Pickover, 15ff. Singapore: World Scientific, 1992.

Kaufmann, Emil. *Architecture in the Age of Reason: Baroque and Post-Baroque in England, Italy, and France.* Cambridge: Harvard University Press, 1955.

———. "Three Revolutionary Architects—Boullée, Ledoux, and Lequeux." *Transactions of the American Philosophical Society* 42 (1952).

———. *Von Ledoux bis Le Corbusier: Ursprung und Entwicklung der autonomen Architektur.* Vienna: R. Passer, 1933.

Kaufmann, Thomas Da Costa. "The Perspective of Shadows: The History of the Theory of Shadow Projection." *Journal of the Warburg and Courtauld Institutes* 38 (1975): 238ff.

Kemp, Martin. *The Science of Art: Optical Themes in Western Art from Brunelleschi to Seurat.* New Haven: Yale University Press, 1990.

Kepler, Johannes. *Harmonices mundi libri v.* Linz: Gottfried Tampach, 1619.

———. *Prodrumus dissertationum cosmographicarum, continens mysterium cosmographicum.* 1596. Reprinted in *Gesammelte Werke,* by Kepler. Munich: Beck, 1937ff.

Kienzl, Barbara. *Die barocken Kanzeln im Kärnten.* Klagenfurt: Verlag des Kärnter Landesarchivs, 1986.

Kircher, Athanasius. *Ars magna lucis et umbrae in X libros digesta.* Rome: Hermann Scheus, 1646.

———. *Musurgia Universalis de natura et productione consoni et dissoni.* Rome: Typographicum haeredum Fratelli Corbinetti, 1650.

Kirwin, W. Chandler. *Powers Matchless: The Pontificate of Urban VIII, the Baldachin, and Gian Lorenzo Bernini.* New York: Peter Lang, 1997.

Kitao, Timothy K. *Circle and Oval in the Square of St. Peter's: Bernini's Art of Planning.* New York: New York University Press, 1974.

Kline, Morris. *Mathematics in Western Culture.* Oxford: Oxford University Press, 1953.

Kostof, Spiro. *The City Shaped: Urban Patterns and Meanings through History.* Boston: Little, Brown, 1991.

Koyré, Alexandre. *The Astronomical Revolution: Copernicus—Kepler—Borelli.* New York: Dover, 1973.

———. *From the Closed World to the Infinite Universe.* Baltimore: Johns Hopkins University Press, 1957.

Kultermann, Udo. *Die Maxentius-Basilika: Ein Schlüsselwerk spätantiker Architektur.* Weimar:VDG, 1996.

Lamy, Bernard. *De Tabernaculo foederis; de sancta civitate Jersalem et de templo eius.* 1720. Reprinted in *A Short History of the Ancient Israelites,* by Lamy. Translated and extended by Adam Clarke. Baltimore: B.W. Sower & Co., 1811.

Lantuch, Katherine A. "The Origin of New Haven's Nine Squares." *Journal of the New Haven Colony Historical Society* 37 (spring 1991): 7ff.

Layton, Michael. *Symmetry, Causality, and Mind.* Cambridge: MIT Press, 1992.

Le Corbusier. "Il faut reconsidérer le hexagone français." In *Architecture et urbanisme.* Paris: Publications Techniques, 1942.

———. *The Modulor: A Harmonious Measure to the Human Scale Universally Applicable to Architecture and Mechanics.* Cambridge: Harvard University Press, 1954.

———. *Le Modulor and Other Buildings and Projects, 1944-45.* New York: Garland, 1983.

———. *Le Modulor 2, 1955.* 1958. Reprint, Cambridge: MIT Press, 1968.

Ledoux, Claude-Nicolas. *L'Architecture considerée sous les rapports des moeurs, de la législation, et de l'art.* Paris: Chez l'auteur, 1804.

Levin, Flora R. *The Harmonics of Nicomachus and the Pythagorean Tradition.* University Park, Pa.: American Philological Association, 1975.

Longer, Johnnes. "Fels und Sphäre: Bilder der Natur in der Architektur um 1789." *Daidalos* 12 (June 1984): 92ff.

L'Orange, H. P. *Studies in the Iconography of Cosmic Kingship in the Ancient World.* Cambridge: Harvard University Press, 1953.

Magnuson, Torgil. *Rome in the Age of Bernini.* Stockholm: Almqvist & Wicksell, 1986.

Manetti, Antonio di Tuccio. *The Life of Brunelleschi.* Edited and translated by Howard Saalman. University Park: Pennsylvania State University Press, 1970.

March, Lionel. *Architectonics of Humanism: Essays on Number in Architecture.* London: Academy Editions, 1998.

———. "'Proportion Is an Alive and Expressive Tool.'" In *R. M. Schindler: Composition and Construction.* Edited by L. March and J. Sheine, 88ff. London: Academy Editions, 1994.

———. "Sources of Characteristic Spatial Relations in Frank Lloyd Wright's Decorative Designs." In *Frank Lloyd Wright: The Phoenix Papers.* Vol. 2, *The Natural Pattern of Structure,* 12ff. Edited by L. Nelson. Tucson: University of Arizona Press, 1995.

March, Lionel, and Philip Steadman. *The Geometry of Environment: An Introduction to Spatial Organization in Design.* Cambridge: MIT Press, 1974.

Marder, T. A. *Bernini and the Art of Architecture.* New York: Abbeville, 1998.

Marino, A. G. "Il Colonnato di Piazza San Pietro: Dall'architettura obliqua di Caramuel al classicismo berniniano." *Palladio* 23 (1973): 81ff.

Markowsky, George. "Misconceptions about the Golden Ratio." *College Mathematics Journal* 23 (1992): 2ff.

Markus, Mario. "Autonomous Organization of a Chaotic Medium into Spirals: Simulations and Experiments." In *Spiral Symmetry,* edited by Hargittai and Pickover, 165ff. Singapore: World Scientific, 1992, 187ff.

Mersenne, Marin. *Harmonicorum libri in quibus agitor de sonorum natura,* etc. Paris: Baudry, 1635–36.

———. *Harmonie universelle: Livre septième des instruments de percussion.* Paris: Baudry, 1635–36.

Middleton, Robin. "Jacques Françoise Blondel and the *Cours de l'architecture." Journal of the Society of Architectural Historians* 18 (1959): 141ff.

Moore, Patrick. *Eyes on the Sky: The Story of the Telescope.* London: Springer, 1997.

Morrice, R. J. "Sanfelice and St. Florian: Indigenous Tradition in Staircase Design." *Architectural History* 26 (1983): 82ff.

Mosser, Monique, and Daniel Rabreau. *Charles de Wailly, peintre-architecte dans l'Europe des lumières.* Paris: Caisse nationale des monuments historiques et des sites, 1979. Exhibition catalog.

Müller, Edith. "Gruppentheoretische und strukturanalytische Untersuchungen der Maurischen Ornamente aus der Alhambra in Granada." Ph.D. diss., University of Zürich, 1944.

Murray, David, ed. *Architecture and Shadow, Via 11.* Philadelphia: University of Pennsylvania Graduate School of Fine Arts; and New York: Rizzoli, 1990.

Neufforge, Jean-François de. *Receuil élémentaire d'architecture.* Paris: Chez l'auteur, 1757ff.

Newton, Isaac. *The Mathematical Papers of Isaac Newton.* Edited by D. T. Whiteside. Cambridge: Cambridge University Press, 1967–81.

———. *Opticks, or a Treatise of the Reflections, Refractions, Inflections, and Colours of Light.* 1730. Reprint, New York: Dover, 1952.

———. *Principia Mathematica.* Vol. 2, *The System of the World.* 1687. Translated by Andrew Motte and revised by Florian Cajori. Berkeley: University of California Press, 1934.

Nicomachus of Gerasa. *Antiquae musicae auctores septem.* Edited by Marcus Meibonius. Amsterdam: Elzevir, 1652.

———. *Musicae scriptores graeci.* Stuttgart: B. G. Teubner, 1995.

Onians, Richard Broxton. *The Origins of European Thought about the Body, the Mind, the Soul, the World, Time, and Fate,* etc. Cambridge: Cambridge University Press, 1951.

Osterweis, Rollin G. *Three Centuries of New Haven, 1638-1938.* New Haven: Yale University Press, 1953.

Ouvrard, René. "Application des Proportions de la Musique à l'Architecture par M.

Ouvrard." In *Cours d'architecture enseigné dans l'Académie Royale d'Architecture,* etc., by François Blondel. 1675. Reprint, Paris: Chez l'Auteur, 1698.

———. *Lettres sur l'architecture harmonique, ou l'application de la doctrine des proportions de la musique à l'architecture.* Paris: Roulland, 1679.

Pacioli, Fra Luca. *De Divina Proportione.* 1509. Reprint, Milan: Silvana, 1982.

Palisca, Claude. *Baroque Music.* 3rd ed. Englewood Cliffs, N.J.: Prentice-Hall, 1991.

Pane, Roberto. *Bernini architetto.* Venice: N. Pozza, 1953.

Panek, Richard. *Seeing and Believing: How the Telescope Opened Our Eyes and Minds to the Heavens.* New York: Viking, 1998.

Park, David. *The Fire within the Eye: A Historical Essay on the Nature and Meaning of Light.* Princeton N.J.: Princeton University Press, 1997.

Pastor, Ludwig. *History of the Popes from the Close of the Middle Ages.* 1891. Reprint, New York: Kraus, 1969.

Pelt, Robert Jan van. "Los Rabinos, Maimónides y el Templo." In *Dios Arquitecto: J. B. Villalpando y el Templo de Salomon,* edited by Juan Antonio Ramírez, 82ff. Madrid: Ediciones Siruelas, 1991.

Pennethorne, John. *The Geometry and Optics of Ancient Architecture.* London: Williams & Norgate, 1878.

Pérez-Gómez, Alberto. "The Glass Architecture of Fra Luca Pacioli." *Architectura.* Forthcoming.

———. "Juan Bautista Villalpando's Divine Model in Architectural Theory." *Chora* 3 (1999): 125ff.

Pérez-Gómez, Alberto, and Louise Pelletier. *Architectural Representation and the Perspective Hinge.* Cambridge: MIT Press, 1997.

Perkowitz, Sidney. *Empire of Light: A History of Discovery in Science and Art.* New York: Henry Holt, 1993.

Pérouse de Montclos, Jean-Marie. "*De nova stella anni 1784* from Newton." *Revue de l'art* 58–59 (1982–83): 75ff.

Perrault, Claude. *Ordonnance for the Five Kinds of Columns after the Method of the Ancients.* 1673. English edition: The Getty Center for the History of Art and the Humanities (Santa Monica, Calif., 1993).

———. *A Treatise of the Five Orders in Architecture,* etc. Translated by John James. London: Benjamin Motte, 1707.

Pevsner, Nikolaus. *Derbyshire.* London: Penguin, 1953.

Phillips, Barty. *Fabrics and Wallpapers: Sources, Design, and Inspiration.* Boston: Little, Brown, 1991.

Pico della Mirandola, Giovanni. *Disputationes adversus astrologiam divinatricem.* Edited by Eugenio Garin. Florence: Vallecchi, 1946–52.

Picon, Antoine *Claude Perrault, 1613–88, ou, la curiosité d'un classique.* Paris: Picard, 1988.

Pinto-Correa, Clara. *The Ovary of Eve: Egg and Sperm and Preformation.* Chicago: University of Chicago Press, 1997.

Pirazzoli-T'Serstevens, Michiele. *Living Architecture: Chinese.* New York, Grosset & Dunlap, 1971.

Poley, Arthur F. E. *St. Paul's Cathedral, London, Measured, Drawn, and Described by Arthur F. E. Poley.* London: the Author, 1878.

Portoghesi, Paolo. *Borromini nella cultura europea.* Rome: Laterza, 1982.

Preussner, Ingrid. *Ellipsen und Ovale in der Malerei des 15. Und 16. Jahrhunderts.* Speyer: VCH Acta Humaniora, 1987, 51ff.

Ramírez, Juan Antonio. "Sinécdoque: Columnas 'Salomonicas.'" In *Villalpando,* edited by Ramírez, 17ff. Madrid: Ediciones Siruelas, 1991.

Ramírez, Juan Antonio, Robert Jan van Pelt, Antonio Martínez Ripoll, and René Taylor. "El Rigor de la ciencia: Los tratados tradicionales sobre el Templo de Jerusalén." In *Villalpando,* 79ff. Madrid: Ediciones Siruelas, 1991.

Raspe, Martin. *Das Architektursystem Borrominis.* Munich: Deutscher Kunstverlag, 1994.

Record, Robert. *The Whetstone of Witte.* 1557. Reprint, New York: Da Capo. 1964.

Reeves, Eileen. *Painting the Heavens: Galileo and the Lunar Controversy.* Princeton: Princeton University Press, 1997.

Robison, Elwin C. "Optics and Mathematics in the Domed Churches of Guarino Guarini." *Journal of the Society of Architectural Historians* 50 (1991): 384ff.

Rocolle, Yves. *2000 Ans de fortification française.* Limoges, 1973.

Rosenau, Helen. *Vision of the Temple: The Image of the Temple of Jerusalem in Judaism and Christianity.* London: Oresko, 1979.

Rykwert, Joseph. *The Dancing Column.* Cambridge: MIT Press, 1996.

———. "Letter from Chandigarh." *TLS,* April 23, 1999, 15.

Schelling, Friedrich von. *Philosophie der Kunst.* In *Werke,* by Schelling. Munich: Beck, 1958.

Scherf, Guilhem. "Pierre Julien et le décor sculpté de l'église Sainte-Généviève à Paris." *Revue du Louvre et des musées de France* 38, no. 2 (1988): 127ff.

Sedlmayr, Hans. *L'Architettura di Borromini: La Figura e l'Opera con un'appendice storico-stilistico.* Edited by Marco Pogacnik. Milan: Electa, 1996.

Serlio, Sebastiano. *Tutte l'opere d'architettura et prospettiva,* etc. Venice: Giacomo de'Franceschi, 1619.

Shubnikov, Aleksei V., and Vladimir A. Koptsik. *Symmetry in Science and Art.* New York: Plenum, 1974.

"Sphären der Revolution: Architektur und Weltbild der klassischen Mechanik." *Architecture Plus* 116 (March 1993): 22ff.

Steinhardt, Nancy. *Chinese Imperial City Planning.* Honolulu: University of Hawaii Press, 1990.

Stephenson, Bruce. *The Music of the Heavens: Kepler's Harmonic Astronomy.* Princeton: Princeton University Press, 1994.

Stewart, Ian. "Broken Symmetry and the Formation of Spiral Patterns in Fluids." In *Spiral Symmetry,* edited by Hargittai and Pickover, 187ff. Singapore: World Scientific, 1992.

Stewart, Ian, and Martin Golubitsky. *Fearful Symmetry: Is God a Geometer?* Oxford: Blackwell, 1992.

Stifel, M. *Arithmetica Integra.* Nuremberg: J. Petreium, 1544.

Streitz, Robert. *Palladio: La Rotonde et sa Géometrie.* Lausanne and Paris: Bibliothèque des Arts, 1973.

Sturm, Leonhard Christoph. *Erste Ausübung der vortrefflichen und vollständigen Anweisung zu der Zivil-Bau-Kunst Nikolai Goldmann.* Leipzig: Richter, 1695.

———. *Sciagraphia templi Hierosolemytani.* Leipzig: Krüger, 1694.

Summerson, John. *Architecture in Britain, 1530–1833.* 6th ed. London: Penguin, 1977.

———. "J. H. Mansart, Sir Christropher Wren, and the Dome of St. Paul's Cathedral." *Burlington Magazine* 132 (1990): 32ff.

Sweeney, Robert L. *Frank Lloyd Wright: An Annotated Bibliography.* New York: Duell, Sloan, and Pearce, 1978.

Taylor, C. "The Geometry of Kepler and Newton." *Transactions of the Cambridge Philosophical Society* 18 (1900): 197.

———. "The New Violin Family and Its Scientific Background." *Soundings* 7 (1978): 101ff.

Thieme, Thomas. "La Geometria di Piazza San Pietro." *Palladio,* n.s., 23 (1973): 129ff.

Thoenes, Christoph. "Ein spezifisches Treppenbeusstsein. Neapler Treppenhaüser des 18. Jahrhunderts." *Daidalos* 9 (Sept. 15, 1983): 77ff.

Thompson, D'Arcy Wentworth. *On Growth and Form.* 1916. Rev. ed., 1942. Reprint, New York: Dover, 1992.

Thompson, R. J. *Instabilities and Catastrophes in Science and Engineering.* Chichester: Wiley, 1982.

Vasari, Giorgio. *The Lives of the Painters, Sculptors, and Architects.* Vol. 1. Translated by A. B. Hinds. London: Dent, 1550, 1568.

Vauban, Sebastien Le Prestre de. *Manière de fortifier selon la méthode de M. de Vauban, avec un traité préliminaire des principes de géometrie,* etc. Paris: Coignard, 1681.

Vegetius. *Flavi Vegeti Renati . . . De re militari libri quatuor,* etc. Lugduni Batavorum: Ex officina Plantiniana, apud F. Raphelengium, 1592.

Vidler, Anthony. "Researching Revolutionary Architecture." *Journal of Architectural Education* 44 (1991): 206ff.

Villalpando, Juan Bautista, and Jerónimo de Prado. *In Ezechielem explanationes et apparatus urbis ac templi hierosolymitami.* Rome: Carolus Vullietus, 1594–1605.

Vogt, Adolf Max. *Boullées Newton-Denkmal: Sakralbau und Kugelidee.* Basel: Birck-häuser, 1969.

Vorob'ev, N. N. *Fibonacci Numbers.* Oxford: Pergamon Press, 1961.

Wagner, Friedrich Christoph. "Symmetrie-Model-Grundlagen der Gestalten." *Daidalos* (March 15, 1985): 123ff.

Ward-Perkins, J. B. "The Shrine of St. Peter and Its Twelve Spiral Columns." *Journal of Roman Studies* 43 (1952).

Washburn, Dorothy K., and Donald W. Crowe. *Symmetries of Culture: Theory and Practice of Plane Pattern Analysis.* Seattle: University of Washington Press, 1988.

Wertenbaker, Lael. *The Eye: Window to the World.* New York: Torstar, 1984.

Weyl, Hermann. *Symmetry.* Princeton, N.J.: Princeton University Press, 1952.

Wilson Jones, Mark. "Designing Amphitheatres." *Römische Mitteilungen* 100 (1993): 391ff.

———. "Principles of Design in Roman Architecture: The Setting Out of Centralised Buildings." *Publications of the British School at Rome* 57 (1989): 106ff.

Wittkower, Rudolf. *Architectural Principles in the Age of Humanism.* 1946. Reprint, London: Academy Editions, 1988.

———. *La Cupola di San Pietro di Michelangelo.* Florence: Nuova Italia, 1964.

———. *Four Great Makers of Modern Architecture.* New York: da Capo Press, 1970.

Wood, John, the Elder. *The Origin of Building, or the Plagiarism of the Heathens Detected.* 1741.

Wren, Christopher. *Tract II on Architecture,* mid-1670s. Published in *Wren's "Tracts" on Architecture and Other Writings,* edited by Lydia M. Soo. Cambridge: Cambridge University Press, 1998.

Wright, Frank Lloyd. *A Testament.* New York: Horizon, 1957.

Zeeman, E. C. *Catastrophe Theory: Selected Papers, 1972–77.* Reading, Mass.: Addison-Wesley, 1977.

Zöllner, Frank. *Vitruvs Proportionsfigur.* Worms: Wernersche Verlagsgesellschaft, 1987.

INDEX